The Underground War

Dedicated To The Memory Of
Lieutenant Colonel Mike Watkins, MBE, RLC

The late Lieutenant Colonel Mike Watkins
MBE, working in the Durand mine chamber.
(*Durand Group*)

The Underground War

Volume 1:
Vimy Ridge to Arras

Phillip Robinson and Nigel Cave

BATTLEGROUND
EUROPE

First published in Great Britain in 2011 by
Pen & Sword Military
an imprint of
Pen & Sword Books Ltd
47 Church Street
Barnsley
South Yorkshire
S70 2AS

ISBN 978-1-84415-976-5

Cover photograph from the collection of Alain Jacques.

Title page photograph: The memorial to the tunnelling officers at the Institute
of Mining and Metallurgy. The original was stolen and, so far as is known, has
never been recovered.

Typeset in 11pt Ehrhardt by
Mac Style, Beverley, E. Yorkshire

Printed and bound in the UK by CPI

Pen & Sword Books Ltd incorporates the imprints of Pen & Sword Aviation,
Pen & Sword Maritime, Pen & Sword Military, Wharncliffe Local History,
Pen and Sword Select, Pen and Sword Military Classics and Leo Cooper.

For a complete list of Pen & Sword titles please contact
PEN & SWORD BOOKS LIMITED
47 Church Street, Barnsley, South Yorkshire, S70 2AS, England
E-mail: enquiries@pen-and-sword.co.uk
Website: www.pen-and-sword.co.uk

Contents

List of Maps, Plans, Diagrams and Tables

Acknowledgements

This book is the result of our collaborative efforts. However, little of it would have been possible without the assistance of numerous people. The compilers of the War Diaries of the different units and formations discussed and the surveyors who produced the plans of the various systems – often under unimaginably difficult circumstances – produced the basic material from which we worked. Compilers and authors of regimental histories and personal accounts provided us with much of the human (and often tragic) detail.

Colonel Jack Sheldon gave freely of his time and knowledge to provide us with information on the German army – as did Herr Norbert Kruger. The late Olaf Grieben, who served as a tunneller on Vimy Ridge, provided contemporary photographs, plans and his personal reminiscences. Various French landowners and farmers, notably Mr and Mrs Delabres of Maison Blanche and others who wish to remain anonymous, gave access to parts of their property or provided photographic material. The Arras Tourist Office was most helpful, as were the authorities at Wellington Cave. M. Alain Jacques, *Responsable du Service Archéologiques d'Arras*, with whom we have worked for many years, provided us with photographs, allowed us to draw on his material and shared his knowledge.

We are grateful to our publishers, Pen and Sword Books, for being understanding while we extended the delivery date of this book several times; we do hope that the wait has been worth it. The Commonwealth War Graves Commission has provided us with information and registers and we have made full use of its excellent website; the cemeteries included specifically in the tours section are eloquent, if silent, witnesses to the outstanding work and dedication of this organisation.

We would like to thank Steve Chambers for the use of photographs and for sharing his very considerable knowledge of the armies of the British Empire. Likewise Simon Jones, for allowing us to draw on some of his research featured in his book *Underground Warfare 1914–1918*. Members of the Great War Forum, wittingly or unwittingly, have provided useful information and expertise. Arlene King, the Veterans Affairs Canada Senior Manager for Commemorative Sites, has been her usual very generous self, not least in allowing her home at Beaumont Hamel to be overrun with maps, plans, books and computers for considerable periods of time. We also thank the several previous Directors of the Canadian Memorial site at Vimy, the past and current

Directors of European Operations and other senior management and staff of Veterans Affairs Canada, with whom we have worked for many years.

Phillip Robinson's wife Mary has put up with long hours dedicated to this book, both at home and abroad and even on holiday. Nigel Cave thanks his brethren and particularly his community in Stresa, Italy, who smile tolerantly at the *pazzo inglese* in their midst.

We owe a particular debt of gratitude to our fellow members of the Durand Group, an eclectic range of personalities who provided a range of specialist skills that have supported our work. The Group largely owes its existence to Lieutenant Colonel Mike Watkins MBE, a world-renowned explosives ordnance disposal expert, who was tragically killed in August 1998 while investigating the O Sector. He has the unique distinction of having a memorial erected by VAC, placed near the exit of the Grange Subway. This book is dedicated to his memory.

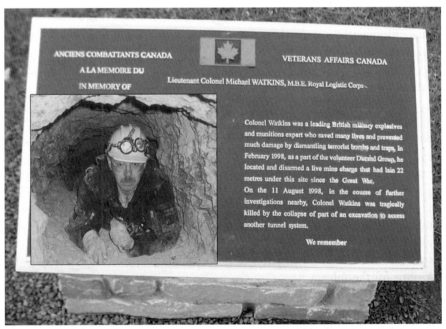

The memorial to Mike Watkins erected by Veterans Affairs Canada.

General Introduction and Advice to Tourers

This is the first in a series of Battleground Europe books on the war underground in the First World War (particularly and above all as it relates to the British Expeditionary Force in France and Flanders). This provides something of a challenge, as there are very few places where the public can access underground workings and the vast majority of the mine craters that characterised significant parts of the old front line have been filled in and have left little or no trace today. Although there are tales and accounts aplenty in this book about what was happening above ground (not least the story of the formation of the British tunnelling companies), the great bulk of it is concerned with the work of the tunnellers and the results of their efforts underground and, consequently, mainly out of sight. One of the reasons why the Vimy Ridge and Arras sector was selected as the first in the series is that there is public access to significant underground workings, the Grange Subway and the Wellington Cave.

At the Canadian Memorial site on Vimy Ridge it is possible (especially if you have the foresight to book a place on what can be a very busy tour) to see a section of the Grange Subway, part of which was designed to be an underground communication trench. But it was more than that: before the 'subway' element was dug there were already underground headquarters and various logistical support elements, such as a water point, which are visited as part of the tour. The subway was added to an existing system which led to deep laterals, many feet below the subway, which themselves connected with different types of fighting tunnels and defensive systems (during the tour you have a chance to look down into the lateral system) and headquarters dugouts. Leading off the subway were saps that led to heavy mortar positions built to be used in the opening of the Battle of Arras on 9 April 1917; another sap was dug to prepare a Wombat mine, also to be used in the attack on 9 April. A tour of the Grange gives an insight into the range of complexities of underground warfare that cannot be seen elsewhere on the British front, and possibly not anywhere else.

At the same time a tour of the publicly accessible parts of the Canadian Memorial site above ground gives a clear indication of the work of the British, French and German tunnellers, and thanks to their often meticulous records, war diaries and personal accounts it is possible to follow the logic of their activities. Those deep, ravaged craters of violently disturbed earth and chalk of

1915–1917 have now become hollows in the ground, rather pleasantly grassed over, smoothed and with the signs of havoc and chaos replaced by the pastoral scene of munching sheep under the shade of innumerable trees. They do, though, have a story to tell: a story of courage, fortitude, remarkable endurance and the triumph of the human spirit. The Vimy Memorial provides a unique visitor experience into the tunnellers' war – other places have parts of what is on offer here but the authors cannot think of a place that provides so many opportunities for a visitor to see something of the underground war. However, to be fully appreciated the site needs to be explained and understood, and in part this is what this book seeks to do.

Also at Vimy many kilometres of the fighting tunnels have been accessed in recent years and examined by the Durand Group, in which process several abandoned mine charges have been investigated, three of which were viable and neutralised. There is therefore an intimate understanding of what lies below the site and how the tunnels relate to what is visible on the surface. The experience here, of which the authors were a part, can also be extrapolated to a personal understanding of other similar mining systems along the front.

In Arras the visitor can access the Wellington Cave (and possibly other underground systems, especially that under the Town Hall, or Hotel de Ville). Wellington Cave was (partially) opened to the public in 2008 and the town of Arras has done a remarkable job with it. However, it shows only one aspect of the war underground; for example, the Wellington was never meant for fighting purposes – effectively it operated as an underground barracks, with communication tunnels leading from it towards the front and to other similar systems. Unlike many of the tunnels, the Wellington Cave was developed (in this case by the New Zealand Tunnelling Company) from a previously existing and huge underground cavity – the consequence of quarrying for chalk to be used in building the town above, a process which commenced back in the early Middle Ages. There are a large number of examples of this type of *souterraine* or cave in Artois and the Somme, admittedly of very different sizes. The point we are trying to make here is that it would be wrong to think that if you have seen the Grange there is no need to see Wellington, and vice versa. They each tell us something about very different aspects of the war underground.

The area between the Scarpe and the northern end of Vimy Ridge was notorious for the ferocity of its mine warfare, particularly for the period between January and July 1916, which involved French, British and German tunnellers. After this, offensive operations by the miners on both sides became less obvious. The number of mines blown fell dramatically (but of course did not cease altogether) and defensive operations became the norm, though preparations for offensive action on a big scale (such as the excavation of subways by the British tunnelling companies) were a feature of the winter of 1916/1917.

This book covers the creation of the subways all the way along Vimy Ridge, which stretches from beyond Souchez in the north almost down to Fampoux, on the Scarpe, in the south. It shows how the British tunnelling companies, taking over from the French in the area from early March to May 1916, set about containing German mining activities and launching their own counter-attacks. It gives a description of each of the subways that were created and the tours section will take you to their location above ground, usually in the area of the entrance. Mining incidents are covered and the story behind some of the existing craters is given; where a particular crater has been filled and restored to other usage – usually agriculture – we seek to take you to or near the spot. Some of the cemeteries where the remains of British tunnellers may be found or where they are commemorated are indicated. Two other *souterraines* or caves are described in some detail – that at Maison Blanche (particularly notable for its magnificent wartime carvings) and one above the Scarpe at Roeux (notable for its graffiti). A lengthy description is also given of the Goodman Subway, much of which has been accessed by the Durand Group.

Some Relevant Reading and Films

This book is supported by two others in the Battleground series: *Vimy Ridge* (1996, reprinted 2009), which covers the fighting on the Ridge from 1915 to its capture by the Allies, and *The Battle for Vimy Ridge – 1917* (2007), which is devoted almost entirely to the period of the arrival of the Canadian Corps and the run-up to the taking of their part of the Ridge in April 1917; this book also has a considerable amount of information on the German side of the wire. Both books provide extensive tours and details about related CWGC and German cemeteries and memorials. Jack Sheldon has written a first-rate book, *The German Army on Vimy Ridge 1914–1917* (2007), which includes a chapter on mine warfare there from the German perspective.

On mine warfare there are several books in print: *Beneath Flanders Field* (2004) is an excellent work on the tunnellers and is profusely illustrated with good diagrams and maps; it concentrates on the miners' war in Flanders, particularly the Ypres Salient and Messines Ridge. Simon Jones's *Underground Warfare 1914–1918* (2010) covers more areas of the tunnellers' war; for example, there is some coverage of tunnelling at Gallipoli, and there are chapters devoted to the extensive French mining efforts and German activities.

On the Battle of Arras there is Jonathan Nicholls' *Cheerful Sacrifice* (1990), which provides a sound overview, personal recollections and is an easy read; it is still in print. On the Canadian Corps' part in the battle, Alex Turner's *Vimy Ridge 1917* (2005) in the Osprey 'Campaign' series provides an accessible, informed and well illustrated (notably the graphics) account.

The Durand Group's investigation of the Broadmarsh Mine in 1997 and some subsequent work in defusing the nearby Durand Mine are the subject of a seventy-minute DVD, *One of Our Mines is Missing!* This has been shown fairly regularly on the History Channel, and can be purchased from the makers, Fougasse Films. In addition, the Durand Group has produced several multimedia DVD reports about the Vimy tunnels, including *O Sector*, *Fighting the Germans Underground* (covering certain German tunnels) and *The Goodman Subway*. We suggest that you use your search engine to find the titles, which often appear on Amazon, ebay or Fougasse Films.

Advice to Tourers

In the earlier volumes of the Battleground Europe series there was usually plenty of advice about hotels and other places to stay; now, with the widespread availability of the Internet, your best bet is to use your search engine to find up-to-date information. The Office de Tourisme d'Arras has a useful website, currently only available in French, though an English version may appear soon. Lists of hotels are given, with a range of prices from the reasonable to the quite pricey, and other useful information. You need to book through the Office if you want to go into the *boves* under the Town Hall, but see the Tours section for further information. Arras has a very fine and historic centre; the damage from the First World War was lovingly restored and the town gives the impression that its characteristic Flemish Gothic architecture has been there for centuries. Arras can be a confusing town in which to drive (which town these days is not?), but the growing popularity of satnav might make the journey somewhat simpler. The advantage of staying in Arras is the wide range of eateries and the pleasant evening strolls that can be taken. There is underground car parking, and parking in the Grande Place is often practicable, but beware the market on Saturday mornings. There are also occasional fairs and other activities there which also preclude most parking. The battlefields covered in this book are also quite easily reached should you be based on the Somme or in Ypres, and there are gites in some of the villages round about. If you want more detailed advice, some of the many thousands of contributors to the Great War Forum – http://1914-1918.invision.zone.com/forums – are likely to give you a wealth of useful tips. The Western Front Association provides a first-class magazine and a bulletin, which come out several times a year between them, sells a number of useful items (for example, DVDs of trench maps) and has its own forum (known as The Forum); there are often branch meetings for local areas of the Association, often involving a talk from a knowledgeable authority on some aspect of the war. It also has a most useful website. We would also strongly recommend another website, The Long Long Trail, http://www.1914-1918.net/, which is packed with a comprehensive amount of information on a great array of aspects of the war.

To reach the area covered in this book, the simplest way is to exit from the A26 péage (signposted Vimy, among others), leading on to the N17 Arras to Lens road and pick up the route from there.

Medical and Vehicle Insurance

We would strongly recommend that you take out travel and breakdown insurance; its cost pales into insignificance if something should go wrong and it provides peace of mind. Make sure that you contact your insurance company if necessary to extend the Green Card provision to comprehensive cover if that is what you have in the UK; in years past we have found that our insurers have made no charge for this service. It is worthwhile having medical insurance as well; at the very least ensure that you have your European Health Insurance Card; you can apply for this online at www.ehic.org.uk or call 0845 606 2030 – there is usually a three-week delay in getting it delivered (though experience indicates it can be a lot less); a temporary number can be obtained at short notice. It is worth bearing in mind that state provision in France does not cover all costs, hence the recommendation for medical insurance. As you are going to be wandering around an agricultural area it would be sensible to ensure that your tetanus jab is up to date.

If you are coming by car you will have the advantage of a flexible tour. The most fundamental thing to remember is to drive on the right – this may sound obvious, but it is quite easy to slip into 'British' habits, especially first thing in the morning or after a stop. The most perilous French regulation (and that of many other European countries) is the rule of priority from the right. If you are on a route marked on signs with a yellow diamond, then you have priority, otherwise be warned that cars can (and often do) shoot out from the right and they are legally correct to do so, no matter how insignificant the incoming road might be; usually, but not invariably, you are warned of this by a black 'x' road sign. This often applies in towns as well, though stop signs are far more common there than in rural areas. Speed limits can be strictly regulated and fines are both on the spot and steep. Do not even think about drinking and driving – the limits are lower than in the UK. You should have a first aid kit, a small fire extinguisher (actually in the car and not in the boot in some countries), a spare light bulb or two for your lights (the police can ask to see it) and a reflective vest/jacket at least for yourself (and preferably one for each of your passengers), also in the car and not the boot. You must have a red warning triangle to put up if you have any form of breakdown. These regulations change regularly, so make sure that you know the most up-to-date ones – you can get the most recent information from the AA website; not all of these are legal requirements yet in France but they are in other EU countries. You should carry your driving licence, proof of insurance, car registration certificate and passport with you at all times (and that includes not leaving them in the car when you go away from it). This can all sound a bit daunting, but we have driven for many years on the continent with no problems.

Clothing and Personal Equipment

This obviously depends to some extent on the time of the year. In the summer the Arras battlefield can be very hot, and so some water and sunscreen are advised. Have a lightweight, waterproof jacket as a minimum; in winter a heavier version is advisable. You will need good walking footgear: if you think you might be venturing into potentially very muddy areas, then take wellington boots, if there is space. (We would recommend a strong plastic bag or similar to put muddy footwear in at the end of a stop so that your car does not become a miniature mud bath itself.) A compass is useful, as are binoculars; a notebook (and functioning pens/pencils) to make a note of any photographs that you take (one field in France looks very much like another when it comes to reviewing them), though the very large storage capacity of modern digital cameras means that you can 'waste' shots on things like street signs and cemetery names to provide an aide memoire. A day sack will be useful in which to keep everything.

Theft, particularly from cars that are obviously tourist, can be a problem in many public parking areas. It takes only a few seconds to smash a window, open the vehicle and seize some of the contents. If you are leaving a car overnight, ensure that you remove everything of value. This may not be practical during the day when travelling between locations but be sure to put valuables out of sight and, if possible, park where there is secure oversight.

Refreshments

If you want to make the most of every day, then it is best to pick up the ingredients for a packed lunch. There is a supermarket close to the Place des Héros in Arras and there is a small supermarket in Vimy and a bakery in Neuville St Vaast; hardly an exclusive list, but we would recommend that you make the most of an opportunity while you can – leaving things until lunchtime might find you searching in vain to find somewhere open. There are reasonable restaurants in La Targette and one near the Vimy Memorial site, just before dropping into Givenchy. These tend to be very popular, so it is best to arrive on the early side of lunchtime. At Notre Dame de Lorette, near the excellent museum, the old, rather forlorn restaurant and bar has been renovated in recent years and you can get a good value meal – but it too tends to be busy. You can also get a baguette sandwich and a drink to the west of the N17 on the Vimy side of the traffic lights at Thélus. Beware August! Many of these places shut down for a few weeks for the annual holidays.

Maps

The maps in this book should enable you to get around the walks and most of the car tours; the major exceptions are the visit to Notre Dame de Lorette (which is well signposted), the cemeteries and Roeux. The IGN 1:25,000 Serie Bleu map 2406 E – ARRAS covers most of the area. The Green Series, 1:100,000, map No. 2 (Lille Dunkerque) includes all parts of the area covered by this book with the exception of Roeux, the relevant part of which is just off the map. We hope that the tour instructions for the visit to Roeux will be adequate. It is worth the investment, should you be seeking to extend your exploration to the south and the battlefields of the Somme, Cambrai and the actions of 1914 and 1918, to invest in No. 4 in the same series. We have occasionally included latitude and longitude coordinates for features to facilitate location by those with GPS satnavs. Coordinates are generally good to better than 10 metres. In most cases we have also included trench map grid coordinates.

Some Warnings and 'Do Nots'

We have indicated in this book several locations of entrances to subways, caves and *souterraines*. There are, we hope obvious, statements to be made about this. Apart from the publicly available systems at Vimy and Wellington Cave, <u>all</u> of the others are private property and are not generally open to the public; Maison Blanche might be, under very controlled and limited conditions (see the Tours Section). Do not start exploring when holes open up in the ground – the underground conditions can be extremely perilous and any entrance is likely to be the most perilous part of all. Any form of excavation without consultation with the appropriate authorities is illegal, even with the consent of the landowner. There are strict rules and regulations concerning the use of metal detectors (basically, do not) and the handling of artefacts; munitions are capable of exploding through movement or vibration. They were designed to kill and they can still do so; particularly dangerous are grenades and gas shells. With less fragile objects, such as unexpended small–arms ammunition, you are likely to be in serious trouble if found in possession of them either in France or the UK. Please observe all restrictions on the Vimy Memorial site and leave all munitions or suspicious or unfamiliar looking bits of rusty material alone.

Potential battlefield hazards: (top left) a spiked man trap; (top right) a spigot mortar bomb; (below left) a Stokes mortar bomb; (below right) a Livens projector gas bomb. All are potentially lethal to unwary visitors.

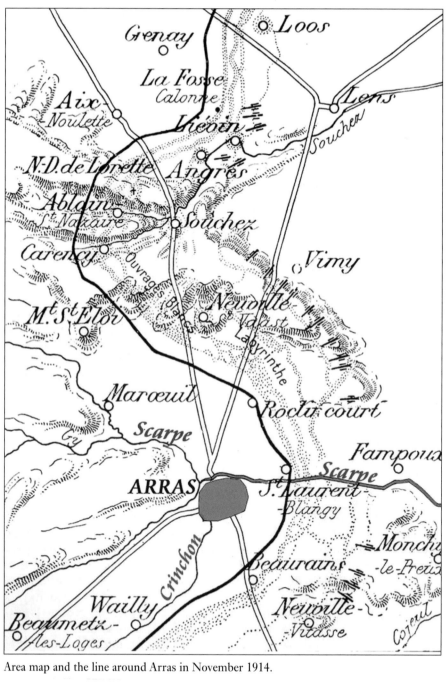

Area map and the line around Arras in November 1914.

Chapter 1

An Introduction to Military Mining

Historical Background

The concept of undermining enemy fortifications dates back well into antiquity. It has been surmised that the fall of the walls of Jericho was the result of an Israelite mining operation. Mining was certainly used by the Romans and became a significant feature in medieval sieges. The technique was to create a large chamber beneath the walls of a stronghold and then burn away the props, resulting in the collapse of the walls above.

With the advent of explosives, mining attack and mining counter-measures became a major factor in siegecraft, a sophisticated science in its own right, influencing besiegers' tactics and the design and construction of fortifications. This extended well into the nineteenth century, with mining operations by both sides at the siege of Sebastopol in 1854–1855 and, rather less well known, during the siege of the Lucknow Residency in 1857–1858 during the Bengal Army Mutiny.

Diagram of the mining technique prior to the use of explosives.

Protracted siege warfare and mining did not, however, play a major part in the Franco-Prussian War of 1870-1871, where the French fortresses were forced to surrender through containment or powerful bombardment. After 1871 the opinion of most artillery and engineer officers of the great military powers was that large-calibre artillery would always defeat fortresses where previously mining might have been the only solution. An unexpected revival of mine warfare during the Russo-Japanese War of 1904–1905, notably during the siege of Port Arthur by the Japanese, led the major European powers to reconsider the application of mining to attacks on fixed defences and the French, Germans and British re-examined their procedures and undertook exercises in mining. In the British case a major siege exercise was undertaken at Chatham in 1907 and a modest mining capability was incorporated into two Royal Engineer Fortress Companies.

Nevertheless the prevailing view was that a European war would be characterised by rapid movement and manoeuvre and would not permit the creation of extensive obstacles and defences. In respect of the experience of the

Russo-Japanese war, a commentator in the *Militär Wochenblatt* in 1910 stated, 'We shall never see a war in Europe like that in Manchuria, still less like that in South Africa. Such extended and strongly fortified positions will never be reproduced in Europe.' It therefore came as something of a shock to all the belligerents in 1914 when, following the defeat of the German advance at the battle of the Marne, and the blocking at the battles of First Ypres (October–November 1914) of the attempted outflanking movements, popularly known as the 'race to the sea', the protagonists became entrenched along the whole line of what became the Western Front. An unprecedented situation of what amounted to mutual siege had developed whereby any offensive action would necessitate direct frontal assault against increasingly strong defences.

The Start of Mining on the Western Front

Almost immediately resourceful commanders began to exploit the possibilities of attacking the enemy defences from underground, although their initial efforts were very small scale by the standards of later mining activities. The French were first into this field, beginning mining operations in the Argonne before the end of October 1914 and just south of the Somme in November 1914. The Germans quickly countered and by late November 1914 both sides had utilised a variety of small mines in support of local offensive operations.

Nor was the British Expeditionary Force (BEF) slow to perceive the possibilities and the dangers. On 3 December 1914 General Sir Henry Rawlinson, then commanding IV Corps, wrote to GHQ suggesting the formation of a special battalion of sappers and miners for such work. Simultaneously, the Dehra Dun Brigade of the Indian Corps attempted, unsuccessfully, to attack a German trench using a 45 lb (20 kg) charge of guncotton placed at the end of a shallow tunnel.

First honours on the British front, however, went to the Germans. On 20 December 1914 they attacked the Sirhind Brigade of the Indian Corps on the Givenchy–Festubert front with ten small mines (effectively bore-hole charges) placed against the forward fire trenches. Though they were small, the physical and morale effect of these mines was considerable and the shaken survivors were driven back to their reserve line.

GHQ instructed the Army HQs (First and Second Army were established on 26 December) to proceed with offensive sapping and mining. However, the RE Field Companies were already overwhelmed with other essential duties. Units made various extempore arrangements, collecting up men with mining experience and forming miscellaneous mining platoons and sections. Meanwhile the Germans continued to extend the use of mining and on 25 January 1915 exploded about twenty on the Cuinchy front.

The Development of the BEF Mining Organisation

In December 1914 Sir John Norton-Griffiths had written to the War Office proposing the formation of special companies of what he termed 'moles'.

Inset: Major (later Lieutenant Colonel) Sir John Norton-Griffiths. (*RE Museum*) Sir John Norton-Griffiths (centre), pictured in about 1915 beside the 2-ton Rolls-Royce he commandeered from his wife. (*From Tony Bridgland*, Tunnelmaster and Arsonist of the Great War, *pl. 26*)

Although but a major in the 2nd King Edward's Horse, a regiment he had personally raised at his own expense, Norton-Griffiths was a Member of Parliament, had been closely associated with Lord Kitchener (the Secretary of State for War) during the Boer War and was the entrepreneurial head of a company of international engineering and mining contractors. At the time one of his firms was engaged in digging tunnels for sewers under Manchester, using a specialist technique known as clay kicking, which allowed small dimension tunnels to be driven quickly through clay. More importantly, certainly in military terms, it was a technique that permitted nearly silent excavation in clay.

Following an interview with Lord Kitchener and a swift reconnaissance in February 1915, Norton-Griffiths was ordered to raise clay kickers and miners for service. The War Office authorised the formation of eight tunnelling companies, originally to consist of six officers and 227 soldiers. As an incentive to recruitment, qualified clay kickers were to be paid 6 shillings per day – three times the pay of a qualified sapper in the Royal Engineers. This disparity in pay gave rise to many subsequent complications, but that is another story.

In what was possibly the fastest-ever formation and deployment of a unit to operations, the first eighteen clay kickers, the nucleus of 170 Tunnelling Company, were enlisted on Thursday, 17 February 1915 in Manchester,

GRAFTING TOOL   CLAY-KICKER ON THE CROSS   THE CROSS

A clay kicker working on 'The Cross'.

processed through the Royal Engineers depot in Chatham, shipped to France and started work at Givenchy on Monday, 21 February. Swiftly converted from civilians to soldiers, they were duly issued with rifles, the use of which was initially a mystery, but they were relieved of ammunition before accidents might occur! The new recruits in these units, aged anything up to 60, did not readily conform to military discipline and the officers commanding the newly formed tunnelling companies had to exercise considerable and pragmatic tact in integrating their often unruly and outspoken charges into the military environment.

The build-up of the mining companies followed quickly, with the enlistment of the few clay kickers available plus men from other mining disciplines, along with a comb-out of Royal Engineer, infantry and other units for suitably qualified personnel. Regular Royal Engineer officers were initially appointed to command, but most of the other tunnelling officers were found by enlisting experienced mineral miners from all over the world and putting them through a brief military training course at the RE depot in Chatham. By June 1915 the eighth tunnelling company (178 Company) had been deployed, but by then the mine fighting had developed in intensity, and the raising and training of further companies proceeded. The first Dominion company in the field, deployed in December 1915, was the 3rd Canadian Tunnelling Company RCE (raised from Canadian units already in France); perhaps because of this, it was the only one of the three Canadian tunnelling companies not disbanded in the summer of 1918.

By the end of June 1916 mining operations were being conducted along almost two-thirds of the BEF front. Likewise substantial sectors of the French Front were subject to intensive mining operations; a particular example where plenty of evidence may be seen today is at Vauquois, northwest of Verdun. By this stage the BEF mining establishment comprised thirty-three tunnelling companies, made up of twenty-five (Imperial or British) Tunnelling Companies RE; three (Canadian) Tunnelling Companies RCE; three (Australian) Tunnelling Companies RAE; one (New Zealand) Tunnelling Company RNZE; and the Australian Electrical & Mechanical, Mining & Boring Company (the ABC, or Alphabetical, Company). A Portuguese mining company was also incorporated into the BEF in 1917, but too late to accomplish much.

The companies were army troops, which is to say their dispositions were decided at GHQ level, and their activities controlled from each army head-quarters. In consequence they generally remained on a particular sector of the front for as long as they were required there, although companies in areas of particularly intensive mine fighting were sometimes switched to less arduous sectors.

As the mining effort and organisation expanded, a staff under Brigadier General (later Major-General) R.N. Harvey was formed at GHQ and each of the BEF armies (ultimately five) had a staff branch headed by a lieutenant colonel controller of mines and a mine warfare school. The establishment of each tunnelling company was finally settled at 568 all ranks under the command of a major and with eighteen other officers, including a medical officer. The table on page 12 shows the organisation of the 3rd Australian Tunnelling Company in about mid-1917, when it was somewhat over strength, with 672 all ranks. Additionally, when in the line, the tunnelling companies frequently had up to 500 infantry attached for labour duties,

Brigadier (later Major General) R.N. Harvey, Controller of Mines at GHQ from late 1915.

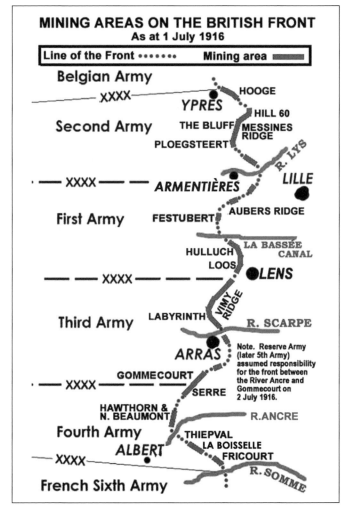

MINING AREAS ON THE BRITISH FRONT
As at 1 July 1916

Line of the Front ••••••	Mining area ▬▬▬

Belgian Army

XXXX

YPRES — HOOGE

HILL 60

Second Army — THE BLUFF — MESSINES RIDGE

PLOEGSTEERT

R. LYS

XXXX — ARMENTIÈRES — LILLE

First Army — FESTUBERT — AUBERS RIDGE

LA BASSÉE CANAL

HULLUCH

LOOS

XXXX — LENS

VIMY RIDGE

Third Army — LABYRINTH — R. SCARPE

ARRAS

Note. Reserve Army (later 5th Army) assumed responsibility for the front between the River Ancre and Gommecourt on 2 July 1916.

GOMMECOURT

SERRE

HAWTHORN & N. BEAUMONT

R. ANCRE

Fourth Army — THIEPVAL

ALBERT — LA BOISSELLE — FRICOURT

XXXX

R. SOMME

French Sixth Army

The mining areas on the BEF front, June 1916.

so their average daily strength was often about 1,000 all ranks. At its peak, in about June 1916, there were between 30,000 and 40,000 men in the BEF engaged on mining and related activities. By extrapolating this figure to the whole of the Western Front, it has been estimated that around 120,000 or more men of both sides were engaged in mining at this stage.

As the BEF expanded and relieved the French along sectors of the front, so they moved out of the clay of Flanders into the chalk areas south from Armentières. In the spring of 1915 they moved into northern Artois, taking over the line to Loos, and in July 1915 Third Army was formed, replacing the French from the River Somme to Gommecourt. Then in March 1916 the First and Third Armies gradually replaced the French Tenth Army in Artois, forming a continuous BEF line from just north of Ypres to the Somme. In central Artois, along the Vimy Ridge to the south of Arras, they inherited an already fiercely contested mining war from the French. It is with this embattled mining area that this book is concerned.

Mine Warfare

In the early stages, mining attack was largely directed towards inflicting casualties and demoralising the enemy rather than achieving a specific tactical advantage. However, it was quickly integrated into the broader battle situation, aimed at fulfilling local tactical requirements. In essence there developed three main forms for mine charges: offensive, defensive and tactical.

As implied by the name, offensive mines were those placed to attack enemy positions. These were in turn separated into Common Mines and Fougasse Mines, the former being so placed as to demolish whatever lay above, the latter to bury an enemy position with debris. Defensive mines were designed to destroy or disrupt enemy mining. This was usually done by placing a camouflet charge close to enemy tunnelling works with the object of destroying the enemy galleries and (ideally) killing their miners. A camouflet is defined as a subsurface charge designed to be contained in the earth and not break surface, although some resulted in craters formed by ground collapse into the void created. Tactical mines served a variety of other purposes. These could include denying ground, creating an obstacle, providing an advanced position, providing high rims for observation or screening off an enemy position and blocking a line of fire.

A variation on the theme included bored mines, in which a charge was laid along a horizontal bore, usually to blow a trench across No Man's Land, occasionally to blow a section of enemy trench. Initially this was attempted by employing a technique known as pipe pushing, whereby a pipe was driven through the earth by a hydraulic ram, but this proved uncertain at best, as solid material along the line could divert the pipe, in the worst case back towards the pipe pushers. Ultimately an Australian hand-drilling machine, known as a Wombat, was adopted. A versatile machine, it served numerous other purposes, such as providing ventilation and chimney shafts for dugouts.

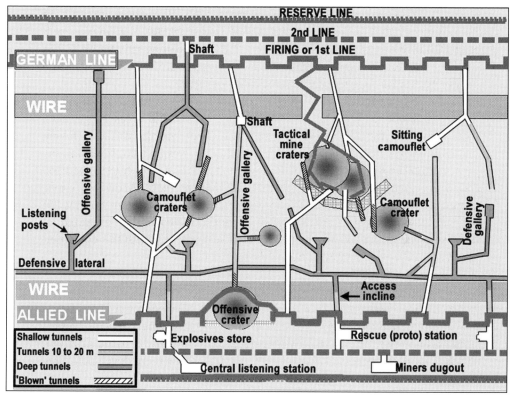

Schematic diagram of a 'mature' mining area.

On the BEF front mine warfare reached its maximum intensity in June 1916. That month British and Dominion miners fired 101 mines or camouflets, the Germans 126: a total of 227. Some sections of the front took on the appearance of a lunar landscape, with a string of massive and often overlapping craters, many over 50 feet deep and 200 feet in diameter. Up to this stage BEF mining activity had been largely reactive, aimed at protecting the infantry from mining attack and retaliating for enemy blows, but as a degree of parity was achieved the defined policy was to establish subsurface defences and only employ offensive mining to fulfil definitive tactical objectives. The tunnelling companies largely focused on driving deep lateral tunnels 60 to 100 feet below (or just ahead of) and parallel to the firing line, with listening posts at frequent intervals. In effect it was a subterranean defensive line from which

A Wombat hand drilling rig.

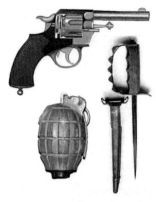

Tunnellers' weapons: a Webley revolver, a No. 36 grenade and a fighting knife. Their principal weapon, though, was explosive delivered in various forms.

they could also drive defensive galleries to meet and counter approaching enemy tunnels.

At times the rival tunnellers quite literally met, most commonly in the clay areas in Flanders, and the miners, entering each other's tunnels, engaged in close-quarter fighting in the pitch dark with knives, revolvers or grenades, or sought to blow in enemy workings with portable charges.

The culmination of the offensive policy, indeed of mine warfare on the Western Front, was the Second Army attack on Messines Ridge on 7 June 1917. On a front of just over 14.5 kilometres and in conjunction with a concentrated artillery barrage from 2,266 guns, nineteen deep mines, with a total of 937,450 lbs of explosive, were fired.

The explosions were clearly heard in London and registered on a seismograph in Switzerland. The German defence was totally shattered, with several thousand German troops obliterated by the explosions; some estimates say as many as 10,000 men were lost. One of the most strongly fortified positions on the Western Front was taken within an hour or so with, initially, few casualties among the assaulting troops.

Mining Techniques and Practice

The conduct of mining operations became a very sophisticated process, creating its own unique tactical and technological innovations. It involved geological and

A 'proto' mine rescue station. Note the cages for canaries.

explosives sciences, especial medical considerations, extraordinary logistical requirements and many other specialist activities. The rescue organisation required that every company had 'protomen', miners trained in the use of breathing apparatus and resuscitation techniques. Listening, to identify and track enemy workings, was brought to a high art by employing various instruments, most notably the geophone, and in some sectors was developed to the extent of having central listening stations linked to an array of seismomicrophones. Precise survey, both on the surface and in the confines of the tunnel, was vital. Ventilation was essential, involving a mix of natural air flow and pumping air through ducts, as also was pumping out water from tunnels prone to flooding. Calculation of explosive charges entailed complex mathematics – and there was much more. It is not intended here to expand this into a treatise on the subject; there are a number of excellent books available, as will be apparent from the bibliography, and some of the details will be covered in successor books in this series.

A listening officer with geophones.

Notwithstanding the techniques and technology, it all came down to the miner on the spot and competent leadership. Manual skills, physical strength, endurance, guile and cold courage of a very high order were required. Nor should we forget the miners' 'friends' – the canaries and white mice used to warn of the greatest

SEISMOMICROPHONE

Seismomicrophones were used for remote listening, The vibration of a lead mass (M), supported by rubber rings, was recorded by a microphone comprising two carbon discs (P1 and P2), which transmitted the results to a central listening receiver.

underground killer, carbon monoxide, given off by the explosives and otherwise undetectable.

As will become apparent in subsequent chapters, the mining techniques of the combatant nations differed in a number of respects. In particular, the construction of extensive defensive laterals appears to have been a predominantly British practice. The French seem to have generally preferred to minimise the amount of spoil to be removed by excavating smaller tunnels, but that imposed some restriction on working at a tunnel face. The Germans often went deeper than the British miners, and instances of tunnels up to 150 feet deep have been found. They had a preference for vertical shafts over inclines and were far more likely to close-timber their galleries (that is, to line them with stout planks), even in sound chalk.

Mining officer - *"What the devil are you men doing here when the canary is dead?"*
Sapper - *"That bird never 'ad any guts Sir."*

Cartoon from 172 Tunnelling Company's Christmas newsletter, 1915.

Explosives

Guncotton and gunpowder were used in the early mines. However, from early 1915 the British mostly employed ammonal. This is a compound of 65% ammonium nitrate, 15% TNT, 17% coarse aluminium and 3% charcoal. It is an inert, slow-lifting explosive. To explode it has to be 'hit' by a powerful detonation wave, usually provided by guncotton primers. These in turn have to be initiated by detonators containing highly sensitive fulminate of mercury.

Major I.A. Jones MBE, of the Durand Group, demonstrating in a tunnel magazine how pairing two ammonal bags facilitated porterage. (*Durand Group*)

Firing was usually with an electrical circuit. For some very large mines gelignite boosters were also employed. The French and Germans used similar ammonium nitrate-based explosives, such as cheddite and wesfalite.

For ease of porterage underground, the ammonal was frequently decanted from 50 lb tins into 25 lb rubberised bags, clamped with wooden slats. Ammonium nitrate has preservative properties that have protected the bags and most of the ammonal recently located in the tunnels under Vimy Ridge remains in nearly prime condition.

Employment of the Mining Companies

The mining companies became very versatile units. As the underground war reached a degree of equilibrium their energies were increasingly directed into the excavation of subways (see Chapter 4), providing underground accommodation in *souterraines* (see Chapter 3), the construction of dugouts and command centres, and facilitating the engineer field companies with hardening defences. Following offensive operations they were frequently employed on the construction of road and rail communications. As experts in handling explosives, it fell to them to seek out and disarm booby traps and delayed action demolitions and traps. They frequently accompanied infantry raiding parties, with the task of destroying enemy mine shafts and dugout entrances. At the time of the German *Kaiserschlacht* and subsequent offensives, from March to June 1918, some were committed to the infantry role and acquitted themselves well, while during the advances of the so-called Hundred Days, in addition to their role hunting explosive traps, many companies added bridging to their other talents.

Captain H.W. Graham encapsulates something of the nature and spirit of the miners and mining companies. He described his experiences on joining 185 Tunnelling Company:

> To begin with, then, none of us were soldiers in the strict sense of the term, but our technical training was what was required in Mine Warfare. We were expected to acquire military knowledge, parade deportment, etc., subsequently during our spells of rest out of the line and of course this we did. A miner, however, gains certain stern qualities in his professional duties during peace time; he is constantly faced with sudden dangers, which have to be tackled without hesitation and with decision, and to avoid suspected dangers in such a way as to imply uncanny caution. At any rate, popular imagination credits us with these attributes, but, lest I be accused of heroics, let me say none of us believed in them! In military matters, who can be surprised then that a Tunneller was often subject to some chaff, but seldom scorn, and, to be sure, on that account, I took advantage to get off parade duties and other tedious work at Rouen [Rouen was a major base camp]. A keener set of men to learn than Tunnellers would be hard to find in a day's march and we were never too proud to be taught the 'other man's' job.

Casualties

Casualties among the tunnellers hardly bear comparison with those among their infantry colleagues. Nevertheless the toll was not light. In all, 181 tunnelling officers lost their lives, including nine from the Canadian companies, twelve from the Australian Companies and three from the New Zealand Company. This amounts to close to 20 per cent of established officer strength. There are no official figures for the number of men from the tunnelling companies who were killed or died in the course of the war, but Peter Barton, a co-author of *Beneath Flanders Fields* and other books, cites a total of 1,516.

An example of the composition of a tunnelling company (3rd Australian Tunnelling Company, March 1917) is given below:

Company Headquarters:

Officer Commanding	Major
Adjutant	Captain or Lieutenant
Medical Officer RAMC	
Company Sergeant Major	Warrant Officer Class 2
Company Quartermaster Sergeant	

36 Other Ranks, including draughtsmen, clerks, drivers, cooks, storemen and batmen

	Mining Sections				
	1	**2**	**3**	**4**	**Total**
Section Commander (Captain or Lieutenant)	1	1	1	1	4
Section Officer (2/Lieutenant or Lieutenant)	3	3	3	3	12
Blacksmiths *	1	1	1	1	4
Carpenters *	1	1	1	1	4
Storekeepers	1	1	1	1	4
Cooks	5	6	6	5	22
Listeners	8	8	4	8	28
Permanent Protomen	2	2	2	3	9
Other trades	7	8	8	6	29
Miners	82	86	94	77	339
Labourers	46	42	41	47	176
TOTALS (all ranks)	157	159	162	153	631

Total company strength: 19 officers and 653 other ranks
* Blacksmiths and Carpenters temporarily employed at Company Headquarters.

Chapter 2

Background to Tunnelling Operations North of the Scarpe

Tunnelling operations form the core of this book, which for the most part is concerned with British tunnelling activity, although some acknowledgement is made to the work of the French, and rather more to the German, tunnellers. In many respects the tunnellers were fighting their own private war on a day-to-day basis, but their work was vital for the protection of the infantry as well as for bigger offensive operations, especially on this sector of the Front.

In 1915 the French launched two major assaults in the area covered by this book: one in the spring, in May, and one in the autumn, commencing in September. 1916 was a year of relative calm on the surface but of considerable activity underground as both sides attempted to win the mine war – or at least to establish some sort of control over the mining activities of the enemy. 1917 was dominated by the BEF's spring offensive and then, as explained elsewhere in the book, mine warfare in this sector almost ceased and tunnellers were assigned to different, though often related, engineering tasks.

What is clear is that tunnelling was significant in the offensives of 1915 and very significant for those of 1917. Obviously they formed only a part in the planning and operational process, so it is important to have a basic idea of the nature, aims and execution of these great, hugely expensive, offensives.

The Background to the Battles of Artois
A few lines might summarise the opening of the First World War on the Western Front. The Germans launched their principal attack through Belgium and Luxembourg, with the aim of enveloping the French army by sweeping around Paris to the west and then driving towards its forces on the border, in effect sandwiching the French army and forcing their submission. For a variety of reasons this plan failed, this first move ending in the halting of the German advance on the Marne and the subsequent withdrawal of the German army to good defensive positions in the area of the Aisne. By mid-September it was clear that if any sort of decision was to be reached it would be by outflanking the enemy to the north, and there followed a series of attempts by both sides to outflank the other, culminating in often desperate fighting around Ypres. After this both sides settled down over the winter, exhausted by their efforts, both physically and in terms of war matériel.

Like any summary, this is all quite true, but the devil, as always, lies in the detail. In particular, this book concerns itself with an area where there was very heavy fighting in the autumn of 1914 but which gets lost in 'a series of attempts by both sides to outflank the other'; the British approach tends then to centre on the First Battle of Ypres to the exclusion, quite often, of the considerable number of Belgian and French troops involved in that action and even to the part of the British II Corps. The British Official History somewhat wryly notes: 'The fighting on the La Bassée front, so far as the valour and determination of the troops on both sides are concerned, was as desperate as that at Ypres, but it never had the same strategic or sentimental importance.'

If the role of British II Corps (and, to some extent, III Corps) gets lost in the coverage of the struggle along the Menin Road, the French army all but disappears in the popular narrative after the Marne – even, to a considerable degree, among the French themselves. In recent years, however, we have been fortunate that Jack Sheldon's coverage of the German army's activities on the Somme and Vimy Ridge has included a significant amount on the fighting of 1914 and 1915, which involved the French in these areas.

Although both sides were, indeed, exhausted by the end of the attempt to outflank each other, this did not mark the end of limited scale offensive fighting. The situation in this sector had left the Germans in control of Vimy Ridge and established on the eastern end of the Notre Dame de Lorette heights. This position provided security for the economically significant Douai plain to the east, industrially rich and home to some of France's most productive coalmines. The position also provided good cover for its artillery and allowed the Germans to dominate Arras to the south, the eastern and southern fringes of which town were also challenged by them.

In December the French launched an unsuccessful attack to take Carency, as part of an attempt by the French Tenth Army to create a suitable line from which to launch a major assault; on the Lorette heights, a gradual process of nibbling at the German positions by XXI Corps achieved some success. Then the Germans launched an attack in early March 1915, taking full advantage of their enormous superiority in trench and heavy mortars and firing a number of mines. Within a few hours they had advanced 600 metres and captured the whole of Spur of the Arabs, running off the Lorette heights. There followed several days of bitter fighting in atrocious weather conditions and with the ground in a horrendous state, at the end of which the French retook the lost ground, at a

Mine crater in Carency. (*Jack Sheldon*)

A French miner at the opening of a new mine shaft, probably in the Carency area. (*Fonds documentaries Alain Jacques*)

total cost of some 3,300 casualties. This small but bitter fight is notable for an early use of mines, in this case as part of an attack. The French continued to chew away at the German positions on the all-important heights, the capture of which would be essential for a successful operation against the German positions on Vimy Ridge, especially its northernmost and highest part.

The Second and Third Battles of Artois

All of this small-scale fighting was the prelude to the launching of the Second Battle of Artois (the fighting in autumn 1914 was the First) on 9 May 1915 by the Tenth Army on a 20-kilometre front; five corps were involved and a considerable weight of artillery was provided. The attack commenced at 10 am; it was notable for the success of the Moroccan Division, which managed to reach Hill 145 and La Folie Farm on the crest of the Vimy ridge. Their efforts are today marked by the Moroccan memorial, not far from Hill 145. But the division lacked support, reserves were held back for too long and units on its flanks were less successful. The line was held, however, on the western side of Zouave Valley, just to the east of the current Cabaret Rouge Cemetery. In the following fortnight the heights of Notre Dame de Lorette were secured and on 16 June General d'Urbal launched another major attack, using twenty divisions, but with minimal results. Again the Moroccans managed to gain the ridge line at Hill 119; again they had to fall back for lack of success on their flanks. This

Zouave soldiers of the French Moroccan Division.

French miners operating an electrical winch at the head of a mine shaft, probably in the Labyrinth area. (*Fonds documentaries Alain Jacques*)

spring offensive had advanced the French line on average 3 kilometres and they had taken 7,400 prisoners; the Lorette Heights were taken, along with some villages, notably Carency and Ablain St Nazaire. The French, too, had used mines successfully, particularly under the German defences before Carency. Some flavour of the type of fighting involved in this battle is to be found in Jack Sheldon's *The German Army on Vimy Ridge*, recording the experiences of the 2nd and 3rd Battalions of Bavarian Reserve Infantry 10 in and around Neuville St Vaast at the start of the battle:

Right in the front line. Reserve Oberleutnant Habenicht, commanding 9th Company, was sitting in his newly constructed dugout when he looked at his watch. It was 10.00 am. 'How many have you counted so far?' '2,000, Herr Oberleutnant,' replied his orderlies. '2,000,' muttered the officer, '2,000 since 7.30 am on this tiny piece of ground!' Seconds later the dugout swayed violently or, rather, it was heaved up into the air, just as though it had been hoisted by a giant hand. 'That was a mine that they have just exploded,' bawled *Offizierstellvertreter* Lobherr, commander of the left hand platoon. A second huge explosion followed. The survivors scrambled out of their dugouts, shouting, 'We are all going to be blown up!' but they retreated quickly because it was no longer possible to count the impact of incoming shells. Red-hot shell fragments, clods of earth, sandbags and other debris flew in all directions, pouring down the steps to the dugouts where the defenders, hardly visible because of the fumes and smoke, waited grimly.

Lobherr kept a look-out himself, but could only risk taking swift glimpses; the scythe of death was swinging dangerously close. All of a sudden, at 11.45 am, all was still – just as if an engine had been switched off. 'Here they come,' he roared, 'everybody out of the dugout!' About fifteen men, their senses reeling, raced to climb the dugout steps. Looking out, their eyes lit upon enemy infantry in immense numbers: several battalions, line after line of them, twelve ranks deep, were approaching at an easy pace, not expecting to meet any opposition.

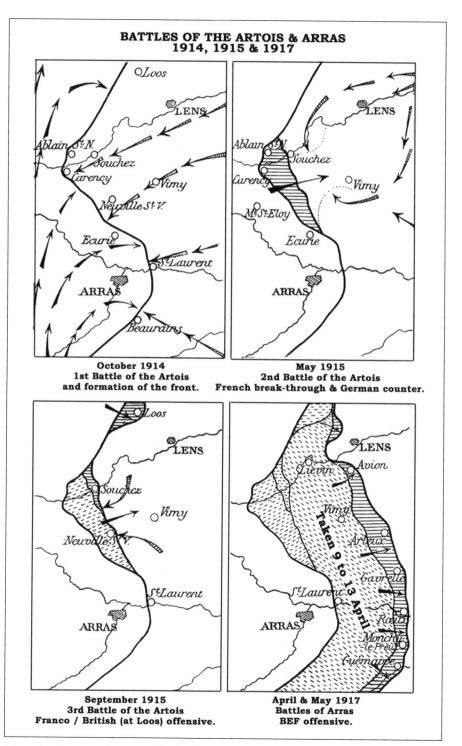

Maps showing several stages of the battles of the Artois and Arras.

The cost had been formidable: some 102,500 casualties (compared with approximately 160,000 British and Dominion casualties for the Battle of Arras in 1917, which lasted about the same length of time but which covered a significantly bigger front).

In September the French launched another offensive in Artois (the Third Battle, 1915), deploying six corps and seventeen divisions, this time with more guns, particularly those of heavy calibre, and with a massive deployment of gas. In addition, the British attacked simultaneously to the north of Lorette, before Loos and Hulluch, and many kilometres to the south the French launched a major attack in the Champagne. It was not very successful; Souchez eventually fell on the 26th but to the south of Neuville St Vaast progress beyond the Labyrinth, which had been taken in confused and chaotic fighting during the Second Battle of Artois, was negligible. In the following days the French advance crept up the western slopes of Vimy Ridge; by the time a temporary halt was called to the offensive, in mid October, the French had lost almost 37,000 men. A final thrust, in November, which lasted about a week, resulted in no appreciable gains but another 12,000 casualties. The fighting of 1915 in Artois had cost France over 150,000 casualties, excluding what has become known as 'trench wastage' in the periods between the major attacks. What had been achieved?

The Germans had been removed from positions that dominated Arras; the French line had been advanced so that it was just short of the commanding heights of Vimy Ridge, overlooking the Douai Plain; and the attacks had removed the possibility of the German army structuring a defence position in depth. For the Germans, they had held the line and they still – more or less – held the crest of Vimy Ridge. The new French positions were difficult, as they could be overlooked by the Germans and lacked a secure supply and communications route. The situation was far from comfortable for either side. Both now engaged in intensive mining operations to gain the tactical advantage and push the other off or further back from the Ridge. In this the Germans were the more successful, epitomised by the series of limited Rupprecht attacks in February 1916 (see Chapter Six).

Street scene in Neuville St Vaast, May 1915. (*Jack Sheldon*)

The British Takeover and Thereafter

The British began to arrive in this sector in early March 1916, taking over the French line at the urgent request of Joffre, whose army was under severe threat from the massive offensive launched by the Germans at Verdun on 21 February. The sector had become a fairly quiet one, with the notable exception of the fierce struggle that was going on under the Ridge. This aspect is well covered in the book and there is little point going over it here. The line north of Arras and up to the French frontier and beyond 'enjoyed' 1916 without great incident (Fromelles, 19–20 July, providing the only major – and tragic – offensive action), as attention was drawn to the long-drawn-out and titanic struggles on the Somme and at Verdun. All this was to change in 1917.

This is no place to go into a detailed exposition of the background to the Battle of Arras, 9 April–16 May 1917. The British part in an offensive masterminded by Joffre's replacement, the dynamic, convincing and articulate (and bi-lingual – he was fluent in English, thanks to an English mother) Robert Nivelle, involved an assault by Third Army, attacking either side of the River Scarpe. The only part of First Army (Horne) that would take an active part on the first day of the offensive was the Canadian Corps (extensively reinforced by the addition of the 5th (British or Imperial) Division and the heavy artillery and other resources of First Army). Their task was to capture the northern half of Vimy Ridge, thereby ensuring that German positions situated there could not disrupt the advance of Third Army (Allenby) to the south.

How did the tunnellers fit into this operation? An enormous effort had been put in by the British tunnelling companies to 'win' the mining war on the Ridge in 1916, and generally speaking they had reached an acceptable degree of success by the early summer. After that neither side wanted to blow mines without good reason, and while it would be a considerable overstatement to say that all was quiet underground from July 1916, there were considerably fewer blows than there had been in the frenetic preceding months. Once the defensive underground systems were established, the tunnellers became available for other tasks. They were now working through chalk, and the possibilities of digging adequately sized tunnels for use by infantry as passageways and for various types of secure accommodation, in a relatively short period of time, were very attractive. Thus the tunnelling companies set about the construction and elaboration

General Sir Henry Horne GCB, KCMG. Horne was GOC First Army at the opening of the Battle of Arras.

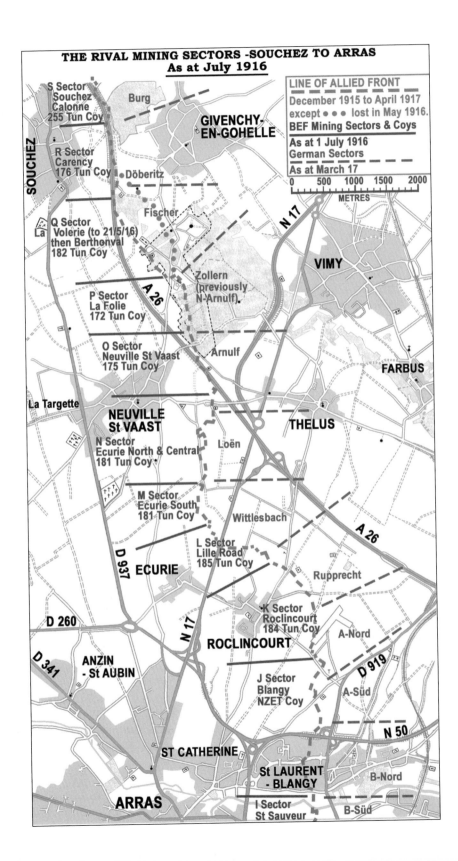

THE RIVAL MINING SECTORS - SOUCHEZ TO ARRAS
As at July 1916

LINE OF ALLIED FRONT
December 1915 to April 1917
except ● ● ● lost in May 1916.
BEF Mining Sectors & Coys
As at 1 July 1916
German Sectors
As at March 17

0   500   1000   1500   2000
METRES

S Sector
Souchez
Calonne
255 Tun Coy

Burg

GIVENCHY-
EN-GOHELLE

SOUCHEZ

R Sector
Carency
176 Tun Coy

• Döberitz

• Fischer

N 17

La

Q Sector
Volerie (to 21/5/16)
then Berthonval
182 Tun Coy

A 26

Zollern
(previously
N-Arnulf)

VIMY

P Sector
La Folie
172 Tun Coy

O Sector
Neuville St Vaast
175 Tun Coy

Arnulf

FARBUS

La Targette

NEUVILLE
St VAAST

Loën

THELUS

N Sector
Ecurie North & Central
181 Tun Coy

M Sector
Ecurie South
181 Tun Coy

Wittlesbach

A 26

D 937

ECURIE

L Sector
Lille Road
185 Tun Coy

Rupprecht

D 260

N 17

K Sector
Roclincourt
184 Tun Coy

A-Nord

D 341

ANZIN
- St AUBIN

ROCLINCOURT

D 919

J Sector
Blangy
NZET Coy

A-Süd

N 50

ST CATHERINE

ARRAS

St LAURENT
- BLANGY

B-Nord

I Sector
St Sauveur

B-Süd

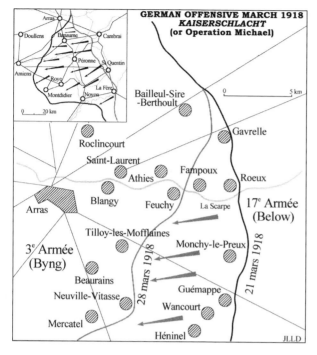

Map showing the German offensive in the Artois and gains in March 1918. (*Jean-Luc Lethos Duclos*)

of a number of subways, extending pre-existing caves or *souterraines* and in general seeking to make use of their numbers and expertise to provide the offensive with as much underground support for the forthcoming offensive as possible. In this they succeeded admirably.

The Battle of Arras had some success, most notably in its earliest stages, when considerable advances were made and the Canadian Corps and British XVII Corps, memorably, captured the whole of the Vimy Ridge extending from Souchez to the Point de Jour just north of the River Scarpe and advanced into the Douai plain beyond. With the line advanced, calm fell over this sector, now some distance behind the front line.

On 21 March 1918 the Germans launched a massive series of offensives, commonly known as the *Kaiserschlacht*; the strongest part of the German assault was targeted at Arras, but Haig's disposition of forces (more men on the front of Third and First Armies and more divisions in reserve, at the expense of Fifth Army, whose front was considered to be less strategically significant) and the strength of the positions ensured that this attack soon ran out of steam (although it did make some notable gains) and the fateful decision was made to concentrate the German attack along the Somme. The tunnellers had played their part, improving dugouts and reinforcing defensive positions, but some of these defences were never needed, including new trenches and dugouts positioned on Vimy Ridge's high ground. In late August 1918 the BEF launched a series of attacks east out of Arras, building on the success of Fourth Army to the south, and the laborious subterranean work of the thousands of tunnellers was never to be needed again in the war.

Chapter 3

Caves and *Souterraines* of Artois

Origins

> Within the Army area of operations and far beyond it – as far as the coast and south down to the regions of the Champagne, Loire and Seine, numerous underground workings, some of considerable depth, exist. The troops are in the habit of referring to them as 'catacombs', but this designation does not correspond to their earlier purpose. These were either underground quarries or places of refuge for the inhabitants during earlier troubled times.

So wrote Padre Jensen in February 1918, in an extensive brief for the German Second Army entitled *Unterirdische Anlangen (Katakomben) in Nordfrankeich (Underground Workings (Catacombs) in Northern France)*.

Padre Jensen's paper lists over 600 such 'catacombs', primarily within the German-occupied areas of northern France. At least as many, and probably a lot more, were situated on the Allied side of the lines. There were certainly many hundreds within Artois alone, but in the absence of consolidated records we can only guess at how many. Described in British records usually as caves, but more commonly today as *souterraines*, they had their origins mostly as underground quarries (*carrières*), extracting for building material the firm chalk, usually found 10 to 20 metres below the surface. This could be 'slabbed' along fault lines and then easily cut into regular cubes. Once exposed to the air it hardened into a soft limestone. Away from the former battle areas, where reconstruction was done with brick, the visitor to northern France can readily observe that many churches and older buildings are made from chalk. There can be few villages that did not have an underground quarry, in most cases with the entrances on church land or in the grounds of the local chateau. In the vicinity of cities numerous underground quarries were developed.

Some of these *souterraines* date back to Roman times, but most are medieval in origin and the workings continued into the eighteenth century, at which stage brick and hard stone largely replaced chalk as a building material. Many were also utilised during troubled times as refuges for the local population and might be expanded to incorporate rudimentary living facilities. At Naours, about 10 kilometres north of Amiens, the local population developed an entire village underground with streets, shops, stables for their livestock, living accommodation, a chapel and even a subterranean town square.

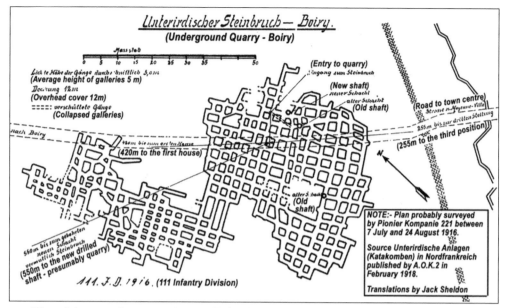

Plan of the extensive *souterraine* near Boiry-St-Martin utilised by the Germans through to March 1917.

The smallest of the *souterraines*, probably carved in the chalk as a family refuge and frequently accessed through a well shaft, might comprise no more than a couple of chambers. Most *souterraines*, those where the main purpose was quarrying the chalk, comprise extensive chambers supported by pillars of chalk, or what might alternatively be described as a grid of corridors between the pillars. Some are massive and genuinely labyrinthine. One such was at Boiry St Martin, about 5 kilometres south of Arras; used as an underground barracks by the Germans, it has approximately 5,500 metres of galleries occupying about 25 acres. This particular *souterraine* was sealed off by the Sapeurs Pompiers in 1995, reportedly because it contained discarded chemical munitions deemed too dangerous to move.

To floor level the quarries were generally 15 to 25 metres below the surface, with an interior height from floor to roof usually varying between 3 and 6 metres. Most featured at least one brick-lined and stepped entrance and they invariably had at least one bottle-shaped *puit* (shaft) for hauling cut chalk blocks to the surface. Those that were developed as refuges might also contain a well for water and square-cut chambers for living accommodation. It is self evident that, close to the front lines, these *souterraines* offered potential as extended dugouts or concealed and secure barracks for troops, headquarters locations and storage accommodation. The engineers on both sides sought them out, although it should be said that in the German-occupied areas the locals attempted to conceal their whereabouts.

Development and Access

Development was not, however, a simple matter of re-opening former entrances. For the engineers of both sides the *souterraines*, once located, had to be inspected for stability. Some were crumbling and clearly unsafe. In those that offered potential, it was necessary to either introduce support to weak areas or block them off, to drive additional inclined entrances to give ventilation and optional exits, to level the floors and remove the detritus of centuries, to signpost the corridors, and then to install the basic requirements of occupation, ranging from lighting (usually from electrical generators) to bunks, latrines, cooking areas and communication centres.

Within Artois the only systems open to the general public are those at Arras below the Hotel de Ville and the Wellington Cave – see Chapter 8. Elsewhere, while the entrance positions of many are known, most have been blocked by infilling; there

German miners shoring in a *souterraine*. (*Fonds documentaries Alain Jacques*)

are, however, a few in private ownership that remain accessible, although for safety reasons occasional entry is restricted to small parties with a valid historical interest and possessing suitable equipment and experience. In some cases, too, the local authorities have secured the entrances rather than infilling them, and an approach to a local mayor may enable entry. But be warned! All are subject to deterioration over time and chunks or slabs of chalk may be delicately poised, ready to fall on the unwary, while in some examples the oxygen levels may be low and there may be dangerous pockets of methane from rotting material.

Souterraines at Vimy Ridge

In the plain immediately west of Vimy Ridge and south of Notre Dame de Lorette there are at least eight *souterraines* that were brought into use during the First World War. Several, such as those at Carency, La Targette and Neuville St Vaast, were initially occupied by the Germans and were the scene of bitter fighting in the 1915 Battles of the Artois as the French drove the Germans back onto the heights of Vimy Ridge. In Neuville St Vaast it is said that the *souterraines* were interconnected and in turn linked to the cellars of houses in the village. A French officer described the fighting:

The passages in which we were advancing were eighteen feet deep, and often twenty-four feet or more. The water was sweating through in all directions and the sickly smell was intolerable. Imagine, too, that for three weeks we were not able to get rid of the dead bodies, amongst which we used to live night and day! One burrow, 120 feet long, took us thirteen days of ceaseless fighting to conquer entirely. The Germans had placed barricades, trapdoors and traps of all descriptions. When we stumbled we risked being impaled on bayonets treacherously hidden in holes lightly covered with earth. And all this went on in complete darkness. We had to use pocket lamps and advance with the utmost caution.

The evidence of this fighting is clearly evident in the Aux [Au] Rietz Cave, situated at the La Targette crossroads, almost immediately opposite the Le Relais restaurant and bar. In places the chalk walls are pitted from the fragments of exploding grenades and scored with bullet marks, while French and German cartridges cases may be found trampled into the floor. Aux Rietz was taken into use by the British after they replaced the French at Vimy and Arras in late February 1916. Captain H.D. Trounce, an American volunteer serving with 175 Tunnelling Company, describes occupying the cave soon after their arrival at Vimy Ridge on 2 May 1916:

Our advanced billets were within 100 yards of the villages of Neuville St Vaast and La Targette. Both of these villages were levelled by enemy fire, nothing remained but a mass of ruins. All the cellars were used by troops as billets. Our men had very curious billets. In this part of France and for some distance south the subsoil is a hard chalk, and this has been quarried underground nearly everywhere, leaving a clay top-soil and good grazing land above. The houses and buildings are constructed of chalk building-blocks with brick foundations. Every house, also, no matter how small, has a cellar.

Spacious chambers in the Aux Rietz *souterraine*, photographed in 1989. Note the supporting chalk pillars. The centre figure is M. André Sergent. (*GPGR*)

Chalk caverns are numerous, and one of the large variety was handed over to us as a billet for our men. Although our company was about 600 strong, we had plenty of room for 400 or 500 extra men in this cavern, and for a long time it took care of over a thousand. It was in decidedly bad condition when it was turned over to us. The air could almost be cut with a knife at that time; however, we put in another upcast and managed to clean it up as well. As it was over 70 feet deep, there was no loss of sleep from enemy shelling activity. Stories were current as to a big fight that had occurred down in this cavern in the previous September, and I should judge that there was some truth in the report, on account of the large French cemetery at the crossroads above [still there] and the number of bodies we unearthed below in the cavern.

In November 185 Tunnelling Company took over the Aux Rietz cave from 175 Tunnelling Company. Then, in the lead-up to the First Army attack on Vimy Ridge in April 1917, it was taken over by the 2nd (Canadian) Division. The history of the 5th (British) Division, which had its 13 Infantry Brigade attached to the 2nd (Cdn) Division for the attack on 9 April, remarks:

The Headquarters of the 2nd Canadian Division, the 5th Division Artillery, and the Heavy Artillery were in a vast cave called 'Aux Rietz', near Neuville St Vaast. It was said to be capable of holding 5,000 men – it certainly held thousands of rats, who made night hideous with their riotous conduct. In the vaulted kitchens the fires lighting up the stalactites and the cooks in their shirt sleeves produced a weird and scenic effect.

The Aux Rietz has had a curious recent history. In the 1970s part of the cave was privately acquired by M. André Sergent, a retired miner who, despite his diminutive stature, had extraordinary strength. With limited assistance, he set about the construction of a nuclear shelter in the cave, manhandling in an astonishing array of equipment and material from the by then redundant coalmines at Lens and Lille. However, as fears of nuclear exchange faded in the

The entrance to the Aux Rietz *souterraine* from Le Relais St Vaast restaurant, 2009.

The interior of Maison Blanche, 2007. The figure is David Hedges of the Durand Group. (*Durand Group*)

late 1980s, he switched his attention to creating safe corridors for visitors, along with displays of the numerous artefacts recovered. So far as is known, this project never fully matured, perhaps because it lacked any alternative exit to the entry stairway and so was not approved on safety grounds. Sadly, André died in the late 1990s.

Located some 1.5 kilometres to the south of the Aux Rietz Cave, along the D937 to Arras, is the Maison Blanche *souterraine*. After 1945 the landowner utilised this for dumping farm rubbish, completely filling the *puit* and almost blocking the brick-clad entrance. However, in 2001 M. Dominique Faivre, an intrepid member of the *Association de Recherches Historique et Archéologiques Militaires* (ARHAM), succeeded in wriggling over the rubbish in the entrance incline and produced a report, drawing attention to the carvings and graffiti within. In 2006 and 2007 the Durand Group, a British-based association specialising in subterranean military features, cleared the entrance on behalf of the proprietors, fitted a secure steel door and installed electric lighting. There is no evidence that this *souterraine* was utilised by the Germans, although it lay behind the German lines until the French forced them out of the Labyrinth in May 1915. However, by early 1917 it had been brought into use by the Canadian Corps for accommodation and linked into the front line and Douai Subway by a series of communication trenches. The history of the 15th Battalion CEF (48th Highlanders of Canada) refers to this *souterraine*:

The 3rd C.I.B. [Canadian Infantry Brigade] was now placed on the right of the Canadian Corps and near the right of the Ridge. The route was not long, so that it was a fresh unit that relieved the 13th in support in the great chalk caves of Maison Blanche near Neuville St Vaast.

Most of the men were on working parties each night, labouring in the front line, supports, and in tunnels being built behind the front line. These, in later days, saved hundreds of men, who sat deep and laughed as concussions shook the shoring and earth trickled down. They slept in the bad air of the Maison Blanche Caves during the day. There were many strange tales told about those caves. One of them would hold an entire battalion and, certainly, they were very old and, perhaps, as the tales went, once sheltered fugitives of the French Revolution and the women and children of Arras during the war of 1870.

Some of the many carvings and extensive graffiti in the Maison Blanche *souterraine*.

Whether or not the *souterraine* sheltered fugitives of the French Revolution, what is certain, as evidenced by the graffiti, is that in May 1940 it sheltered Belgian refugees. Aside from the scribbled graffiti of the 1940 refugees, the cave is remarkable for the extraordinarily skilful carvings made by the Canadian occupants in early 1917. One such sculptor was Private Ambler, who had been a stone carver before enlisting. In 2007, under arrangements made by the Durand Group, his son, with other family members, visited and viewed the artistry of their father. Intermingled with the carvings, drawings and often poignant inscriptions, there is a letterbox sculpted out of the chalk and inscribed with the names of Privates W.P. Beckett and T. Mason of 2 Company, 48th Highlanders (of Canada). Were they perhaps responsible for the company post? In any event, they both appear to have survived the war. (See the Tours section about the possibility of accessing this *souterraine*.)

Nearby are four other *souterraines* taken into use by the Canadian Corps. Just 2 kilometres to the northeast the Zivy cave connected to the subway of the same name. On 9 April 1917 Brigadier General Rennie of 4 (Cdn) Brigade had his headquarters here. Further north, in Zouave Valley, 182 Tunnelling Company connected three caves to Tottenham Subway. None is presently accessible but, if Maison Blanche is any guide, they are probably rich in evocative graffiti.

On 9 April 1917 Brigade Major D.E. Macintyre DSO MC of 4 (Cdn) Brigade was located in Zivy Cave. He was one of the main organisers of the huge Canadian pilgrimage that came to Europe in 1936 for the unveiling of the Vimy Memorial and subsequently wrote a book, *Canada at Vimy*, about his wartime experiences, threading it with an account of the pilgrimage. He describes the interior of the cave in a vivid description that could doubtless serve for other, similar, underground shelters on both sides of the line:

Zivy Cave was fitted out with bunks, tables, cooking stoves, telephones, electric lights, running water and anything else that was essential. It would have to accommodate two brigade headquarters and five battalion headquarters, as well as about 400 men, to be held there as a reserve. [Advanced Brigade HQ was moved from Junction Trench to the Cave during 7 April.] The saturated ground above us leaked its moisture through the roof of the cave in a tiresome dribble on everything below – tables, beds and floor – so that there was always an inch or two of greyish white slime underfoot. Scattered about on the floor, men could be dimly seen by the candlelight, their grotesque shadows dancing on the adjoining walls. Some slept, fully clothed, their weapons near at hand, ready to surge upward at the first alarm. Others cleaned their arms while their comrades played cards or made tea over small fires. Numbers of soldiers with their army clasp knives carved their names and unit numbers in the firm chalk of the walls … There was a constant movement of men entering or leaving the cave. The sound of talking, coughing, spitting and shuffling feet went on without ceasing.

Sometimes a wounded man would be brought in by the stretcher bearers and, if his pain was greater than he could bear, his piteous cries would cause the wakeful to turn their heads and sleepers to turn restlessly.

Carrying parties would arrive from outside and dump their loads; reliefs struggled up to the line and tired, mud-covered men came back to snatch a little rest. The smell of foul air, mud, cooking, sweat, urine, chloride of lime, tobacco and candle smoke filled the atmosphere and was almost overpowering. And over and beyond all this there was the continuous, sullen rumble of gun fire, like a thunderstorm. But with all these discomforts, it was a thousand times better than being outside.

On the other side of the line the Germans were likewise adopting such underground quarries. Their records show caves located at Arleux, Bailleul sur Berthoult, Givenchy en Gohelle, Mericourt and Thélus, though, as far as is known, none is now accessible.

Arras to Roeux

The New Zealand Tunnelling Company War Diary illustrates how widely spread these underground quarries were. In the course of advancing from Arras to Roeux, over ground taken from the Germans in April and early May 1917, a distance of about 6 kilometres, they recorded finding twenty caves of various dimensions, most of which were taken into use for accommodation and other facilities. It is worthy of note that *The New Zealand Tunnelling Company 1915–1919* records that between May 1917 and March 1918, in addition to extensive work on road reconstruction, the company constructed 180 dugouts and nearly a hundred concealed machine-gun nests, as well as trench-mortar emplacements, observation posts and underground communication galleries. Furthermore, if perhaps less relevant, the Company's rugby team never suffered a defeat and won the championship of the region.

Much the biggest complex developed by the New Zealanders, following on from the advance, was that at Roeux, where, drawing on their experience in the

German soldiers attending a concert in a souterraine, probably in the area of Neuville St Vaast, 1915.

Some of the extensive graffiti in the Roeux caves.
(*The Proprietor*)

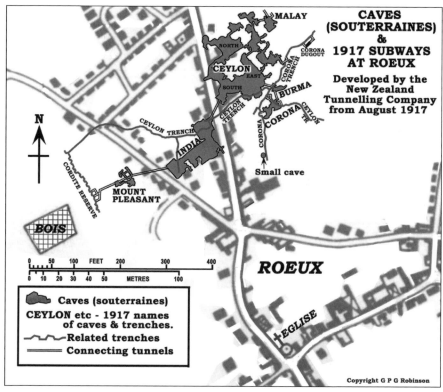

The Roeux caves and subways superimposed on a current map. (*GPGR*)

Roeux *souterraine* detail: India cave.

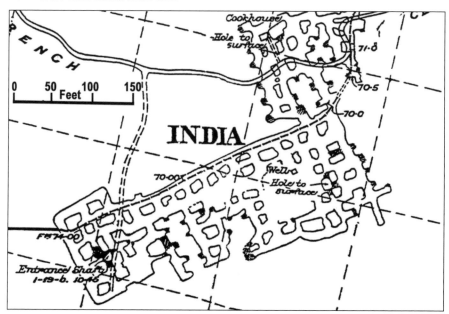

The consequences of building over *souterraines*: the Mairie at Beaumetz lez Cambrai collapsing into an extensive cave in 2008.

Arras caves (see Chapter 8), they linked four small and two large *souterraines*, extending from Mont Pleasant Wood east to within 450 metres of the forward trenches, and equipped them effectively as subterranean barracks. After completion, at about the end of December 1917, they were mostly occupied by troops of the Guards Division, who left a rich legacy of graffiti, including carvings, fine drawings and cartoons done in indelible pencil (which is remarkably enduring), poetry and whimsical comments. These *souterraines* were overrun and abandoned during the *Kaiserschlacht* offensive, which commenced on 21 March 1918, but, perhaps surprisingly, there is no evidence that they were subsequently taken into use by the Germans.

The Roeux caves remain accessible through a single entrance into India cave but, almost certainly for reasons of safety, the site is not open to visitors. The proprietor is understandably reticent and material for this book was provided on the understanding that neither his name nor the exact location of the entrance would be disclosed.

After the War

As already remarked, there are few villages or towns in this part of the Pas de Calais without at least one *souterraine*; many have several. Rebuilding after the First World War and more recent expansion has resulted in housing and commercial buildings being erected over these often-forgotten underground quarries. Inevitably, from time to time, collapses occur, though to the knowledge of the authors none in recent years with fatal consequences. At Beaumetz lès Cambrai, where the whole centre of the village is situated over a *souterraine* (utilised by 252 Tunnelling Company in March 1918), the front of the Mairie started to collapse in early 2008 and was evacuated pending probable demolition. No doubt more will be revealed in this dramatic manner in the years ahead.

Chapter 4

The Subways on the Artois Front

Development

The consolidation of the Western Front line from the North Sea to the Swiss frontier by the end of 1914 placed the protagonists in a position of what amounted to mutual siege. Barbed wire and skilfully placed machine guns rendered unsupported infantry assault ineffective. Ever-increasing reliance was placed on artillery to neutralise the defence, break up offensive action and inflict attritional damage on the enemy. The approaches to front-line positions were subjected to frequent artillery and mortar bombardment. Conceptually it was only a small step to look to what might be termed as subsurface communication routes.

With their focus on defence, broadly speaking, on the Western Front, the Germans began at an early stage to develop subterranean communication passages and supporting facilities that were largely impervious to artillery fire. French and British engineer resources were, however, largely committed to supporting offensive preparations, the priorities being roads and railways, camps, water supply, gun positions, dugouts and the advancement of trenches. As British resources expanded – in particular with the addition of the tunnelling companies – increasing attention was given to constructing concealed routes forward for the infantry and placing short-range weapon systems, such as mortars and flame-throwers, close to the enemy firing line. For the opening of the Battle of the Somme on 1 July 1916 approximately fifty tunnels were constructed, though all but two were in effect Russian saps – shallow tunnels constructed only a few feet below the surface; many of these were subsequently converted into deep communication trenches through the removal of the top cover. In most cases they were driven from the firing line into No Man's Land, rather than providing a covered and safe approach to the firing line. Even the two deeper tunnels prepared by 252 Tunnelling Company in the Beaumont Hamel area were primarily intended to establish Stokes mortar positions close to the enemy lines and to provide a secure passage for telephone cables and runners. Both were too narrow and restricted for use by fully equipped troops.

From late 1916 the mining companies were increasingly diverted to the construction of subways, in particular where the German positions overlooked the Allied lines, for example at Hill 60 (in the Ypres Salient), Auchy, Hohenzollern, Hulluch, Loos and Vimy Ridge. These generally extended back from the firing line to the reserve lines, sometimes further, and in places ran parallel to the front and were interconnected. In the Hulluch area by late 1917 it had become possible to walk several kilometres underground between different parts of the line. The most extensive system was that at Arras, described in Chapter 8, though the St Sauveur and Ronville caves and tunnels might be better defined as underground cantonments interconnected with infantry tunnels to the forward trenches.

Not a great deal is known by us about the German subways on the Central Artois front – there could be plenty of information tucked away in the remaining German archives – but these will be considered later.

Anatomy of a Subway

Subways varied greatly, depending on the ground, the intended purpose and local divisional or corps requirements. In broad terms most were driven with between 24 and 30 feet of head cover, this being deemed adequate protection against all but super-heavy artillery or armour-piercing naval shells. The main passageway was usually about $3\frac{1}{2}$ feet wide and $6\frac{1}{2}$ feet high, so that a fully laden infantryman could walk along it. Invariably there were a number of entrances-cum-exits, necessary for ventilation and usually designed so that laden stretcher bearers could descend. Most were lit, albeit dimly, with electric lighting, powered by a generating station situated near the rear of the tunnel. Timber (and sometimes concrete) supports were placed as necessary, though in chalk tunnels, which were naturally more stable, they were used sparingly. Almost invariably chambers and dugouts were cut into the sides for HQs, logistical and administrative facilities, medical posts, sanitary purposes and sometimes sleeping quarters. A tunnel major and his small staff enforced strict rules regarding their use and traffic control, and common procedures were adopted, such as having telephone lines on one side of the tunnel and electric cables on the other.

Major H.R. Dixon MC, the GHQ Assistant Inspector of Mines at the time, described, in an unpublished post-war memoir, the Hythe Subway at Loos, constructed between December 1917 and March 1918. He regarded this, in his own words, as probably the 'most elaborate of all':

Reference was made in an earlier chapter to the subway constructed under Hill 70 at Loos. This was mainly the work of an Australian Coy, and was possibly the finest example of this class of work ever executed. Hill 70 is a long hog-back to the north of the village of Loos, and was one of the only gains we continued to hold after that famous battle in the autumn of 1915 [sic. At best, only partially true; Hill 70 was secured by the Canadian Corps attack of August 1917]. At the time of my last inspection of this work the Eighth Corps, under an old Sapper in Sir Aylmer Hunter-Weston, the Hunter-Bunter of so many war yarns, was holding this front, and in the detailed development of the subway, and its subsequent maintenance, the Corps Commander took the greatest interest, with most beneficial results.

The rear entrance to the subway was in direct connection with our light railway system, which in its turn communicated direct with a railhead for that area. The tunnel ran under the highest part of the hill towards the front line for some 700 yards. In branches off it were large and comfortable dugouts, cook-houses, wells and water-bottle filling stations, various Aid-posts and a casualty-clearing station, or, to be strictly accurate, a forward dressing station. In the forward portion were cleverly hidden Trench Mortar battery and Lewis and Vickers machine-gun positions, Company and Battalion HQs with rocket posts adjoining, and away out under our own wire was a special observation chamber, from which a large periscope was arranged in among the wire, camouflaged to look like an old tree stump. This instrument was of special design, and looking into the eye-piece one had the whole of the German lines in view over a wide area, and their working parties were spotted at once if they ventured to do work outside their trenches. Telephone communication with all the other parts of the system enabled swift action to be taken if the enemy were seen.

But the most interesting features of this fortress lay in the measures taken for protection against gas attacks or heavy gas shelling and the concrete work which was carried out. Every entrance to the surrounding trenches was fitted with a gas curtain, made from an army blanket, specially treated to prevent gas passing through it. These were arranged on rollers, above a sloping frame, so that a pull of a string would fasten them tightly in position over the door. To ensure that no gas or contaminated air could enter the system owing to damage or failure to close any door, a powerful electrically driven fan could in emergency provide the air for the whole system. This was drawn through an enormous box-respirator, and the pressure caused in the galleries when the fan was at work was such that air could not get in to the galleries, even at an open door. The power station for driving the electric fan and the lighting plant was installed and run by the Australian AE&MM&B Company and was necessarily quite an elaborate affair in itself.

The tactics to be adopted in the event of an attack had been very carefully thought out, and the garrison, which comprised a whole brigade of infantry, had very special training in the use of the many new devices employed. Chief among these was the scheme of concrete doors. In the main galleries were doors made of solid concrete 3 feet thick, mounted on rails. By means of snatch blocks and ropes, they were normally pulled clear of the gallery into chambers cut for them in the chalk, but the rails on which they ran were arranged to slope towards the gallery, where they ran below the level of the floor, and if need arose the door could be run into position by a single pull of the rope, which released it at once. These doors were provided with loopholes. All the lights in the main galleries were set in recesses cut in the side, so that while the gallery was clearly illuminated throughout its length, it was impossible for an enemy to see the lamps and shoot them out.

At the foot of the steps leading down from each trench entrance was an ingenious trapdoor, also made of concrete, arranged on a pivot across the gallery so that when a bolt was pulled out the outside end turned downwards into a hole 20 feet deep, into which the pursuing enemy or his bombs could drop, while the inside part of the door rose into place and blocked the gallery. These doors were also provided with loopholes. It was a sad day for the garrison officer responsible if the Corps Commander (Hunter-Weston) ever found one of these doors not in working order owing to mud.

Many other subways were constructed at other parts of the front on similar lines, but perhaps Hill 70 was the most elaborate of all.

The Subways on the Central Artois Front

The Hythe tunnel was constructed in early 1918 when a German offensive was expected, so that elaborate defensive features were built into it. Those along the Central Artois front, started in October 1916, were initially intended to be subsurface communication trenches. However, as cited in a report by Lieutenant Colonel G.C. Williams, the Controller of Mines in First Army,

> Subways were originally constructed to facilitate the passage of Infantry from Reserve Trenches, through badly trench-mortared areas, to forward positions during times of normal trench warfare. On the Canadian Corps Front, some Subways were in the course of construction for this purpose. Early in January [1917] it was decided to increase the numbers of these subways and elaborate them for use during offensive operations, and the following accommodation points were included in their construction:
>
> • Dugouts to house large bodies of Infantry
> • Cookhouse
> • Latrines
> • Brigade battle headquarters
> • Battalion headquarters
> • Tramways for carrying ammunition and stores
> • Electric light, and power stations
> • Forward dressing stations
> • Trench mortar ammunition stores and emplacements
> • Water filling points
> • Signals stations.

The same applied to Third Army, covering the southern half of Vimy Ridge and around Arras, where likewise the tunnelling effort was diverted to subways. The scale of that effort may be judged from the table overleaf:

Central Artois Subways as at 9 April 1917

Sector	Subway Designation	Length in Feet (Metres)	Tunnelling Company	Corps – Div Front
'S' Souchez – Calonne	Rotten Row Bois en Hache	500 (150) *350 (107)*	255	1 Corps 24th Div
'R' Carency	Souchez Coburg Gobron	1,700 (520) 1,335 (407) 870 (265)	176	Cdn Corps 4th Cdn Div
'Q' Berthonval	Blue Bull Vincent Tottenham Cavalier	1,530 (466) 1,665 (508) 4,611 (1,408) 3,360 (1,024)	182	
'P' La Folie	Grange Goodman/Pylones	4,029 (1,228) 5,649 (1,722)	172	Cdn Corps 3rd Cdn Div
'O' Neuville St Vaast	Lichfield	1,590 (485)		Cdn Corps 2nd Cdn Div
'N' Ecurie North	Zivy	2,523 (789)	185	
'N' Ecurie Central	Bentata	2,229 (680)		Cdn Corps 1st Cdn Div
	Douai No. 33 Subway	2,118 (646) *900 (274)*		
'L' Lille Road	L 29A L 28B L 27 Subway L 26 Subway L 21A Subway Barricade	*250 (76)* *400 (122)* *1,700 (518)* *600 (182)* *1,300 (396)* 1,194 (364)		XVIII Corps 51st (H) Division XVIII Corps 34th Division
'K' Roclincourt	Fish	1,000 (305)	184	
'J' Blangy	No subways ?	N/A		XVIII Corps 9th Division
'I' St Sauveur	St Sauveur	37,000 (11,280) of passageways	184, 176 & NZET NZET	VI Corps 12th Division VI Corps 3rd Div
'H' Ronville	Ronville			
Southern Arras	Not known	Some short subways but 'neutralised' by German withdrawal	179 & 181	VII Corps 14th, 56th, 30th & 21st Divisions

Notes:
1. Figures in italics are approximations derived by measuring plotted subways off mining maps.
2. The total length of the passages in the Ronville and St Sauveur systems in Arras was obtained from a report by Brigadier General Harvey, the Controller of Mines at GHQ. This figure is probably for the length of passageways cut and excludes routes through the caves.
3. Excluded are a number of relatively short subways constructed south of Arras but neutralised by the German withdrawal to the Hindenburg Line in early 1917. These were, nevertheless, connected to the abandoned German lines and remained a useful communication facility.
4. So far as can be established, the subways designated by letters and numerals, as distinct to those with names, were developments of mining tunnels. It would appear that No. 33 Subway was for the purpose of laying a Wombat mine (though this was not blown). L 29A was a mining rescue station. No information has come to light on the L 28B and L 21A Subways. L 27 and L 26 were mining galleries especially enlarged for the passage of infantry but lacking most of the facilities in the named subways.

The scale of the endeavour, over the six months from October 1916, is remarkable. Excluding the passages linked with the Arras caves, the total tunnel footage is around 41,400 feet (12,640 metres). This entailed excavating approximately 880,000 cubic feet of mostly chalk with a mass of about 44,000 imperial tons (25,000 cubic metres and 45,000 metric tonnes). Contemporary tunnelling company figures also indicate that the excavation of related dugouts and chambers in the tunnels added about half as much spoil again, a staggering total of roughly 66,000 tons. Adding in the footage for the tunnels linking the Arras caves, the volume and mass would be roughly half as much again.

Brigadier General Harvey, having remarked on the diminution in enemy mining activity after 1 July 1916, noted,

> Only towards the end of the preparatory period [early 1917] did the enemy begin to show uneasiness, by resuming activity in his mine systems, and this was most apparent in the VIMY RIDGE and GRANGE Sectors. His nervousness will be easily appreciated by anyone who examines our lines from the enemy's observation points on the PIMPLE and BROADMARSH Crater. All down the front from the VIMY RIDGE southwards, enormous piles of spoil bags, which grew daily, can be seen. The amount of chalk to be handled from the subways was so great that, even if the working parties had had the desire to spread the bags, and endeavoured to render the heaps inconspicuous, it is doubtful whether they could have done so. The covering of these heaps with camouflage was quite out of the question; it was tried at the commencement of the work, but the amount of spoil speedily outran the camouflage.

A great deal of credit belongs to the infantry and pioneers who were pressed, somewhat reluctantly, into providing labour for moving the spoil from underground to the dumps and carrying parties for the huge supply needs; the work being mostly on the surface, it was a task made hazardous by artillery and mortar fire. Daily, each tunnelling company employed anything from 200 to 500 men on this labouring role. The Engineer field companies also contributed significantly, mining many of the dugouts under tunnelling company supervision, laying trench trolley-ways, installing water, electrical and sanitary resources, and constructing or modifying machinery and other facilities in their workshops. All along the front the Australian Electrical and Mechanical, Mining and Boring Company (the 'Alphabetical Company') were engaged on installing and maintaining plant, electrical systems and ventilation, while further back Canadian and British forestry companies felled and prepared timber, of which there was never enough.

There was a lively rivalry between the tunnelling companies seeking to outdo each other on maximum footage driven in a day, and several claimed that distinction. This is not the place to adjudicate. Lieutenant Colonel Williams, the Controller of Mines for First Army, wrote that the records of progress were constantly being broken, the greatest eventually being 14 metres forward drive on a single face in 24 hours.

A common enquiry among visitors to the Grange Subway is how many subways there were along the Canadian Corps front. There are several 'correct' answers. On 9 April 1917 there were twelve, if Goodman/Pylones is judged to be one subway rather than two connected, or thirteen if Pylones is deemed a separate subway in its own right, and optionally fourteen if the somewhat obscure No. 33 Subway is included. Then on 12 April the 4th Canadian Division replaced the 24th Division at the Pimple, adding the Souchez Subway to whichever of the above totals is chosen!

The Grange Subway

Apart from the Wellington Cave in Arras, the only place on the Western Front – at least known to the authors – where visitors can see something of these subways is the forward end of the Grange tunnel in the Canadian Memorial Site at Vimy. Although now reinforced throughout with concrete and other supports, well lit, and variously sanitised for public safety, it does nevertheless provide a valuable insight into the nature of the subways and what was involved in their construction.

The original conservation was initiated in 1926 at the inspiration of Major (later Colonel) D.C. Unwin Simpson of the Royal Canadian Engineers, the Resident Engineer for the construction of the Vimy Memorial from 1926 to 1936. This work (and that on the neighbouring conserved trenches) was a means of keeping the labour force occupied during an extended delay when delivery of limestone for the construction of the memorial was held up for some months. Something of the original state of the subway can be seen in pictures taken in the 1930s and, as may be seen by comparison with recent

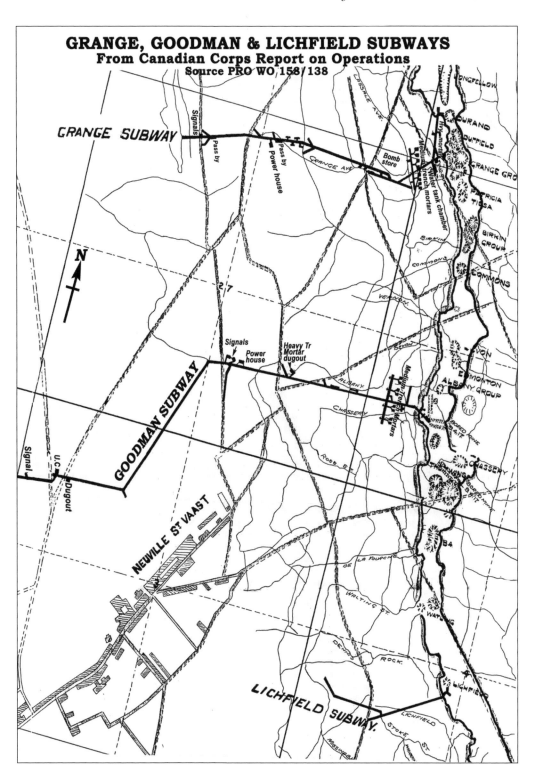

GRANGE, GOODMAN & LICHFIELD SUBWAYS
From Canadian Corps Report on Operations
Source PRO WO 158/138

The entrance to Grange Subway from the main defence line, pictured in the early 1930s.

The sign above the door reads: ENTRANCE TO GRANGE SUBWAY, REOPENED NOVEMBER 1926, BATTLE-FIELDS MEMORIAL COMMISSION.

The sign on the door reads: 'NE PAS DESCENDRE SANS LE GUIDE.' (*From a postcard*)

(Left) View along the main tunnel of the Grange Subway in the early 1930s. Note the absence of any supporting structures and the unprotected artefacts. (*From a postcard*) (Right) The main tunnel through the Grange Subway in 2008. Note the extensive supports and bright lighting. (*VAC*)

photographs, much further engineering has been necessary to maintain it in a safe condition.

Full details on the Grange Subway can be found in the Tours Section of this book.

The Goodman Subway

Although not open to visitors, the Goodman Subway, strictly a combination of two subways, the Goodman and the Pylones, has been entered in recent years. Part of it was accessed in 1988 by a Royal Engineer team via the La Folie tunnels. Then in 2003 the Durand Group excavated and laddered an 8-metre deep vertical shaft into the tunnel. Over the next couple of years they cut through several collapses to expose 1,325 feet (404 metres) of the forward end of the tunnel, investigating and surveying a little over a quarter of the full length.

The survey (see overleaf) shows that it had many of the characteristics of the Grange. There are passages to mortar pits near the firing line, an incline connection (today slightly perilous) to the deep mining system, bays off the main passageway, a dugout that housed the battalion HQs of the 4th and 5th Canadian Mounted Rifles situated opposite an exit, and what was either a latrine or kitchen. (It was at this exit that Captain Brisco, a section commander of 172 Tunnelling Company, had his fatal rendezvous with a German shell.) There was also a water point, although in this case it took the form of a reservoir for around 50,000 gallons, pumped in from a nearby well. Continuing to the rear there are more bays, a heavy mortar position and, beyond a collapse that has not been penetrated, a generator powerhouse and a signals station that may have housed a radio transmitter, though this is not certain. The rear entrance into what was actually Pylones Subway is situated on the northern outskirts of Neuville St Vaast.

Except that the tramway and most of the timber supports were salvaged some time after April 1917, the tunnel remains much as it would have been at

The excavated shaft into the Goodman Subway. (*Durand Group*)

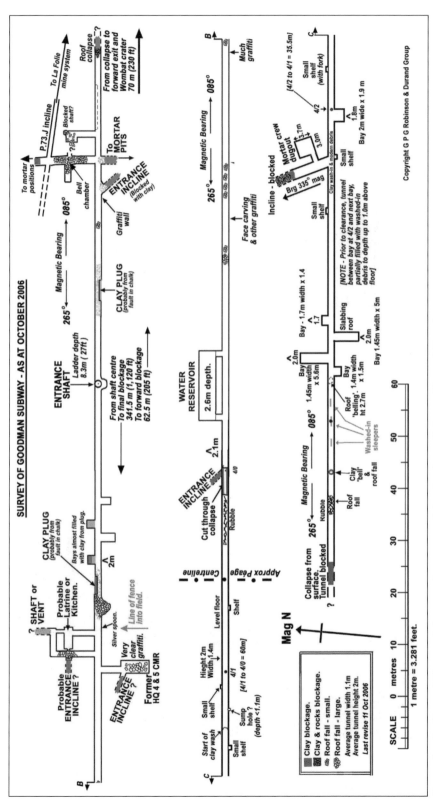

Survey by the Durand Group of the opened-up parts of the Goodman Subway. (*Durand Group*)

A section of the Goodman Tunnel in 2004. Note the cables on the floor. Originally these would have been attached to the walls or timber supports. (*Durand Group*)

the time. Along with military detritus, such as discarded water containers and mess tins, the tunnel has a liberal sprinkling of primed grenades and abandoned small-arms ammunition. What sets it historically apart from the Grange, however, is the extensive graffiti, mostly written with the ubiquitous indelible pencils, and some carvings, made predominantly by Canadian troops. These have all been recorded by the Durand Group and work is in hand to commit the material to a DVD, along with such records as may be found of the individual soldiers. It is probable that the Grange was equally adorned but the writings and carvings were chiselled out by souvenir hunters in the past or 'lost' in the course of successive safety engineering works. In this context Unwin Simpson reported that the Grange Tunnel suffered from the visits of German troops during the Second World War and that some of the Canadians' fascinating wartime graffiti was deliberately obliterated.

The Goodman Subway fell within 8 (Cdn) Brigade's sector. Their procedure was distinctly different from that adopted by 7 Brigade in the Grange. The

Goodman Tunnel carving and graffiti. The inscription reads: 'Pte J Hoover, B Coy, No 721767, 43 Battalion, BEF, France'. (*Durand Group*)

Clearing a blockage in the Goodman Subway, 2006. (*Durand Group*)

feeding-through of the assaulting troops was done on the night of 8/9 April according to a rigorous movement schedule, as shown in this extract from 8 Brigade instructions dated 2 April 1917:

GOODMAN TUNNEL
This subway is under the control of Lt Col LANG, with HQ in TUNNEL under BAY STREET, to whom all matters of traffic must be referred.

For IN traffic only, except for Runners and parties of one or two officers who may go against the traffic.

For the purpose of ventilation, when this TUNNEL is being used for the accommodation of many troops, no man will be allowed on the steps of the exits, and the men in the TUNNEL must sit down to allow more space for the free passage of the air currents.

SPECIAL TRAFFIC INSTRUCTIONS FOR Y/Z NIGHT
TABLE A: To be followed if Zero hour is within one hour of dawn.

4 CMR	Companies from PYLONES start to leave PYLONES at 1.30 am. Tail clear of PYLONES by 2.30 am. Tail clear of BAY STREET at 3.30 am. Tail clear of TUNNEL at 4.30 am.
2 CMR	Company from CENOT CAVE start in at BAY STREET at 3.30 am. Tail clear of BAY STREET at 4.30 am.
5 CMR	Leading two Companies go into TUNNEL at WEDD STREET at 2.30 am. Head stop at BAY STREET and rear two Companies follow into PYLONES and pick up material to be carried.

Head of leading Company start forward from BAY STREET at 4.30 am. Stop at PS Line. Rear two Companies file out of PYLONES and take up position with head at BAY STREET.

The various battalion war diaries show that they conformed to this closely timed progression with only a couple of minor delays.

Another particular was the blowing of a Wombat mine from the head of the tunnel just after zero hour (5.30 am). 8 Brigade Operation Order Number 8 of 7 April states:

The 172nd Tunnelling Company will blow two bored communication trenches, one from the extension of GOODMAN TUNNEL, the other South of CHASSERY CRATER at Zero plus 30 seconds. The troops in the assembly trenches will be warned that these 'blows' will shake them considerably, but that, if they keep their heads down under cover from pieces of flying mud, they will be quite safe.

As an adjunct to this, after the Wombat blow 172 drove a short tunnel into the Wombat crater so that telephone cables could be run forward, sheltered from

The Wombat crater at the head of the Goodman Tunnel in 2006. It is 150ft long and about 15ft deep. (*Durand Group*)

damage by enemy artillery and mortar fire. The Wombat craters remain today; that from the Goodman was cleared of undergrowth in 2006 by the Durand Group. These are unique features, not apparent anywhere else on the Western Front.

Technical Features

On 9 March 1917 Captain R.S.G. Stokes, from the staff of the Controller of Mines at GHQ, visited 172 Tunnelling Company and produced notes on his discussions and observations. The edited extract below indicates something of the technical considerations involved.

Went up to Goodman Subway with Capt. Dick Cleland (Adjutant) - then with Capt. Brisco. The new connection to Pylones Trench is being 'raced' with two faces going. There was about 500ft to do and about 40ft per day is being advanced in the two faces. This should be through for certain before the end of the month.

Goodman Subway
To be finally 3600ft long; it is now lit electrically, but current off 12 hours daylight in area not to interfere with IT. [Internal Tramway?]
These are strong and easily fixed up. Lamps are wholly encased – no reflector. Lamps – 20 C[andle] P[ower], 220V.
Present work in Goodman (in addition to Pylones and rear connection) consists of:
Medium T.M. emplacements - three pairs.
Magazines therefore.
Various stores.
Chamber for Wombat drilling from extreme end of Subway – to blow communication crater. Chamber started.

An absolute minimum of timber has been used in these subways – more logging would, in many parts, be desirable if it were at hand.

Magazines for each pair of medium T.M. emplacements are standardised at 1,000 cubic ft.

Grange Subway
A similar programme, but the gallery itself is completed.

Also: Three pairs of Medium T.M. emplacements with ammunition store [ultimately four pairs]
One Heavy T.M. emplacement.

This subway is lit electrically all the time – a very good illumination which must influence very definitely the attractiveness of the communication to the infantry.

There are fourteen exits to Grange Subway.

Wombat Hole
Another chamber is being cut for a Wombat hole – to the left of Durand Crater – for blowing a communication crater.

Standby Electric Lighting
The leads are to be taken through the main lateral system, connecting the two subways so that either plant can serve both subways in case of trouble.
FS Lanterns

Wombat Drill Holes
Five holes are to be drilled near Watling Crater, with Australian team. Only one hole will be drilled at a time.

The question of charging, detonation and length of tamping an uncharged hole (to give minimum work after blow, when opening up from gallery into crater) will require settlement in detail. I think C[ontroller] of M[ines] First Army (from whom we obtained cordeau detonnant by special request) has made arrangements but Corps do not know yet exact plans. The holes have to be drilled first. I think Third Army has been on the right track and First Army in the wrong in this matter.

First Army have scheme for 3ft cylinders of stove pipe, with wooden plug ends & repositioning links of cordeau detonnant.

Exits
Done in 1 in 1, 1 in 2 & 1 in 1½. Brisco prefers 1 in 1½.
Grange Subway
At the fire trench exit, bags are taken out and dumped behind the Duffield Craters. During recent armistice to collect our dead and wounded after 2nd Can [Div] unsuccessful raid, party of enemy came over to our rim of craters and fraternised with men at this dumping site. (Reported by Symes to C.E. Army who visited the place.) [In fact he is probably referring to the disastrous

raid in force by 11 and 12 (Cdn Brigades) of the 4th Division on 1 March 1917.]

Defence of Exits

These are special garrison posts or chambers for command of loopholes and in some cases automatic closing doors.

<u>Enemy Activity</u>

The Broadmarsh mine is now charged, 23,500 lbs at 61 ft and enemy is working close & higher. In Z enemy are very close and much talking heard.

Subways in the Carency and Berthonval Sectors

Between them 176 and 182 Tunnelling Companies drove seven subways into Vimy Ridge north of the Grange, all except Souchez on the front of the 4th (Canadian) Division. Souchez, the northernmost, was utilised by 73 Brigade of the 24th Division until its line was taken over by 10 (Cdn) Brigade on 12 April 1917 (incidentally, not to be confused with the 73rd Battalion CEF, The Royal Highlanders of Canada, who were also deployed on the northern end of the Ridge). It was not, it would seem, the most salubrious of the tunnels. On 12 April the 102nd Battalion CEF (The North British Columbians) of 12 Brigade were ordered up to support the 44th and 50th Battalions for the assault on the Pimple, both of which had their HQs in the Souchez Subway. According to their War Diary,

> Being uninitiated into the conditions in the new area the Bn. passed over the Souchez valley in broad daylight. That no casualties were incurred was not the fault of the Hun gunners, who plastered the valley with shells, but was rather due to the mud, which for once proved a blessing. The ground was so soft and the mud so deep that the shells buried themselves before exploding. HQ was in the tunnel, a subterranean sewer but all was ankle deep and sometimes knee deep in water instead of sewerage. The Battalion Orderly Room was a fair-sized chamber raised above the water level, but as it had to serve the four battalions of the 10th Brigade, there was only standing room for our HQ staff, who were neither welcomed nor needed.

The A26 péage, cutting through the former Canadian lines along the north end of the Vimy Ridge, has changed the battlefield topography, particularly so in the area of the Pimple. Nevertheless the steeper western slopes, used today only for grazing, still show the lines of the communication trenches, while the track from Souchez to Neuville St Vaast along the Zouave Valley retains almost exactly the 1917 alignment. The positions of the former entrances to all the subways along the valley can be quite readily discerned.

Coburg Subway, approximately 550 metres south of Souchez Subway, had its rear entrance situated close to the bottom of the slope on what at the time was

The entrance to Coburg Subway in 1917.

known as Tunnellers Ridge, a warren of dugouts and mining entrances. Gobron Subway, a further 275 metres on, was situated well up the slope of the Ridge. For the attack on 9 April they were respectively occupied by the 73rd Battalion and the 72nd Battalion (Seaforth Highlanders of Vancouver) CEF. As with most of these northern subways, detailed plans have not been located but 176 Tunnelling Company's War Diary has a fulsome description:

Gobron Subway, which was on the right of the Company's front, was 618 ft in length, and off it were a 50′ × 9′ × 6½′ Medical Aid Post, fitted up with brackets for a double tier of stretchers placed longitudinally down either side, an apartment for the M.O. and his medical stores and an operating table. The Subway also contained a battalion HQ, a station for electrical power generating plant, a bomb store near the forward exit, a chamber for water tanks and eight recesses for urinals, spaced evenly over its entire length. It was eventually found that the power plant was not available, and the subway was lighted [sic] by hurricane oil lamps at 4ft intervals protected

The entrance to Gobron Subway in 1917.

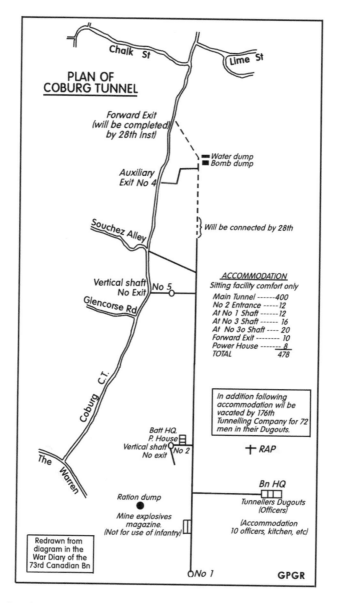

PLAN OF
COBURG TUNNEL

Chalk St

Lime St

Forward Exit
(will be completed
by 28th inst)

Water dump
Bomb dump

Auxiliary
Exit No 4

Souchez Alley

Will be connected by 28th

Vertical shaft No 5
No Exit

Glencorse Rd

ACCOMMODATION
Sitting facility comfort only

Main Tunnel ------400
No 2 Entrance -----12
At No 1 Shaft ------12
At No 3 Shaft ------ 16
At No 3o Shaft ---- 20
Forward Exit -------- 10
Power House ------- 8
TOTAL   478

In addition following
accommodation will be
vacated by 176th
Tunnelling Company for 72
men in their Dugouts.

Coburg C.T.

+ RAP

Batt HQ.
P. House
Vertical shaft No 2
No exit

The Warren

Bn HQ

Ration dump

Tunnellers Dugouts
(Officers)

Mine explosives
magazine.
(Not for use of infantry)

(Accommodation
10 officers, kitchen, etc)

Redrawn from
diagram in the
War Diary of the
73rd Canadian Bn

No 1

GPGR

by guards of expanded metal. This subway was provided with two entrances and three forward exits.

Coburg Subway, in the centre of the [176] Company Sector, was 873 ft long, having its two entrances at the foot of the Ridge in the ZOUAVE VALLEY, and its two forward exits just behind the support trench, with two others slightly further back. Connected to the subway was the advanced HQ of the Company's officers, which, just prior to the operations, was handed over to the Infantry and was used ultimately as a battalion and, later, as a brigade Battle HQ. The Subway also contained the Company's explosives magazine, an electric power station, forward bomb reserve store, water tanks chamber and urinal recesses. Lighting, as in the case of Gobron Subway, was by means of protected hurricane oil lamps. The average depth of cover was about 50 ft. The size of both subways was 6'-6" × 3'. Signal Stations were established in both Subways and connection between them and another battalion HQ in Souchez Tunnel was maintained by cables laid from the Subways along the main mine lateral gallery, which extended along the whole of the Company's front. This was an important factor in ensuring uninterrupted telephonic communication between brigade and the HQs of the battalions on the right and left during the operations. The main passage of both Gobron and Coburg Subways was utilized for the purpose of storing in each a battalion of assaulting troops. The men filed in to the tunnels between 9 and 10 o'clock on the night of the 8th, and began to move out and take up their positions in the assembly trenches at 5 o'clock on the morning of the 9th.

Blue Bull Subway, only 250 metres south of Gobron but at the base of the Ridge, had a special distinction as the terminus for the narrow gauge railway that ran from the main logistics base at Ecoivres, across the plain and into and along the Zouave Valley. Shortly after dusk every night the train, laden with stores, rations, ammunition and men making for the front, chuffed its way over Mont St Eloi Ridge and, defying the searching German guns, distributed largesse along the way. Repair teams stationed along the route rapidly remedied

A light railway at Brielen near Ypres, similar to that employed from Ecoivres along the Zouave Valley.

any strikes on the trackway, while as far as is known the train itself never suffered a hit. At Blue Bull the entire train is said to have disappeared into the tunnel, where unloading was completed. With a new cargo of salvage, the dead, the wounded, and men coming out of the line, the train would later emerge to return to Ecoivres, collecting further 'cargo' as it traversed the area. Local myth has it that the engine and trucks remain today inside the tunnel, although this seems somewhat unlikely in the opinion of the authors. The site of the trackway, viewed from the Souchez to Neuville St Vaast track, is still apparent and many of the fencing supports used by local farmers were probably salvaged from it.

This tunnel, just north of another warren of dugouts on Hospital Ridge, where 12 (Cdn) Brigade had their Battle HQ, shared the characteristics of the other subways but had a working electrical lighting system. Prior to the assault it was occupied by the 38th Battalion CEF. As with some of the other subways, Blue Bull was

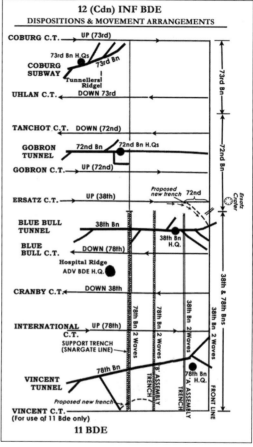

Schematic diagram by HQ 12 (Canadian) Infantry Brigade showing the allocation of tunnels to assaulting troops.

driven well out under No Man's Land, not specifically to debouch troops at the point of assault but more to provide a secure passage for runners and telephone cables. Lieutenant A.D. Lumb (later a major and an MC winner, who went on to command 175 Tunnelling Company) relates:

The 182nd Tunnelling Coy were engaged in putting in the long 'Blue Bull' subway, starting from outside of the ridge and designed to come out in No-Man's-Land, to form safe passage for attacking troops and wounded coming back. In one of the adits [essentially an incline] we had risen from a lead cover of 60 ft. to 4 ft. from the surface, about midway between the opposing front lines, which were at this place 200 yards apart and, as the attack started at dawn by the Canadians, our orders were to cut through to the surface. When we broke through to the surface we found a German standing over the

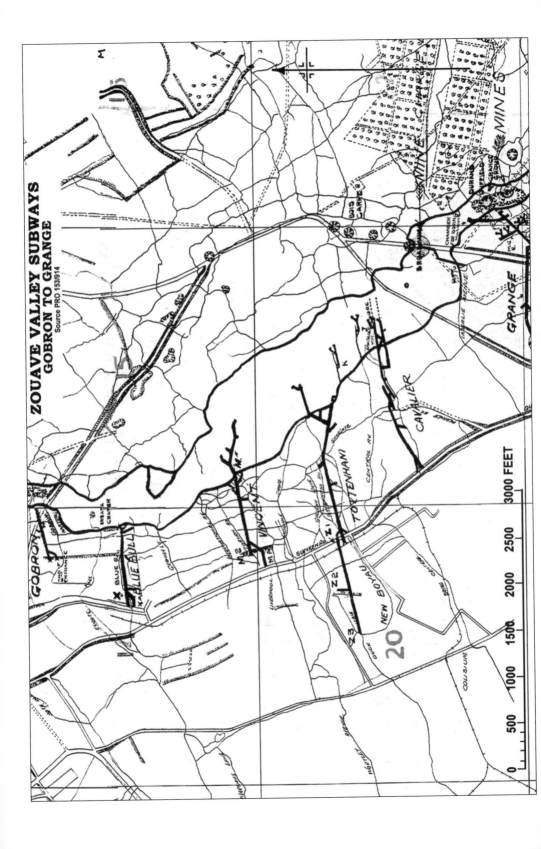

ZOUAVE VALLEY SUBWAYS
GOBRON TO GRANGE
Source PRO 153/914

top. We at once seized him and pushed him down head first through the hole. The wretched man howled for mercy, thinking his end had come, and in very broken English tried to tell us how he was a Canadian and not a German.

This was not Lumb's only prisoner of the day. A while later, in the German line, about twenty of the enemy surrendered to him. They were ordered back but no sooner did they appear on the trench parapet than a German machine gun opened fire on them. That was too much for them and they broke into a frantic run, hotly pursued by Lumb, cursing and vainly waving his revolver. Lumb's reward for his 'bag' was a complaint that he had 'directed' the prisoners to the wrong battalion HQ.

Vincent Subway, some 450 metres south of Blue Bull and about 275 metres north of Zouave Valley cemetery, had its rear exit on the Souchez–Neuville track. Constructed by 182 Tunnelling Company, and occupied on 9 April by the 78th Battalion CEF (The Winnipeg Grenadiers), it had much the same characteristics as Blue Bull, though lacking a railway terminus. It also extended into No Man's Land.

The War Diary of 12 (Cdn) Brigade contains detailed instructions for the management of the Coburg to Vincent tunnels, starting with specifying the officers in charge. Plans of each subway were provided and fixed to noticeboards, but regrettably none of these seems to have survived in the archives. Personnel to be detailed by each battalion for its own tunnel are specified as: a. 1 Officer or 1 NCO of Sergeant or above to be in charge of all Police Posts and sanitary men in each tunnel; b. A Police Post of two men to be at each entrance or exit of each Tunnel; c. Four men to be detailed for sanitary duties in each tunnel.

Detailed instructions were set out for traffic control. In essence, prior to the attack, these restricted movement against the flow of troops moving forward to runners, individual officers and medical personnel. Once the assaulting troops had deployed, priority was largely accorded to the evacuation of the wounded. In Vincent and Blue Bull a rudimentary traffic light system was installed under control of the officer in charge of the tunnel. Red lights were switched on for 'Up' traffic only, red lights off for 'Down' traffic only.

Tottenham and Cavalier Subways (referred to in some Canadian accounts as 'Tubes') were largely completed by 182 Tunnelling Company well ahead of the date of the planned attack, in the case of Cavalier on 13 January 1917. This probably explains why they were then fitted out to provide extensive accommodation. These two were probably the most intricate of all along this part of the front, excepting of course the Arras caves.

The original rear entrance to Tottenham started just by the Souchez–Neuville track, about 70 metres past the current junction with the track that runs beside the Zouave Valley cemetery. The approaches were, however, under observation and subject to frequent harassing fire, so the passage was extended under Zouave Valley into the ridge on the western side, thereby making Tottenham the second longest of the subways. The main passageway picked up one small *souterraine* and a branch tunnel was run out to two more, each of which was fitted out for accommodation, HQ and other facilities. Two of the forward exits emerged in No Man's Land, about the centre of what is now Canadian Cemetery No. 2; it is to be hoped that the passages below the cemetery were made secure against degradation and collapse!

The Cavalier Subway extends from the west side of the A26 péage into the Canadian Memorial Site, with three exits in the former No Man's Land between 5 and 90 metres south of the circular Givenchy Road Canadian Cemetery. With the passage of time the Subway is making itself evident with at least two ground collapses in the fields just outside the Memorial Site and one presently developing within the site itself. Fortunately good plans of both the Tottenham and Cavalier have survived and illustrate the extensive facilities incorporated (see opposite).

These two subways had their first major test at the time of the disastrous brigade-sized raid by the Canadian 4th Division on the night of 28 February/1 March 1917. The details of the raid itself, and the armistice called on 2 March by Hauptmann von Koppelow of Reserve Infantry Regiment 261, need not concern us here. This raid is well covered in a number of the reference works, and from the German perspective in Jack Sheldon's *The German Army on Vimy Ridge*, and in his (and Nigel Cave's) *The Battle for Vimy Ridge*. A 4th Division post-raid report stated that 'All Subways were largely used, and proved of great value, especially in the evacuation of wounded and in getting cases quickly away from the shell area.' One feature of the raid was the extensive discharge along the line of asphyxiating gas from cylinders, some from the Support Line behind the forward tunnel exits. The wind was also fickle and some gas was blown back across the Canadian lines. The 4th Division report relates how this was handled:

All Subways were hermetically sealed. Sets were removed at the foot of the inclines and two thicknesses of sandbags containing clay were built in. Each bag was worked in and apertures sealed by wet clay.

A small hole was drilled through the Barrier thus made, a pipe being pushed through, leading to a Strombos Horn Cylinder [an iron cylinder of compressed air] on the Subway side of the Barrier.

After the second wave of gas, two men were sent above ground to each exit. They raised the gas curtains and kindled a fire at the bottom of the incline. The compressed air from the Strombos Horn Cylinder was then liberated, thus blowing the passage between the Barrier and the exit free of gas. This was found to be most efficient.

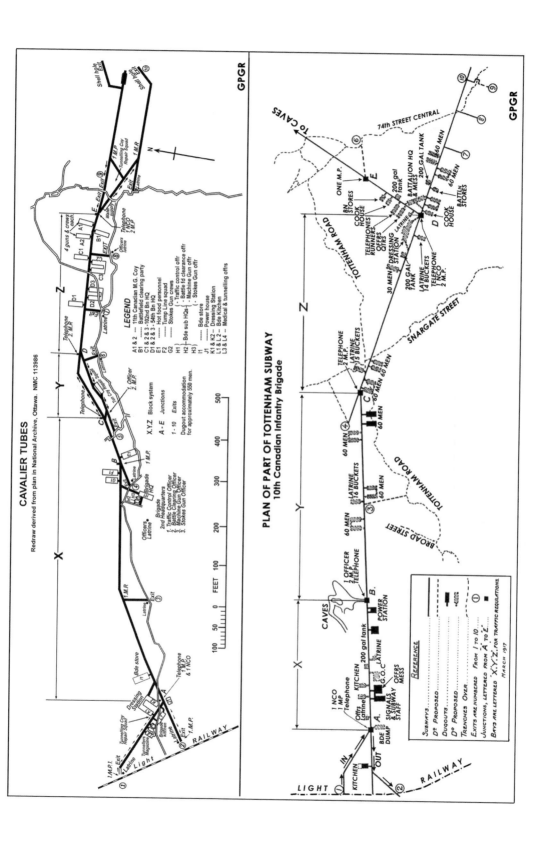

CAVALIER TUBES

Redraw derived from plan in National Archive, Ottawa. NMC 113986

LEGEND

A1 & 2 — 11th Canadian M.G. Coy
B1 — Battlefield clearing party
C1 & 2 & 3 -102nd Bn HQ
D1 & 2 & 3 -54th Bn HQ
E1 — Hot food personnel
F2 — Tump Line squad
G2 — Stokes Gun crews
H1 — Traffic control offr
H2 — Battle fd clearance offr
H3 — Machine Gun offr
I — Stokes Gun offr
J1 — Bde store
K1 & K2 — Power house
L1 & L2 — Dressing Station
L3 & L4 — Bde Kitchen
— Medical & tunnelling offrs

X,Y,Z   Block system
A - E   Junctions
1 - 10   Exits
Dugout accommodation
for approximately 550 men.

100 50 0 FEET 100 200 300 400 500

Brigade
2nd Headquarters
1. Traffic Control Officer
2. Battle Clearing Officer
3. Machine Gun Officer
3. Stokes Gun Officer

GPGR

PLAN OF PART OF TOTTENHAM SUBWAY
10th Canadian Infantry Brigade

REFERENCE

Subways
D° Proposed
Dugouts
D° Proposed
Trenches Over.
Exits are numbered from 1 to 10.
Junctions, lettered from A to E.
Bays are lettered X.Y.Z. for Traffic Regulations.
March 1917

GPGR

It only needed a few minutes to demolish the Barrier and get the exit into working order. In all, about fourteen exits were so treated. No ill-effects from the gas were felt in any Subway.

The Subways between the Canadian Memorial Site and Arras (O to J Sectors)

As shown in the table on page 38, south of the Goodman there were a further five Subways on the Canadian Corps front; from north to south these were Lichfield, Zivy, Bentata, Douai and No. 33 Subway, though the authors have not been able to establish the purpose of No. 33 and whether it rates inclusion. Setting aside the uncertain nature and status of No. 33, the others were similar in characteristics to those already described, except that Zivy was linked to the *souterraine* described in Chapter 3. For the attack on 9 April 1917 Zivy accommodated the HQs of 4 (Cdn) Brigade, the 18th Battalion CEF (Toronto), the 21st Battalion CEF (Eastern Ontario) and D Group Machine Gun Company,

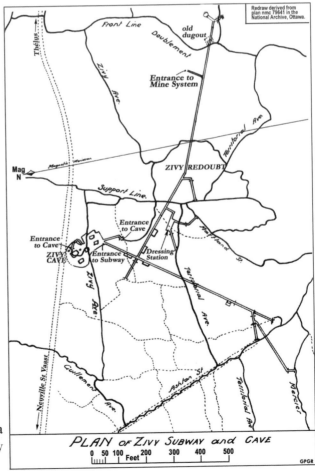

See also the panorama showing the site of Zivy Cave on page 203.

PLAN of ZIVY SUBWAY and CAVE

along with a company of the 20th Battalion CEF (Central Ontario) and an RAP (Regimental Aid Post). Employed also as a communication hub, it would have been a busy place.

At least seven subways were situated in the XVIII Corps area, on the right flank of the Canadian Corps. These mostly seem to have been developments of mining tunnels, so were probably only employed for the passage of infantry rather than fitted out for command and control. The exceptions are Fish Subway, in the 34th Division area, electrically lit and with brigade and battalion HQs; and Barricade Subway, unusual in that it was well behind the front line. Situated just north of the intersection of the Arras–Lens road and the Ecurie–Roclincourt road, it was intended to evade an enemy artillery hot spot, a precursor perhaps of modern pedestrian subways at busy road intersections.

The ascending slopes on this southern part of Vimy Ridge are gentle – to the eye almost level ground – and have been fully restored to agriculture, along with some commercial development. A visitor with trench and tunnelling

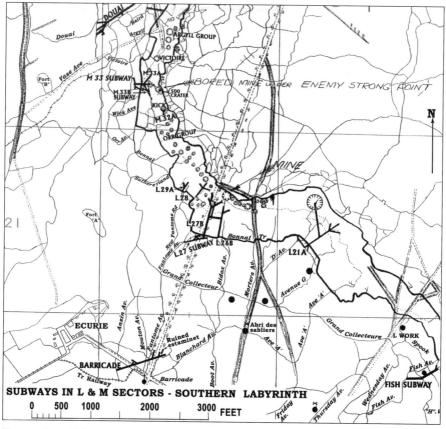

Extract from HQ First Army 1:10,000 scale plans showing the subways in the L and M Sectors and their alignments in relation to the trenches.

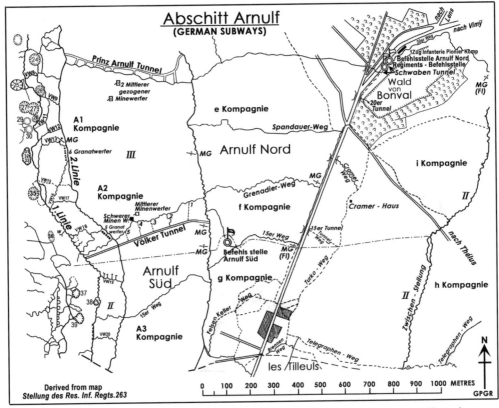

German subways in the Prinz Arnulf Sector, notably the Prinz Arnulf and Volker Tunnels, but also showing several short tunnels, including the Schwaben. German terms are explained in the glossary.

maps, allied to the excellent 1:25,000 *Carte Bleues*, could identify with reasonable precision the locations of all these features. But there is nothing on the surface today to indicate their presence.

German Subways

Although extensive research in the Munich archives by Norbert Krüger and Jack Sheldon has uncovered much material relating to German mining, nothing of any significance has yet been found concerning German subways on this particular front. Two were identified by the British First Army on the Canadian Corps front and marked on the mining plans. The longest of these, the Prinz Arnulf Tunnel, situated almost directly opposite the forward exit of the Goodman Subway, extended from just within the Canadian Memorial site to a right-angle bend in the Rue Canadienne (about 225 metres south of the track to the 3rd Canadian Division memorial). Certainly in place by January 1916, it was probably constructed by *Das Koenigliche Bayerische 12 Infanterie-Regiment*.

About 425 metres long, it parallels – and had many exits into – the Prinz Arnulf communication trench, which ran through what is now the *Forêt Dominial de Vimy*. The rear entrance connected with a light railway, traces of which are still evident in the forest. So far as the authors can ascertain, its sole function was to provide a safe passage for troops and it was not expanded to include command and logistical facilities, nor developed for defence. The tunnel was overrun by 8 (Cdn) Brigade within 30 minutes of the opening of the attack on 9 April, providing a rich harvest of prisoners. Tunnellers of 172 Company inspected it immediately after it was taken, and it was while returning to Brigade to report it free of booby traps and demolition devices that Captain Richard Brisco was killed by a shell.

Volker Tunnel, about 275 metres in length, had its forward exit about 135 metres southeast of the present Lichfield Crater Cemetery. As with the Prinz Arnulf Tunnel, 5 (Cdn) Brigade captured it almost immediately after the opening of the attack on 9 April. Captain Cooper of 172 Tunnelling Company 'obliged' several German prisoners to disclose the locations of several demolition charges and with his men re-opened blocked entrances to bring it back into use. Rumour had it that it was later connected to the Lichfield Subway, but no evidence has been found to support this. Today there is nothing to indicate the presence of the tunnel, which lies below flat agricultural land. The new (2010) Thélus by-pass cuts across it, but surprisingly the road engineers made no effort to investigate what might lie below the carriageway. It is to be hoped that this does not provide an unwelcome surprise to future traffic!

German accounts make reference to a number of short tunnels in the area (for example the Schwaben) that were essentially underpasses at artillery 'hotspots', and it is probable that there were other tunnels, similar to the Prinz Arnulf and Volker, elsewhere along the front. Alexander McKee, in his book *Vimy Ridge*, provides a tantalising glimpse of what may have existed. Referring to the advance of the 1st Royal West Kents (part of 13 [Imperial or British] Brigade, attached to the 2nd Cdn Division), he wrote: 'The Telegraph Weg was the important communication trench leading across the attack triangle and linking the German reserve units in the area of Farbus with the immense tunnel and dugout command post system at Contour 135, otherwise known as Telegraph Hill, between Thélus village and Thélus Mill to the north [sometimes called Hill 140].' McKee goes on to quote Captain Nisbet of 1/RWKs, attached to the 29th Battalion CEF: 'By 10 a.m. the Canadians were in possession of the village of Thélus. Nearby we descended a deep shaft and to our surprise found that it led to a vast underground system of dugouts and tunnels. So unexpected and rapid had been the advance that the inhabitants were blissfully cooking or awaiting their breakfasts.'

This does beg the question of how exactly to define a 'subway'. It was common German practice to interconnect dugouts by tunnels, while in their

Construction of an officer's dugout of 2nd Battery KB FAR 1 at Vimy in early 1916. Left to right: Reserve Hauptmann Danzer, Kanonier Trillich and Leutnant Karl Leibenger (died of wounds at St Mihiel on 12 February 1917). (*Jack Sheldon*)

support and reserve lines they constructed numerous lagers, effectively underground barracks holding complete companies or more, and in the forward areas frequently connected to dugouts in the line. On and around Hill 145, the site of the Vimy Memorial, German trench maps show the *München-Lager* between the 2nd and 3rd Lines. On the hill's crest lay a double trench system, incorporating the *Obere Hangstellung*, supported on the reverse slope by the *Untere Hangstellung*, a twin tunnel system for sheltering the reserves, plus, further north, the *Hanseaten-Lager*. At the *Untere Hangstellung*, just over the scarp slope east of the Vimy Memorial, there remains today a concrete structure with a geared windlass for hauling trench trolleys up the slope to the lager. An engine would have been housed below, though whether this remains in place intact is not known.

These tunnels frequently enabled the defenders to emerge after the assault troops had passed over and engage the following waves, but were also traps for the men sheltering within from the barrage. Sergeant Roland Irwin DCM of the 1st Canadian Mounted Rifles, quoted by McKee, said that

Zwischen gave up a lot of prisoners; it also gave up the German Regimental Commander, and you never saw a madder man. He had started his Easter breakfast of bacon, eggs, toast, cereal and coffee with – if you please, fresh Danish butter and canned cream – 'Carnation' brand – from just 150 miles south of my home in Vancouver. The case was stamped 'Belgian Relief Fund'. Well, he never even got started and Al Swanby really enjoyed it, while Heinie private soldiers

View down a well-constructed German dugout shaft. Note weapons at the ready on the stairway. (*Fonds documentaries Alain Jacques*)

The well-revetted entrance to a German bunker or dugout system. The occupants were evidently humorists. The inscription above the door translates as 'Rat House', that to the left as 'Dancing Every Saturday' and that to the right as 'Dance Hall'. The partially obscured word within the entrance appears to be 'Herbergement', probably meaning 'Rooms to Let'. Below that is the word 'Rabies'. (*Fonds documentaries Alain Jacques*)

laughed their heads off. [It should be remarked that although a relatively senior officer may have been captured, the only regimental commander taken that day was Oberstleutnant Brunner of Bavarian Reserve Regiment 2, off to the south.]

For both sides there was of course a much deadlier and nerve-wracking side to the business of clearing these underground systems: 'Fred Zuehlke lost an arm when he went single-handed down a big dugout. A German officer shot him at a bend in the stair. It was his last shot!'

Captain Thain MacDowell, OC B Company of the 38th (Ottawa) Battalion CEF, was awarded a VC for his actions in capturing and then holding one such large dugout or lager. It was located in Baby Trench, just on the east side of the junction with Cyrus trench – today in a field just 225 metres from and slightly north of Givenchy en Gohelle Canadian Cemetery (see page 193). With two runners, Privates Hay and Kebus, MacDowell was looking for a suitable place to use as a command post. Ahead of them were some German machine guns and MacDowell promptly knocked out one of the machine gunners by throwing a bomb that killed him. His colleague decided to make himself scarce and disappeared into a hole in the ground. The Canadians quickly followed up the vanishing German and discovered a major enemy fortification.

MacDowell called on the 'unseen' to surrender but there was no reply and so, with his two runners posted at the two entrances, he began to investigate. He descended a stairway. After fifty-two steps he rounded a corner into the main room of the underground fortress and was suddenly confronted by a large group of the enemy. He called back up the steps, using a voice full of great authority, to 'supposed' colleagues waiting at the head of the tunnel. The Germans were seemingly convinced and immediately raised their hands in a gesture of mass surrender; they even piled arms in the centre of the room when ordered to do so. MacDowell was then able to send them out of the tunnel in small groups of about ten at a time, a process which quickly stopped when his runners, not knowing the men had been disarmed, shot the first batch. Of the prisoners, mostly Prussian Guardsmen of 11th Regiment RIR, MacDowell wrote, 'I am afraid that only a few of them got back as I caught one man shooting one of our men after he had given himself up. He did not last long, and I am afraid we could not take any back except a few who were good dodgers as the men chased them back with rifle shots.'

Although he was wounded in the hand, MacDowell continued to hold the position for five days and had to endure some heavy shellfire. In a series of four situation reports to Battalion HQ, explaining the circumstances of his much depleted and exhausted company and seeking reinforcements, he described the dugout:

> While exploring this dugout, Kelty and I discovered a large store of what we believe to be explosives in a room. There is also an old sap leading away down underground in the direction of No. 7 Crater. It has a winch and cable for hoisting. This was explored down to a car [?] but no further, as it may be wired. Would you get in touch with brigade as quickly as possible and ask that a party of either 176th or 182nd Tunnelling Company come up and explore these. We have cut all wires for fear of possible destructive posts. The dug-out has three entries and will accommodate easily 250 or 300 men with the sap to spare. It is 75 feet underground and very comfortable. The cigars are very choice and my supply of Perrier water is very large.

Perhaps more information on these German tunnels and lagers may be obtained through further archival search, and doubtless with the passage of time some will reveal themselves. It is doubtful, though, whether any cigars that may have remained will be 'choice' any longer.

Chapter 5

The Pimple to Broadmarsh

Carency and Berthonval (La Volerie) Sectors

British Takeover in the Artois

On 21 February 1916 the Germans launched a massive attritional offensive against the French salient at Verdun, the primary objective being, if the notorious Falkenhayn memorandum is to be believed, to force France out of the war by bleeding its army dry in defending prestigious ground. By the beginning of early March the French command was in desperate straits as the battle sucked ever more men and resources into what was to become the most lengthy battle of the entire war, finally stuttering to an inconclusive halt in December 1916. The consequences of the offensive were wide, impacting on the Franco-British plans for an offensive on the Somme in mid-1916, but more immediately there was a need to reinforce the battered formations around Verdun. Joffre's Tenth Army was still situated between the British First Army in French Flanders (from Loos to the frontier, approximately) and the Third Army on the Somme. He appealed to Haig to release the Tenth Army and to fill its part of the line from the resources of the BEF – not such a difficult operation, in the sense that such a move had already been considered as part of the preparations for an offensive later in the year. In an almost overnight rush, and largely achieved within the first two weeks of March, the First Army extended to the south to the area of Vimy and the Third Army to the north, thereby taking over the whole of Tenth Army's front. Fourth Army, under Rawlinson, was formed on 1 March and in due course took over the Third Army sector from the Somme to Foncquevillers. There was now an unbroken BEF front from just north of Ypres to the Somme. The struggle for Vimy Ridge, extending from Souchez to the River Scarpe (which flows west–east through Arras), suddenly became a British responsibility.

The Arrival of 182 and 176 Tunnelling Companies on Vimy Ridge

One of the first British units to arrive on the Ridge was 182 Tunnelling Company. In *War Underground*, Alexander Barrie expressively chronicles the situation that faced the tunnellers upon their arrival in the La Volerie (or Q) mining sector – which was located largely within the present Vimy Memorial site. After a highly successful local German attack in May 1916, which pushed the British line back about 500 metres, it was renamed the Berthonval Sector.

French dead in the area of Note Dame de Lorette or Zouave Valley.

When the commander of 182 Company, Frederick Mulqueen, arrived on the Ridge on 12 March, he found the situation there somewhat different from that which he had anticipated. In the autumn of 1915 the French had pushed their way almost to the top of this northern part of the Ridge. What no one had told Mulqueen was that the French had been pushed well down the western slope in the intervening months, not least by a surprise attack a few days before the end of February 1916.

The situation was far from pleasant. On that first visit Mulqueen found himself in Ersatz Trench, a name retained from its previous German occupants. Many of the casualties of the particularly fierce fighting that had taken place between the French and the Germans in 1915, a consequence of determined French pushes, still lay around, most noticeably the corpses of the Algerian Zouaves, highlighted by their distinctive red pantaloons; their memory was perpetuated by the naming of the valley to the west of the Ridge in their honour. The tactical situation in the sector was not at all good from the perspective of the Army which came to take over the line from the French. A theoretical defensive position, consisting of three lines, existed clearly on the trench maps but barely did so in reality. Essentially the position consisted of poorly constructed trenches linking up shell holes and craters, and occasionally not even that. In addition the ground was in a very poor state – thick, glutinous mud being the chief characteristic, making movement extremely difficult and tiring.

A French trench at Souchez, in late 1915 or early 1916.

Mulqueen was taken to the surprisingly comfortable dugout of a French engineering officer, a subaltern, in command of this sector of mining. Despite language difficulties – both men knew only a few basic phrases and words of the other's language – some sense of the situation underground was arrived at, gestures and maps filling in the gaps left by lack of verbal understanding. An entente cordiale was soon established:

It was apparent that there had been a good deal going on underground. German miners were very active and the French had fought back with spirit. The subaltern spoke freely about it all, backing up his words with clear air reconnaissance photographs; afterwards he showed his visitor round the mines. But they, too, were not quite what the British were used to.

The ground near Vimy consisted of about eight feet of watery clay resting on chalk. At a depth of thirty feet the chalk became so hard that it had long ago been dug out in places for use as a building material. Many rambling tunnels had been left as a result. The subaltern told how they had used them to blow up the German lines twice within the last five weeks. He was sure, he said, that the enemy had been badly hurt. But Mulqueen's main reaction was an acute unease. It occurred to him at once that the Germans might find their way into these strange, uncharted, ready-made tunnels just as the French had done; then, he knew, he would have to watch out for trouble. An examination of the system did nothing to ease his mind. The mines were not

EXTRACT FROM WORK OF THE R.E. IN THE EUROPEAN WAR, 1914-19.
GEOLOGICAL WORK ON THE WESTERN FRONT.
FIGURE 19 - NE. TO SW. SECTION ACROSS VIMY RIDGE

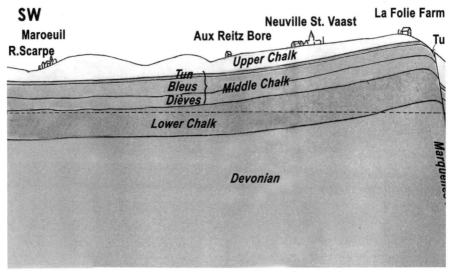

SW SECTION

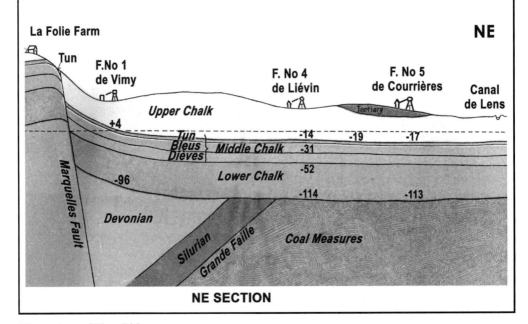

NE SECTION

The geology of Vimy Ridge.

easy to enter. Two in particular – FS and G5 – both positioned well forward, were especially difficult. The entrances, which had been badly damaged and narrowed by shell-fire, reminded Mulqueen more of rabbit holes than anything else.

When he did manage to climb through, he found himself in a dark, oppressive, down-sloping passageway that was disturbingly eerie. He shone his torch on the roughly cut walls and weird-shaped shadows flickered and danced before him. Moving further into the mine he passed through a number of large chambers, where the air was heavy and foul-smelling; everything ran or dripped with water. Mulqueen found it all most unpleasant. And before the two men parted the Frenchman revealed that German miners were probably well forward in this

Transfeld Crater shortly after it was blown in early 1916. Note the soldier (circled) at the top of the crater. (*GPGR*)

sector. It was not what he said so much as his tense, strained attitude that told Mulqueen the truth. He returned to his unit with much to think about. And that day the Germans fired a heavy camouflet that wrecked the whole of one of the galleries to be taken over. It looked like an omen for the future.

Much the same situation confronted 176 Tunnelling Company, commanded by Major Edward Momber (who by the time of his death, in June 1917 in the Salient, had won a DSO and an MC), when they replaced the French 23rd Division's engineers on 19 March 1916 on the left flank of 182, in the Carency Sector.

Vimy Ridge and the Mining Situation at its Northern End
To place in context the situation of 182 and 176 Tunnelling Companies, the important, dominating feature that is Vimy Ridge needs to be described. It extends about 16 kilometres from Souchez in the north almost to Fampoux on the River Scarpe. At its northern extremity, the location of the Carency mining sector, it takes the form of a sharp ridge with steep slopes on either side, known as the Pimple. In early 1916 the French were holding the western heights with the Germans on the other side, No Man's Land effectively being along the crest. Going south, into the La Volerie/Carency sector, taken over by 182 Company, the Ridge becomes an escarpment with a steep drop on the German side but with relatively gentle slopes to the west. Here, through almost to its highest point at Hill 145 (sometimes known as Hill 140), where the Canadian monument stands today, the Germans held the crest, with the French lines just below.

The Pimple viewed from Notre Dame de Lorette in late 1915, looking across Souchez.

South of Hill 145 the escarpment becomes progressively less pronounced, and in the late 1915 fighting the French had been checked before the crest and then forced back onto the lower slopes. For the Germans, however, their position on the northern heights was tenuous. Lacking depth or room to manoeuvre, they could only hold their line by packing the front-line trenches with infantry, a situation vulnerable to concentrated artillery and mining attack. One way for them to improve matters was to take the offensive underground.

It was fortuitous for both 176 and 182 Tunnelling Companies that, shortly before they took over, the German miners had expended much of their effort in a concentrated mining attack that destroyed many of the French galleries. They were thus accorded a short breathing space and went to work with vigour, to a large extent abandoning the French 'rabbit holes' and developing new tunnels from behind the forward line. The objective was to block the enemy's underground advance and then go on to the offensive. Initially the War Diaries report little more than digging and listening activities, but about 7 April the rival miners 'collided'. For the next six weeks there is scarcely a day without reports of the blowing of one or more camouflets or mines. Looking back on this period in later life, Mulqueen described this time as one full of 'rude shocks': 'Our men were buried and our nights made sleepless. We were striving to overcome a situation that threatened to overwhelm us.'

182 Tunnelling Company in La Volerie Sector, April–May 1916

On 18 April, just after midnight, the Germans blew the Neuer Transfeld mine, situated near P.79.K., destroying 30 metres of the gallery and permanently entombing four men, 2nd Corporal Mayer DCM and Sappers Roberts, Robinson and Watt. (These men are commemorated on Bay 1 of the Arras Memorial to the Missing, though curiously enough they are shown as being from 173 Tunnelling Company, which at that time was operating at Loos. Perhaps they were attached.) The Neuer Transfeld Crater is clearly visible today in the Canadian Memorial site – see the tour guide. The following day 182 Company retaliated with a 4-ton mine charge that destroyed a section of the German line on the crest of the Ridge. A succession of punishing blows from the enemy followed. Dire as the situation was for the tunnellers, it was in many ways worse for the infantry holding the line, living in constant fear of annihilation or burial. The tunnellers began to come in for heavy criticism.

Mulqueen was summoned by Lieutenant General the Hon. Sir Julian Byng (later commander of the Canadian Corps but then commanding XVII Corps) and taken to task for failing to provide better protection. Mulqueen tried to convince him that they were doing the best they could with the men and the time available. Helpfully, shortly afterwards, the men of 182 were relieved of a part of the line further south by 175 Tunnelling Company and were thus better able to concentrate their resources.

Some of the heavy mine fighting in the La Volerie sector, principally in the area today on the southern side of the road to Givenchy within the Canadian Memorial site and the private woodlands to the north of the Moroccan Memorial, was described by Hauptmann Erich Karitzky in the history of *Reserve Jäger Battalion 9*; this is followed by a description of the same events from the British perspective:

From the middle of April there was considerable turmoil in the positions. Mining preparations were well advanced on both sides. Listening posts and mine galleries were now very close to one another. The first blasts occurred in neighbouring sectors. On 16 April the British blew a mine under Bavarian Infantry Regiment 24 then, on 18 April, the Bavarians retaliated at the Transfeld Crater [see tour guide]. On 19 April the British set off a mine to our right in the Reserve Infantry Regiment 86 sector. On 20 April there were two tit for tat blasts by the Bavarians and a further one on 24 April. On each occasion there was the usual fight for the crater and heavy artillery fire from both sides, which spilled over into our area. What a pleasant neighbourhood!

In Gallery 12 in our sector the sound of enemy mining was detected on 25 April. Reacting swiftly, a forty *Zentner* [$40 \times 50\text{kg} = 2$ tons] camouflet was blown in the right hand branch at 1.00 pm. This set off a British charge, which was apparently located right next to it so, instead of a camouflet, a crater forty metres in diameter and ten metres deep (Crater IV) was created. Thanks to the daring actions of Reserve Leutnant Schmeling, commander of 1st Company, the crater was seized and preparation for defence began. Reserve Leutnant Schuiz and twenty-four Jägers rushed across from Sap 2 to the crater, occupied the threatened western lip and defended it in a battle with hand grenades.

During the day work began on preparing the edge of the crater for defence and by that night, despite two further attacks with hand grenades by the British, it was protected by a barbed wire obstacle. In that way we secured the crater as an advanced post sixty metres in front of our positions. The following morning, the 26th, there was a further explosion in the Reserve Infantry Regiment 86 sector, which provoked another violent exchange of artillery fire all along the line. The explosions continued when another mine was detonated away to our right near *Funfwegekreuz* [Five-Way Junction, located on The Pimple] which was held by Infantry Regiment 163. At that moment they were conducting a relief in the line, which was made extremely difficult because of the weight of artillery fire coming down on the positions and the rear area. This fire continued on 27 April.

On 28 April, Gallery 12 in our sector was finally ready to be blown. It had been charged with 120 *Zentner* [120 × 50 kg = 6 tons] of explosive. Simultaneously the Bavarians were to blow a nearby gallery containing 50 Zentner [2½ tons]. At 8.30 pm we blew Crater VIII, located only eighteen metres from Crater IV, which had been produced on 25 April [respectively Jäger and Nero craters – see tour guide]. It was fifty-two metres in diameter and eleven metres deep. The Bavarian crater was thirty-two metres in diameter and eight metres deep. Immediately after the explosions, artillery fire poured down on the sector. Despite the fire, Leutnant Nielsen and his riflemen rushed to the western edge of the crater and threw back the enemy, who had arrived simultaneously, with hand grenades and held the position until reinforcements arrived. Our machine guns played a not unimportant role in ensuring that we held on to the crater.

After about two hours the artillery fire reduced somewhat and for the remainder of the night the place was a hive of activity as the crater was prepared for defence, making use of copious quantities of trench stores carried forward by the companies in support. By morning the new Crater VIII and Crater IV had been linked via Sap 3 to the previous front line trench. The morning was quiet, but heavy fire for effect came down on the entire battalion position during the afternoon, with the craters being given special attention. All the trenches suffered badly, in particular the route forward to the craters and the approach routes from the rear. At 8.00 pm it was necessary for a platoon of 3rd Company to take over the craters. The 15th Company had been weakened by all the casualties it had suffered.

During the night the destructive fire of the enemy was interspersed with three attacks using hand grenades, but all were beaten off. The artillery fire continued to be heavy all night. Total losses during these days of fighting for the craters amounted to twenty killed and seventy-nine wounded. From 30 April to 5 May things were relatively quiet. The enemy artillery concentrated on the rear areas, which was fortunate; at the front much maintenance and improvement of the positions was required. Examination of enemy corpses revealed that we had been opposed during the past few days by the Worcestershire Regiment [in fact 3rd Battalion, Worcestershire Regiment, 7 Brigade, 25th Division].

182 Tunnelling Company's reference to these events is laconic, and also contains inconsistencies in respect of blows and timings. For example, their War Diary states that both Nero and Jäger craters were blown together at 3.40 am on 27 April, whereas both the German account and that of Johnston below agree that Jäger alone was fired at 7.30 pm (British time) on 28 April.

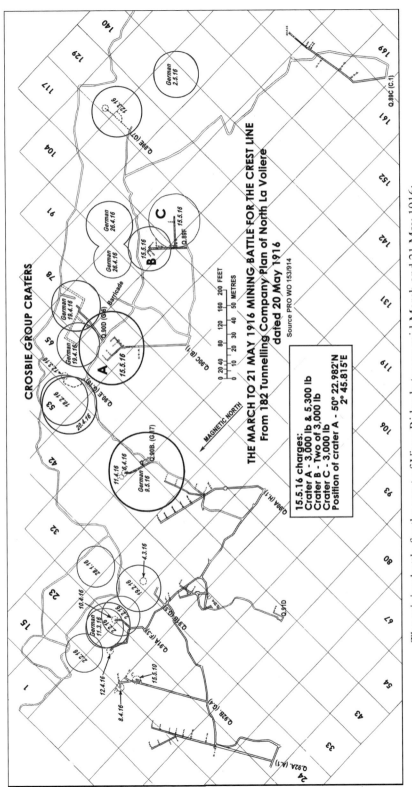

The mining battle for the crest of Vimy Ridge between mid-March and 21 May 1916; derived from 182 Tunnelling Company plan of tunnels and craters dated 20 May 1916.

Interesting comparisons can be drawn from the diary of Alexander Johnston, the Brigade Major for 7 Brigade (25th Division). Johnston was subsequently promoted to brigadier general commanding 126 Brigade in September 1917, a meteoric rise from subaltern in three years; it was, however, an appointment that he enjoyed for only a couple of days before suffering a serious wound which marked the end of his active participation in the war. A brave man, he collected a DSO and Bar and an MC; his most interesting edited diaries have been recently published.

April 28th. Round the trenches all morning with the Gen[eral]. and Birch [the GS01 of the Division, a senior staff appointment]. At 7.30 pm again the earth was shaken to its foundations, and we knew that yet another mine had gone up. We soon heard that it was at the end of the line where the left company of the Regiment [3/Worcesters] was. Apparently the 13/Cheshires on the left were pushed out of their trenches and our left was consequently completely in the air. The Regiment therefore double blocked Centrale [a trench] and started to bomb from right to left along the outpost line. It was, however, so wrecked by the mine explosion and the shelling that they could not have stayed there and, having bombed the Huns out, they came back to a trench of ours about thirty yards behind, where they had the situation well in hand, though they got rather badly shelled. The battalion on our left had gone back to their support line and by 1 am things had quietened down and the Bosche had certainly had enough of it. However, the new crater [it was named Central Crater, after Central Avenue, and Jäger Trichter by the Germans] was alongside of the other at the head of Centrale [Nero Crater] and the two made a sort of wall looking down this main communication trench, which would be very serious if the Huns got an MG or a sniper's post on it. The Division therefore ordered a counter-attack to be made in conjunction with the 74th Inf Bde on the left: there was a lot to arrange, and the latter are a long way away so that in the end the counter-attack, which could not have started before daybreak, was postponed.

April 29th. Very busy all day making arrangements for the attack. Had a long look at the craters from an OP, then went up into the trenches and to the head of Centrale and had another good look at the place to be attacked. The whole ground is just one mass of craters and shell holes, and it is almost impossible to say where anything is. Our guns, a 9.2 inch, two 8 inch, six 6 inch guns, two batteries of Hows [howitzers], two 4.7 guns and two brigades of 18 pounders began shooting steadily at 2.30 pm and then increased to rapid fire at 7.30 pm. We did not get definite orders for attack till the afternoon, there was a fearful lot to arrange and everything was too hurried. However, all the arrangements for the infantry were up to time and the assault by half a company of the Regiment started at 8.15 pm. [The attack was launched from Bertrand Trench, the support trench to the Front Line.]

Directly they left our trenches they were met by very heavy machine gun fire from both flanks and in front, while they got punished by artillery fire from the north; they lost heavily but, in spite of this and the roughness of the ground, they managed to get close up to the lip of the crater and Parks [sic – Captain T.G. Parkes, commanding A Company. He survived the war and was to win the MC and Bar] and a couple of men actually got into it. They found the craters full of Germans in a consolidated position who were waiting for them and threw showers of bombs on to them. Like ourselves, the artillery had been rather rushed; they had not had time to get properly registered, and they had not damaged the enemy's position in the slightest. In fact their bombardment had been worse than useless, merely told the Germans we were coming; a whole platoon was wiped out, and the attack had failed. It was decided to make another attempt at one in the morning: there was no artillery preparation, and the men just crawled up under cover of darkness in the hopes of surprising and rushing the German trench. Again three or four of them got up to the lips of the crater, but machine gun fire opened on all sides again, in spite of our artillery making a barrage on either flank as soon as they heard the show start, and the attack had to come back to where it had started from again. Our losses for so small an operation had been pretty heavy: the enemy's shelling had been very severe – some of our front trenches being quite flattened out. Eventually things simmered down, and all our wounded were got in by daybreak. Managed to lie down and get a rest at about 4 am.

176 and 182 Tunnelling Companies on the Offensive

The Germans had to a large extent expended their immediate underground capabilities and, in the brief pause that followed, 176 and 182 Companies went on to the offensive. On 3 May 176 Company at the Pimple blew three mines with total charges of 21,000 lbs of explosive, the craters formed being named Momber (after the OC of 176 Tunnelling Company), Love (after the OC of 3rd London Field Company RE), and Kennedy (after the CO of the 21st (Surrey Rifles) London Regiment), whose troops successfully rushed and held the craters. Then, at 8:30 pm on 16 May, 182 Company struck, springing five mines under the German lines on the crest 450 metres to the north of Central Crater. It was a carefully conceived scheme, with two of the mines on the right flank overcharged to throw up high lips screening the infantry assault from enfilade fire from the higher ground at Hill 145. Moments after the firing, men of the 11th Lancashire Fusiliers and the 9th Loyal North Lancashire Regiment raced across, protected by a box barrage; the only Germans to be found were dead. These craters were named after Lieutenant Colonel J.D. Crosbie of the Fusiliers, who commanded the assault. They still exist in the privately owned forest area to the immediate north of the Canadian Memorial site.

The aggression on both sides grew in intensity. Alex Johnston's diary reports that on 18 May, in what amounted to a skirmish, the 10th Cheshires lost

Canadian Memorial Site – Vimy. The view south from just uphill of the Neuer Transfeld Crater, looking towards Broadmarsh Crater (on the left at the bend of the road). The road to Canadian Cemetery No. 2 is just visible on the extreme right.

Broadmarsh Crater. The crater to which he was referring in fact is probably from a British camouflet fired on 5 May and in much the same position, or slightly southeast, of the Broadmarsh Crater of today. Some inconclusive grenade fighting by the Cheshires followed, in which Johnston re-organised the defence. The following day a company of 8/Loyals (directed by Johnston) put in a well organised counter-attack at dusk and not only recovered the lost ground but wrested the Neuer Transfeld Crater from the German defenders. This minor success was to be short-lived; a storm was about to break around the incoming British 47th Division, then in the process of replacing the 25th Division.

The German Attack, 21 May 1916

For the full story of the German attack on 21 May 1916 see Nigel Cave's book *Vimy Ridge – Arras* and Jack Sheldon's *The German Army on Vimy Ridge*. The attack had a particular connection to the British tunnelling effort in that one of its declared objectives was to relieve the German defenders of the constant threat of mining attack by seizing the entrances to the British galleries, although another consideration was certainly to give depth to the German defence on the northern heights. This attack was the brainchild of General von Freytag-Loringhoven, Deputy Commander of the German Supreme Command, under Falkenhayn, who in mid-April had been given temporary command of the 17th Reserve Division to gain battle experience; owing to the sickness of the IX Reserve Corps' commander, he took on that command as well. Preparations were exacting in their detail and, in addition to IX Reserve Corps artillery, the attack frontage of 2 kilometres was to be engaged by all the guns of the

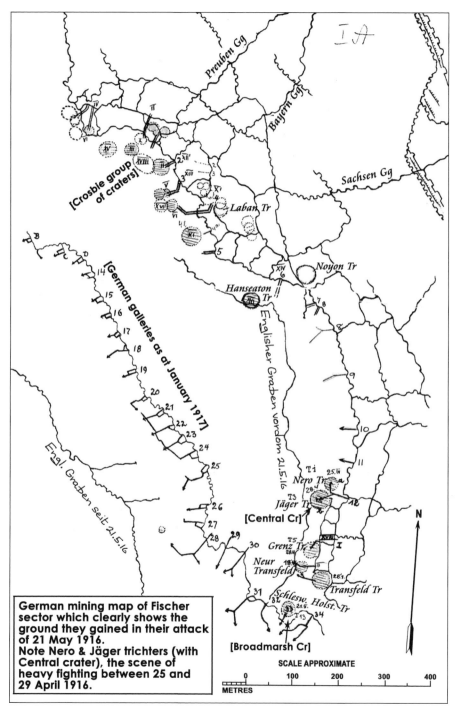

Sketch map of the German Fischer Sector lines, craters and tunnels as in January 1917. This covers the former Franco–British La Volerie Sector and subsequent southern half of Berthonval Sector. *(GPGR)*

Broadmarsh Crater in the summer of 1916. It had been developed for defence. Note the mine shaft entrance indicated by an arrow. (*GPGR collection*)

Broadmarsh Crater in 2009, photographed from the same perspective as the 1916 photograph. Note the subsidence behind the figure, indicating the location of a dugout entrance.

neighbouring IV Corps and those of the Guard Reserve Corps that were in range. Reinforced by nine batteries of heavy howitzers, the fire plan would be undertaken by around eighty batteries. The bombardment opened at about 3:30 p.m. and the infantry assault was launched at 7.45 p.m. [British time]. In bald terms the defenders were driven back around 450 metres, almost to the base of the Ridge, although to the north, from Momber Crater to the Pimple, the line held. Hastily conceived counter-attacks did no more than add to the casualty toll and with preparations well in hand for the Franco-British attack on the Somme, Haig vetoed Wilson's proposals for a set piece attack to recover the ground lost. (Ironically, perhaps, Henry Wilson was also enjoying a brief period as a Corps commander (IV), moving him away from higher staff duties.)

Included in the German plan was the blowing of a mine at the southern hinge of the attack; this was to result in the Broadmarsh Crater, known as Schleswig Holstein Trichter to the Germans (Trichter = Crater). Reserve Leutnant Krüger, 5th Company Footguard Regiment 5, described the firing of the mine:

At 9:44 pm we poured out of our dugouts and raced towards our jumping off point. 9:45 pm! A severe shock shook the earth and a wave-like motion began below our feet. There was a great noise from deep down then, slowly, the earth in front of us began to heave upwards into what looked like a great mountain. Suddenly it burst open and great flames, crowned with a whitish-grey smoke cloud, leapt upwards. Gradually the smoke cleared and, like a

Artist's impression of Lieutenant Richard Brandham Jones of the 8th Loyal North Lancashire Regiment in the action that resulted in the award of a posthumous VC.

shower of meteors, clods of clay and lumps of chalk rained down upon us. It was a man-made earthquake! Gigantic! Dreadful to behold!

It was here, fighting from the Neuer Transfeld Crater, or between it and the newly formed Broadmarsh Crater, that Lieutenant Richard Brandham Jones, 8th Loyal North Lancashire Regiment, won a posthumous VC. He so inspired the men in his platoon that even after he had been killed and their supply of grenades had run out, they continued to resist, throwing empty bomb boxes and lumps of flint. The nine survivors of the platoon were finally forced to withdraw at 10 pm, having contained the German attack for over 2 hours. Leutnant Krüger's account testifies to the heavy casualties inflicted at this point and the intensity of the fighting: 'We formed a long human chain to pass thousands of hand grenades forward to where they were being thrown constantly. Explosions were continuous.'

Of the events of 21 and 22 May the 182 Company War Diary recorded:

On these dates the trenches containing all our mines, with the exception of P.79.B., were taken by the enemy after a very heavy bombardment lasting from 3 o'clock in the afternoon of the 21st to 2 am on the morning of the 22nd. The following is an account of the attack written by the mining officer in charge of the left sector:

Sir,

I have the honour to report that, after heavy trench mortaring, the enemy sprung a mine to the left of Q Trenches at 3 pm on May 21st 1916.

A violent bombardment commenced at 3:20 pm, which lasted twelve hours.

About 5 pm a runner took shelter in our dug-out and reported 27 men and 1 officer alive in the front trenches and 30 men holding the supports.

As soon as possible Lt Robinson reported to Battalion H.Q. The Colonel's orders were to send a party of our ex infantry men under an officer to report to him, the remainder of the company to stand to.

2nd Lt Dale had already taken 25 men and was standing in reserve at the foot of Granby Street. This was reported to Battalion, who were satisfied.

At 12:50 am the bombardment became very violent and at 1 am a party under Lt Robinson left for our HQ with the intention of reporting the situation to you.

At about 1:30 am on the 22nd the first counter-attack was delivered and failed completely.

Reinforcements came and a second counter-attack was made at 2 am, the men going up over our dugouts in extended order. This attack was partly successful, as it drove the enemy back to Boilelet trench.

During the whole time the Valley was subjected to heavy shelling, a large percentage composed of tear shells.

I reported to Battalion at daybreak and was ordered to standby and keep the men under cover. I had occasion later on to visit Battalion HQ to report a gun firing up the valley. During the morning a party of men under an NCO was sent to the Bois-de-Bray for rations. The party returned safely in the afternoon.

Owing to the earlier trench mortaring by the enemy, few men were on shift when the bombardment commenced.

Casualties reported were:-

1 killed, 14 missing, & 3 wounded [German records indicate that fourteen men of 176 & 182 Companies were captured]. Of these, 2 missing have returned.

The Cyclists [attached to 182 Tunnelling Company] were furnishing fatigues and lost 6 missing, 3 wounded and 2 dead.

Two of our dugouts were hit and this accounted for the 3 deaths and the majority of wounded.

Following instructions from yourself and Brigade Headquarters the Company was moved out at 9 o'clock in the evening and reached St Eloi without further casualties. A sergeant and 5 men were left to guard the dugouts.

A relief due out on the morning of the 22nd took a report of the situation to you. I also reported their casualties to the Cyclists.

I have the honour to be, Sir

Yours obediently

R.B. Fisher

2nd Lt RE

From May 22nd to 26th the whole Company remained at Headquarters, but on the latter date part of the Company was sent to the Right sector to charge the remaining mine left in our hands, viz P.79.B., with a view to blowing and holding a crater in front of P.78 trench. 6,000 lb of ammonal was laid and tamped by May 28th but on further consideration with the Division it was decided to withdraw this charge and substitute a sitting charge of 500 lb to blow up the trench if again retaken by the enemy. This was done and the leads laid along the trench to Battalion Headquarters and buried. [Judging by a small isolated crater that exists today at that location – trench map ref S21d58, 50° 22.470'N 2° 46.021'E – it appears that this charge was subsequently blown, but the authors have not found any reference to this in the War Diaries.]

These dramatic events on the right flank of 176 Tunnelling Company in the Carency Sector seem to have largely left them untouched, except that one sapper and four attached infantry were reported as missing. Their War Diary does not even make reference to the German attack!

182 Tunnelling Company and the Berthonval Sector

Although the Germans certainly gained important ground, their capture of 182 Tunnelling Company's galleries did not avail them much in halting or hindering British mining operations. On 5 June, after a week constructing new infantry dugouts, 182 resumed mining from their new positions in what was now termed the Berthonval Sector; initially they started seven galleries, many more were to follow. Free, initially, from German counter-mining, they progressed quickly, and even picked up several lost La Volerie galleries. But the nature of the mining activity had changed. Both the British and the Germans had adopted a largely defensive posture and neither side sought to provoke the other underground in this sector. Furthermore, by October 182 and 176 Tunnelling Companies had interconnected a continuous lateral through the Berthonval and Carency sectors over 750 metres long, making any undetected approach to the British, subsequently Canadian, lines from underground almost impossible.

From the beginning of June there are no reports of any firings until the Germans blew a mine on 10 August, followed by a camouflet on 12 August and another on 30 August – the last such recorded on the Berthonval front. Through to April 1917 182 Company fired just one camouflet (on 27 August) and two interconnected mines on 27 November, thereby forming Montreal Crater, marginally south of Momber. However, they report the laying of seven precautionary mine charges, apart from those employed in blowing Montreal Crater, totalling 95,000 lbs of explosive. Given that there is no record of these being salvaged, it may be supposed that many, or all, of these charges still lie in position beneath the Ridge. Remarkable also is the lack of 182 Company casualties, in marked contrast to the tunnelling companies on their flanks. After 1 June 1916 the first reported fatalities are of one miner and seven Canadian infantry, who died of carbon monoxide poisoning on 26 March 1917.

The underground stalemate suited the company. From late September front-line manning was largely reduced to listening and the majority of the company, reinforced for a time by a section from 173 Tunnelling Company, were diverted to the construction of underground communication and accommodation tunnels – see Chapter 4.

The Germans in the Berthonval Sector

For information on German mining in their Fischer Abschnitt (Sector), which covered most of Berthonval and a small part of the La Folie Sector to the south, the authors are indebted to the late Herr Olaf Grieben for information, plans

Two of Leutnant Grieben's mining pioneers in front of Tunnel no. 23, probably photographed during the summer of 1916. One of the two, probably the man in the tunnel entrance, has been identified as Pionier Piefke. Note the 'drill' working dress, and that the man in the trench is wearing extempore head protection made from a sandbag. The trench is deep, dry and well revetted. (*GPGR collection*)

and photographs provided in 1988. Grieben arrived at Vimy Ridge in June 1916, then aged 18. As a mining officer of the 9th Company Reserve Engineer Battalion (and later as its Adjutant) he was intimately involved with establishing a new mining system along the new Berthonval Sector front line (see plan on page 77). This plan also clearly illustrates the previous crater line, the extent of the German gains, and the fact that they appeared to have been developing a lateral along this front – an unusual departure for the Germans. Their front was well covered by regularly placed shafts, varying in depth from 25 to 40 metres. It was apparent that any mining attack by 182 Company would first necessitate a protracted underground offensive to penetrate the German works.

Of the German procedures Grieben wrote:

The three mining platoons rotated the duties, each platoon spending twenty-four hours at a time on the position. They would, for example, leave their billets at 6.00 pm, carry out mining tasks from 8.00 pm one day until 8.00 pm the next, then return to billets, arriving at 10.00 pm. On the other hand the duty engineer officer spent three days continuously forward. His duties were to maintain liaison with the infantry battalion commander of the sector and to divide the remainder of his time between supervision of mining and maintaining a listening watch.... In consequence he was constantly on the move, by day as well as night. This involved moving above cover, because the trenches were in a state of collapse and the going was extremely difficult. Decision-making

German officers listening in a trench for sounds of underground activity.

Leutnant Olaf Grieben doing his rounds in January or February 1917 in the German forward trench about 50 yards north of Broadmarsh Crater. Note the parlous state of his trench. (*GPGR collection*)

was difficult, especially when reports from the listening parties indicated that there was a risk of a British mine explosion. This meant that, as a precaution, the infantry had to be moved out of the danger area, which in turn carried the risk that the British would spot what was happening and rush to capture the unoccupied position. It was only when I was older that I came to realise what responsibility I had borne [ie as Adjutant], aged only 18½.

Photographs provided by Grieben well illustrate his point about the difficulty of moving around the trenches, at least in the winter of 1916/17, when they deteriorated under both the weather conditions and continuous harassment from the 4th (Cdn) Division, which had taken over the sector (see also page 219).

Shortly before he left the Vimy area, Grieben was caught out by a raiding party and was lucky to escape:

On 27 January 1917, the Kaiser's birthday, there were special rations and everyone was in good spirits. I was down in Gallery 23, discussing listening reports. There was a constant increase in the sound of battle (artillery and mortar fire). Suddenly a voice bawled down into the gallery, 'Herr Leutnant, the Tommies are in the trench!' This was followed by a thumping sound coming down the stairs and I leapt back. But what was bumping down from step to step was not the man who had shouted; instead it was a British demolition charge, probably with a delay fuse. It rolled down the horizontal gallery and came to rest in full view of the entrance chamber to the gallery. Every one of us down in the dugout was filled with horror. If it had detonated, our lives would all have been snuffed out. But it did not; it was a dud. All of us rushed out of the other entrance! Not a shot was fired. The man who had shouted lay there, his skull smashed in by a trench cosh. [Gallery 23 is situated about 90 metres to the right of the road leading to Canadian Cemetery No. 2, just short of the parking bay at the cemetery.]

That a certain pride of endeavour among the miners was shared equally by both sides is well illustrated by an extract from a detailed account of mining operations on this part of Vimy Ridge by Reserve Leutnant Otto Riebike, 2nd Company 28 Engineer Regiment.

War underground is numbered amongst the most terrible types of fighting which occurred during the World War. There are few who can really imagine what took place in the bowels of the earth when the Army communiqué contained the terse words, 'We have blown a mine'. It was in fact a microcosm of the most monstrous style of warfare imaginable and was conducted by a few men in narrow, airless galleries, filled with chalk or clay dust who, at the cost of endless demands on their nerves, gave it all their strength and energy. This was the domain of the sappers; men of steel, both physically and mentally. It was utterly different from the experience of those who confronted the enemy under starry skies or in broad daylight.

It was necessary to be well informed to know where the engineers were conducting their war. Nothing special betrayed the way into their underground galleries. They just looked like the entrances to normal mined dugouts. The huge quantities of spoil, the white chalk or the yellow clay, which were removed from the earth at night were carefully buried in shell craters and thus put out of sight. Barely a light coloured stone or heap of spoil remained which could not be explained away. The sappers closed on the enemy armed with picks, spades, chisels and drilling machines. The spoil was carted away in sandbags or miners' trucks and day and night the mines swallowed props and shuttering timber which had to be brought forward from far to the rear. The entrance to the underground labyrinth opened out from one or other of the forward trenches into a steeply descending gallery or shaft. There, deeper than a house, was the workplace of the sappers, who climbed in and out using ladders.

Perhaps this can stand as an epitaph for all the military miners of the time, whatever their nationality?

Carency Sector – 176 Tunnelling Company

The situation for 179 Tunnelling Company in the Carency Sector (at the northern end of the Ridge) was completely different. As already stated, here the opposing trenches were mostly close to the crest of the ridge, with steep slopes on either side. The mining battle continued unabated as both sides sought to deny the other the advantage of the crest. Between 1 June 1916 and the capture of the Pimple on 12 April 1917, 176 Company blew fifteen mines, using some 175,000 lbs of explosives, and seventeen camouflets, with charges totalling over 43,000 lbs. The biggest single mine was a triple charge, employing 49,550 lbs of ammonal, at the Pimple on 1 June, fired between the existing Newer Cut and Mildren Craters. In turn the Germans blew eleven mines and nine camouflets. At the Pimple itself the crest disappeared into a long string of overlapping craters, with frequent infantry tussles to hold the rim on the 'home side'. Casualties were commensurate, with 176 Company losing two officers and forty-two soldiers killed or died of wounds, 106 others wounded and thirty-six men

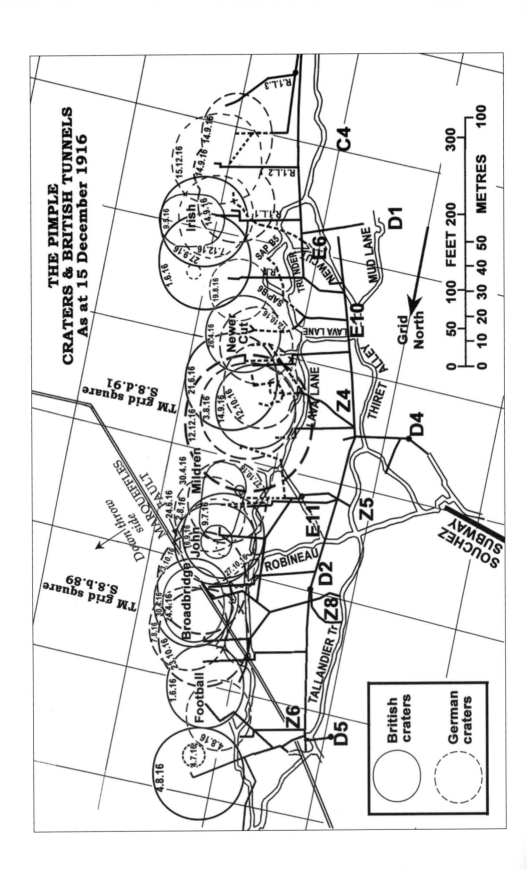

THE PIMPLE
CRATERS & BRITISH TUNNELS
As at 15 December 1916

hospitalised with gas poisoning from carbon monoxide, a total of 186 all ranks. The officers in question were 2nd Lieutenant Frederick Malcolm McIntyre, who died of wounds on 1 May 1916 (buried in Hersin Communal Cemetery Extension, I.F.1), and Captain Raymond Burke Williams MC, who was killed with two other miners by a blow 60 metres south of Kennedy Crater (S9c.14.09) on 19 September 1916; he is commemorated on the Arras Memorial. Major Edward Marie Felix Momber DSO MC, the Officer Commanding, was wounded on 26 June 1916 and was succeeded by Captain (later Major) G.A. Harrison DSO MC from 173 Tunnelling Company. (Momber was wounded again on 18 June 1917 and died two days later; he is buried in Lijssenthoek Military Cemetery.)

The tit-for-tat mine fighting is graphically described in various German accounts. *Offizierstellvertreter* Hugo Gropp, of Reserve Infantry Regiment 76, relates that on taking over from his predecessor on the Ridge he was assured that all was quiet. Having made his rounds he settled into a comfortable dugout, to be abruptly disturbed by an agitated platoon runner informing him that, 'The British are below us in a gallery'. Reluctantly he decided he had to go to check for himself and descended a confined stepped incline to a narrow gallery measuring only 60 by 80 centimetres, reputedly 50 metres below ground: 'There was nothing but the eerie silence of being far from any living being. It was a vile feeling. It would be preferable to be wallowing in the thickest mud imaginable in an open trench.' Fearful that the silence portended a mine blow, he scrambled back to the surface but then, in the company of another officer, returned to listen again. This time they heard above them the distinct sounds of heavy objects being pushed along a gallery. They reported back to the *Kampftruppenkommandeur* (Commander of the Forward Troops) and orders were issued to blow a camouflet immediately. The support battalion and engineer officer were alerted and explosives brought forward hastily from the engineer depot, then passed into the depths by a chain of men, one to every third of the hundred steps. By 6 pm all was ready; the infantry pulled back from the

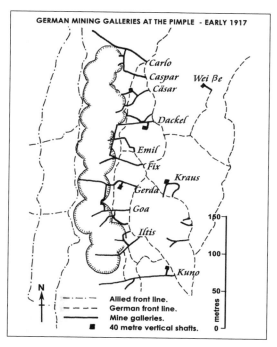

GERMAN MINING GALLERIES AT THE PIMPLE - EARLY 1917

Carlo
Caspar   Wei βe
Cäsar
Dackel
Emil
Fix
Kraus
Gerda
Goa
Iltis
Kuno

N

— · — · —   Allied front line.
— — — —   German front line.
————————   Mine galleries.
■   40 metre vertical shafts.

150
100
50
0
metres

German officers about to fire a mine charge.

danger area and stood to. As the mine was fired the artillery opened up on the British trenches:

> The earth rocked, was heaved upwards violently, swayed about, then was thrown clear of the surrounding earth. Standing upright, I watched a pillar of earth being shot into the air, then all of us who were near the entrance to the gallery were on our backs, knocked down by the shock, as though struck by lightning. Then, just as if a hurricane had struck, everything which had been hanging on the walls of the dugout – gas masks, belts of ammunition, coats and personal equipment – was hurled out of the dugout, as though it had been shot out of a pistol. Luckily nobody was standing directly in front of the entrance; he would have been torn apart.
>
> As quickly as it had appeared, the ghost disappeared once more. The explosive gases had heaved the earth upwards, but then opened a way into the gallery and vented near to where we were standing. We scrambled to our feet and helped to re-establish the correct manning of the company position. The explosion had not created a new crater. This was fortunate, because it meant that we did not have to fight for possession of it. Of course there was a price to pay. The Tommies wanted revenge and were soon pounding our position with mortar fire and all calibres of artillery.

The date of this blow is uncertain but it seems probable that it was one of the two fired on 15 June or (more likely) 21 June, neither of which did much damage to 176 Company workings. Whatever the case, 176 Company hit back hard with a 12,000 lb mine at Z5 on the Pimple on 28 June, and on 3 July with a double mine, totalling 15,000 lbs of ammonal, on the southern edge of Momber Crater (S.15.a.10.65). Hugo Gropp was on the receiving end of the 3 July charges:

On 3 July the Company was manning the front-line trenches and receiving the constant greetings of the enemy artillery. It went on all day long, broken only by pauses of differing lengths. That evening the air was filled with a howling, roaring sound, like that of Woden's wild warriors. Countless steel greetings poured down from the enemy. The clock showed 11.45 pm when, suddenly, something weird and dreadful happened. The earth rocked. On the right flank of our sector the ground writhed in wild anguish. A yellowish-black cloud rose into the sky, whilst all around clods of earth, mixed with pieces of timber and metal, rained down over a wide area. The earth had received a gaping wound.

Where once our sap head had been located, a crater now yawned, sixty metres wide and twenty metres deep. Some members of the garrison of the sap were flung into the air, others were buried. Twenty metres of trench were levelled and two mine galleries were buried, together with the engineers who were working in them. Two sections of our men were also buried by falling debris. We were all filled with paralysing horror, but the moment demanded action. 'Volunteers!' bawled the voice of Leutnant Pietzker, 'Follow me!' Together with his brave little band, he raced for the northeast lip of the crater that had just been formed. A little later he was followed in the same way by Leutnant Morgenroth, whilst sections from 1st Company rushed over to assist. They arrived in the nick of time.

The enemy had occupied the western edge of the crater immediately after the explosion. Ready to do battle, the opponents were lined up, barely eighty metres apart. Back in the trench gallant work was being carried out in an attempt to save living beings from death by suffocation. Unfortunately our efforts were in vain. At 1.50 am British hand grenades were thrown and their artillery resumed its destructive work. The enemy then attacked our right flank and the left flank of the 2nd Company. Our infantry immediately produced its own defensive fire, as large numbers of hand grenades were thrown at the attackers. The machine gunners joined in, creating a hail of iron of their own. The enemy had to fall back, but our casualties were very heavy that night: fifteen killed and ten wounded.

The Final Act, 9 April 1917
On 9 and 10 April the northern heights of Vimy Ridge, apart from the Pimple, were taken by the Canadian Corps, and the slopes on their right flank, to the south, by XVII Corps. Two days later, on 12 April, the Germans were driven off the Pimple by 10 (Canadian) Brigade in conjunction with an assault on their left flank by 73 Brigade of the 24th Division, which took the remainder of the

German miners entering a gallery at the Pimple. (*Jack Sheldon*)

Lorette Spur and Bois en Hache. As observed in the extract from the 176 Company War Diary below, it is interesting to note that the assault on the Pimple only just preceded an intended German offensive. The company was also responsible for the last of the mines to be blown on the northern end of the ridge. Of events on 9 April the War Diary says:

The work of the Company during the latter half of March and up to the 9th of April consisted to a great extent in preparations for the General Offensive, which began on the latter date. The task allotted to the Company was provision of the two Infantry Subways, Gobron and Coburg, with suitable accommodation off both, and the preparation of three mines Z1.R1L1 upper and lower and C3.R1L1. The two first named mines were respectively 60 ft and 110 ft below surface. The upper blow was for the purpose of providing a Crater to form a strong point and for purposes of defilade on the extreme left flank of the Front of Attack. The deeper charge was to deal with the enemy galleries, and thereby protect the new flank to be formed from a subsequent blow [by the enemy]. The mine in C3.R1L1 was to smother, by Fougasse effect, a machine gun position on the Eastern lip of Kennedy Crater that might come into play against the Left Flank of our assaulting troops. The camouflet in E5.R1L1 was simply in the way of a routine operation against an enemy gallery that was thought to be charged against us ... Precisely at Zero hour – 5.30 am – the mine in Z1.R1L2 [the writer appears to have confused the tunnel references] was blown and was followed six seconds later by the mine in C3.R1L1 and the camouflet, whilst simultaneously our batteries and machine guns opened on their barrage lines and the assault was launched. An interesting feature in connection with the mining on the Company's Front is the anxiety that our underground operations were causing the enemy, as disclosed by the capture of a German Order by the 79th Reserve Infantry Brigade, 79th Reserve Division, dated 5 April 1917. This document gives details of an attack, which was to be delivered by the 16th Bavarian Division shortly after the 5th April 1917, on a frontage of about 3,200 yards south from the Souchez River, that is on the Sector for the safety of which this Company was responsible. The purpose of the attack, which was to capture and hold the objective, was to obtain a better defensive position, and to 'remove the mine danger'.

Although 182 Company had several mines prepared, these were not employed in support of the attack. Their War Diary entry for 9 April is notably laconic: 'At 5 am a general attack was made, all objectives attained'. The War Diary does, though, contain an extensive report on the subsequent reconnaissance of the German workings and covers a variety of facets, including an assessment of German mining tactics, shafts, ventilation, haulage, spoil dumping, listening equipment, charges and explosives, rescue apparatus and survey instruments. The company assessed that the German system was defensive in purpose, with deep listening posts at regular intervals (which conforms to the information from Olaf Grieben). The shafts were generally inclines at 45° or 30° but often driven below the water table, with resultant flooding of the galleries. These and the galleries were close timbered and with a few exceptions very confined, being just 1.22 metres high by .61 metres wide. Spoil was mostly manhandled, except for three shafts where a monorail had been employed, and one location where a start had been made on a communication tunnel (subway) equipped with a trench trolley on rails. Overall 182 Company was not particularly complimentary about the German efforts! Of the galleries they entered – and many were not accessible – they found two that had clearly been charged ready to blow (S15c.37.56 and S15c.31.64) and two others that were in the process of being charged (at S15c.49.51 and S15a.14.39). The gallery to one of the charged mines had collapsed, while the other was already tamped. There is no evidence that these were subsequently cleared.

As First and Third Armies advanced onto the Douai Plain the tunnelling companies followed, mostly concerned with the construction of roads and dugouts. The fighting tunnels were abandoned to the attention of salvage parties. Later, in the 1920s and into the 1930s, the entrances were in-filled in the course of battlefield restoration, but below the in-fill the tunnels remain, a hidden and silent witness to the endeavours of courageous men.

Chapter 6

The La Folie Sector

Introduction

Situated entirely within the Canadian Memorial Site, the La Folie (or P) mining sector encompasses almost all the features of the mining war. The craters on the surface, within the area open to the public and extending south through the Memorial Site forest (not accessible to visitors), are a visible testimony to the intensity of that conflict, while guided tours through part of the Grange Subway (see Tours Section) give visitors a glimpse of the subsurface works of the miners and, at one point, a sight down an incline into the depths.

That tantalising glimpse into what the Canadian guides refer to as 'The Sap' is a tiny part of the British La Folie system, extending to over 3 kilometres of tunnels in the chalk. It remains today in almost the same condition as it was left in April 1917. Seven inclined entrances from the main defence line trenches, most still with their wooden trolley rails, connect to a lateral of just over a kilometre in length situated just forward of the main defence line. In turn, the lateral connects to fighting and listening galleries at depths of 18 to 30 metres below the surface, and by shafts and stairways upwards to many of the earlier fighting tunnels, driven before the lateral was put in place. This lateral, used as a conduit for telephone and electrical cables, also connects to the Goodman Subway, of which some 600 metres has been accessed in recent years (see Chapter 4). Two unused mine charges and a camouflet charge remain in place, each of which was neutralised by removal of the initiation systems between 1997 and 2003. Numerous features such as gas doors, ventilation pipes, supporting timbers, rails, miners' tools and a plethora of discarded tins and containers litter the tunnels, albeit in varying degrees of deterioration, while several seismomicrophones have been recovered.

The La Folie Sector confronted the German Arnulf North mining sector and the southern fringe of the Fischer Sector. German mining plans show around twenty-five tunnel entrances, almost all into a single shaft or incline, though branching in many cases into a 'Y', generally sunk to a depth of 30 to 35 metres (in many cases below the water table, giving rise to flooding difficulties). With a couple of exceptions it was not German practice to connect the tunnels laterally. However, one such system, at the southern end of the La Folie sector, had three entrances interconnected at a depth of around 33.5 metres; accessed in 2005, it was investigated in detail by the Durand Group.

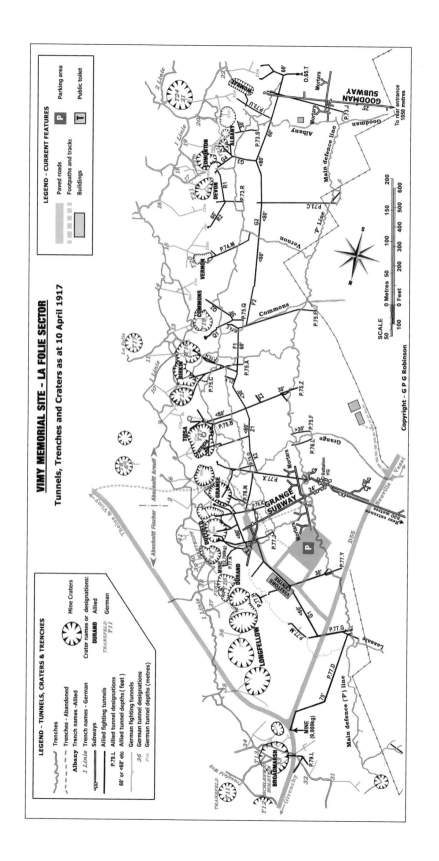

VIMY MEMORIAL SITE - LA FOLIE SECTOR
Tunnels, Trenches and Craters as at 10 April 1917

LEGEND - TUNNELS, CRATERS & TRENCHES

Trenches
Trenches - Abandoned
Albany Trench names -Allied
1 Linie Trench names - German
Subways
Allied fighting tunnels
P.79.L Allied tunnel designations
60' or <60' etc Allied tunnel depths (feet)
German fighting tunnels
36 German tunnel designations
71m German tunnel depths (metres)

Mine Craters

Crater names or designations:
DURAND Allied
T11 German

LEGEND - CURRENT FEATURES

Paved roads
Footpaths and tracks
Buildings

P Parking area

T Public toilet

Copyright - G P G Robinson

SCALE
0 Metres 50 100 150 200
0 Feet 200 300 400 500 600

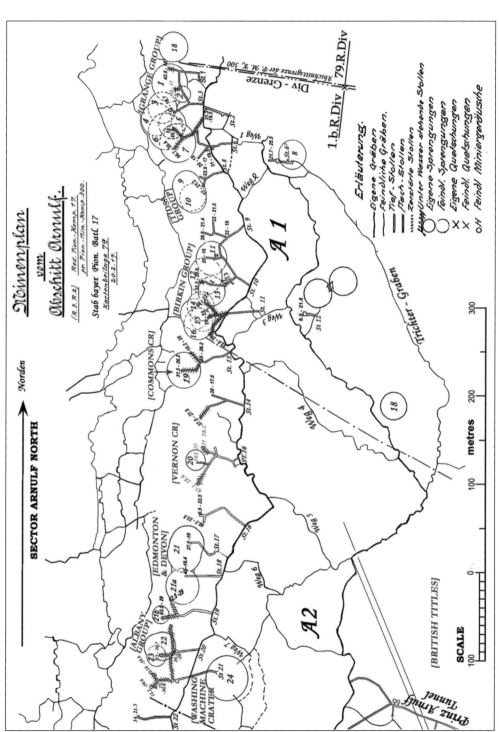

(For translation of legend, see page 135.)

A major German subway, the Prinz Arnulf Tunnel, is also situated in the La Folie sector, though all but the forward exits lie under the *Forêt Domaniale*, outside the Canadian Memorial site. Additionally there are an unknown number of shallow French and German galleries driven during the fighting on the Ridge at the end of 1915, along with numerous dugouts, some of which were interconnected by short tunnels.

With the trench lines, saps and craters still visible (albeit those in the forest area are largely concealed by thick undergrowth), and the British tunnel system beneath accessible, along with some German tunnels, this sector is a unique and historically priceless microcosm of the war waged on the surface and underground.

The French Period, October 1915–March 1916

Following a preliminary bombardment of hitherto unparalleled ferocity, the French Tenth Army opened the Third Battle of Artois on 25 September 1915, in conjunction with the BEF offensive at Loos, just to the north. Fourteen French divisions, with three in reserve, went into the assault between Angres, just north of Souchez, to Roclincourt, on the northern outskirts of Arras. Relative success attended XXI and XXIII Corps on the northern flank, where the latter initially gained most of the crest from the Pimple to just short of Hill 145, although they were subsequently forced back to positions just below the top. III Corps, attacking between Hill 145 and Farbus, almost broke through the defending Grenadier Regiment 11 and Infantry Regiment 51 at La Folie Farm, but the advance was checked on 2 October by Footguard Regiments 2 and 4, which were rushed in as reinforcements. On 11 October the French made a final concerted effort to gain the precious 200 to 275 metres to the crest, but in three days of bitter fighting the exhausted remnants of the Guard Corps and the newly arrived 1st Bavarian Division restored the German line.

With the ground reduced to a quagmire and his troops worn out, on 14 October General d'Urbal, commanding Tenth Army, ordered a suspension of the offensive and instructed the troops to consolidate. French losses amounted to 48,230. Overall German casualties are not known but, as an indication of the ferocity of the fighting, the German Guards Corps lost 117 officers and 7,327 other ranks over about two weeks.

In the La Folie Sector the French were not allowed much time to consolidate. On 30 October a regiment of the 1st Bavarian Division launched a surprise attack between Artilleriegraben and 11er Weg, driving the French back a short step into what is today the forest area of the Canadian Memorial site. This was probably the last of the small counter-offensives on this part of the Ridge not involving a major contribution from the miners of one side or the other. Already to the south, from Thélus to Roclincourt, the rival engineers were again locked in battle underground, and those within the La Folie Sector followed suit.

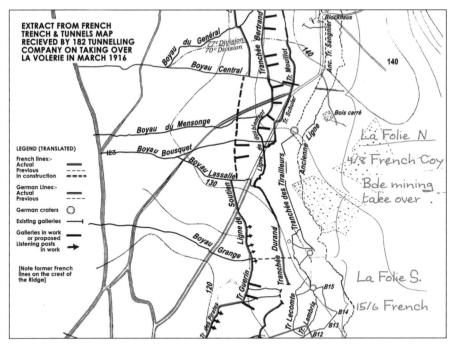

French trench map of the northern part of La Folie Sector, *c.* February 1916.

Hereafter almost all significant offensive action by either side was accompanied by a mining attack.

In January 1916, in order to increase the depth available to the defence and to distract attention away from German offensive preparations near Verdun, a series of minor attacks under the codename Rupprecht was launched in I Bavarian Reserve Corps area on the Ridge. The first of these, Rupprecht I on 23 January, accompanied by the firing of four mines (two others failed), drove the French from their forward line near and south of Thélus. Rupprecht II followed nearby on 24 January; Rupprecht III extended into the La Folie Sector on 26 January and Rupprecht IV into the La Volerie (Fischer) Sector two days later. The latter included the blowing of the Transfeld Crater and another large mine in the vicinity of the subsequent Crosbie Craters (see Chapter 5).

Rupprecht III, mounted by the 50th Reserve Division, involved the use of four mines of hitherto unprecedented size, the northernmost being situated in the La Folie Sector, 150 metres west of the forward exit of the Prinz Arnulf Tunnel. German accounts are not specific but indicate 'several hundred *Zentner*' of explosive (around 20,000 to 30,000 lbs). There was much debate over the possible consequences. What might be the size of the craters? What would be the effect of the debris and should the assault troops be withdrawn from the front line? What would be the best time to attack – in daylight or at night? The assaulting unit, Reserve Infantry Regiment 230, had to make most

The German La Folie Crater prepared for defence. It was probably blown as part of Rupprecht IV. (*Jack Sheldon*)

The former German La Folie Crater in 2010.

of these decisions itself in the absence of any precedent. Finally it was decided to attack at 7.30 am on the 26th. A member of the 11th Company described what happened:

Our company was in support during the explosions and the following assault so, finally, after a great deal of hard work, we took up our positions in the second trench. Once more there was time for reflection as it gradually became light and each man occupied himself with the anxious question, 'What does the day hold for me?' I believe that many a comrade made his peace with God and prayed hard with all his heart. So there we stood in the early hours of 26 January 1916, leaning against the damp wall of the trench, man by man, our gas masks ready on our chests and we waited tensely for the explosions. Suddenly there was an order from the company commander. In a hurry he rushed around from man to man, 'Open your mouth!' Everyone stood there, mouths gaping. The odd nervous one ducked down while others strained to see in all directions through the morning mist. Still more stood there in silence, staring forwards.

Everywhere the tension was acute as we waited, feverishly, for the violent crash that everybody knew was about to happen. Suddenly the word raced along the line of men who stood there with fixed stares and their mouths forced even wider open, 'Stand by!' and, almost immediately, a noise began, down in the deepest of depths – a violent, dull, underground roaring. The earth heaved and shook and a pillar of fire roared up into the sky. With great rattling and crashing sounds the debris dropped back to earth. The morning fog dispersed and the tension was broken by the shouts of 'Hurra!' of the assaulting troops mingling with the notes of the buglers blowing 'Advance at the double!'

Four massive craters had been blown and occupied by us. However, under concentrated mortar and artillery fire, it was necessary a short time later to withdraw from Crater 4 [IV]. At that, we in support were moved further forward. It was a ghastly move through mud-filled trenches under heavy artillery fire, as we climbed over the bodies of our fallen and wounded comrades. The drive for self-preservation did not, however, leave us with much opportunity to express our sympathy and we simply had to plough through the corpses. As evening approached on 26 January we received orders to retake the lost crater. We knew only too well what a difficult task we had been given, but we soon found ourselves lined up in a wrecked trench, up to our knees in mud, our bayonets fixed and our teeth chattering.

The moon cast a pale, ghostly light on the ploughed-up ground and the mysterious deep, water-filled, shell holes. In the distance a machine gun fired the odd burst, but otherwise all was quiet. To the left we could hear the dull report of exploding mortar bombs and fiery trails, arcing through the sky, pointed the way that Death had taken. Over there the high lip of the crater, bathed in the silvery-white moonlight, beckoned to us and bid us come. 'Stand by!' – the word was passed swiftly from mouth to mouth down the line of soldiers. Hand grenades were clasped tightly and rifles were held in an iron grip. The peep of a whistle sounded shrill in the still of the night and there was a confused rush as, with jaws clenched, everyone launched themselves forward.

But the Frenchmen had been lying in wait. Mortar bombs crashed down all round, machine guns chattered and hand grenades barred our way to the crater. Shouts of anger and pain filled the air, but it was no good, we had to pull back. We found ourselves, much reduced, huddled in a sap. Now and again a further attempt was made, but it was all in vain. Filled with bitterness, we attempted to recover our dead and wounded but, even in that endeavour, we had very little success. Many of our dear comrades had to lie where they had fallen – and over all this the moon cast a silver light on friend and foe, cold and heartless.

We passed the following day in the mud and water of the front-line trench. Finally we were relieved and the company pulled back into Schwaben Tunnel. It was a hard road back, through the pitch-black night and the flattened trenches. Many a man was trapped up to his hips in the mud, but helping hands pulled them free and we plodded our way to the rear and rest.

Leutnant Sprengel of the 5th Company Reserve Infantry Regiment 230 is more forthcoming about the failure of the attack on Crater IV:

Over from the Crater IV area came the sounds of another very heavy grenade battle. I was not long in doubt as to what was happening. The noises drew closer and suddenly the remainder of 6th Company leapt into my crater. There were barely twenty of them and I could not make them stay. A *gefreiter*, whom I met later, told me that I had shouted at them, 'If your heart is beating inside you, Stay!' Three heeded my words and remained to hurl grenades at the French until our arms ached from the effort. The French pressed forward, much further than usual, until they were landing grenades in our crater – something they otherwise would never have achieved. A man standing on my right received one full in the face. The reinforcements arrived and everything quietened down. I spent the entire night sitting next

German working party in a crater that, if not Trichter 24, has very similar features to it.

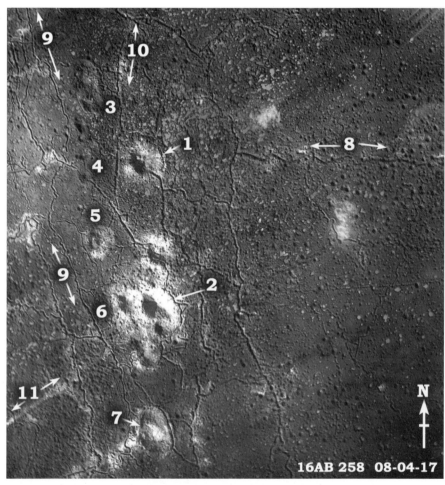

Aerial photograph dated 8 April 1917 of southern La Folie and northern O Sector terrain, showing the 'Washing Machine' to the B4 craters.

Key:
1. Trichter 24 ('Washing Machine Crater')
2. Trichter 26 (the largest crater on the ridge)
3. Trichters 21 and 21a (Edmonton and Devon Craters)
4. Trichters 22 and 23 (Albany Craters)
5. Chassery Crater
6. The Twins
7. B4 Craters
8. Prinz Arnulf Weg
9. Canadian forward (observation) line
10. German forward defence line
11. The 'Sunken Road': old road to Neuville St Vaast

to my friend S., who had deployed the remains of his company in my area. He was down to twenty men from 170.

Crater IV (Number 24 on the Arnulf Sector tunnelling plan) is the second largest remaining on the Ridge, at 45 metres diameter and 8 metres deep. It is, though, dwarfed 180 metres to the south by the crater from a German blow on 2 March 1916 – Trichter 27 on the Arnulf plan, at 50 metres across and 12 metres deep. Excluding several of the water-filled craters at Messines, it is exceeded only by the Lochnagar Crater on the Somme and those at Vauquois near Verdun. Although situated within the Canadian Memorial site, Trichter 27, like the castle of Sleeping Beauty, is almost impenetrably shrouded in brambles and thick undergrowth.

Crater IV (or Crater 24, depending on which plan is viewed) was partially cleared by the Durand Group in 2003. A domestic appliance found at the bottom lent the crater the sobriquet 'Washing Machine Crater' (although the appliance was later identified as a gas cooker, the name stuck!). The Durand Group's excavations and archaeological work in the crater uncovered, along with a great deal of battlefield debris and munitions, the bodies of two German soldiers, regrettably without any means of identification.

The French success at Crater IV (Washing Machine Crater) was short lived. Despite the endeavours of the miners of *15/6 Companie du 7er Regiment du Genie*, on 8 February the Germans struck again with four mines, these craters today being situated along the eastern edge of the Beech Avenue in the Memorial Site forest. The accompanying attack forced the French 90 metres back to their support line trenches and into what was shortly to become the British P line (principal or main defence line). With that the Germans captured almost all of the French mining galleries in the sector.

Extracts from a report by the 1st Field Engineer Company of *Pionier Bataillon 1, No. 8* describes some of the captured French galleries and bears out the 'rabbit hole' comments by the British tunnellers (note that all measurements are in metres):

Tunnel 1. French name G.11, stairway shaft 0.65 × 0.80 lateral clearance. Incline of 20 degrees, without a mine vestibule. Tunnel length 18 m.

Tunnel 2. Inclined shaft, 1.00 × 1.00 horizontal clearance, incline of 30 degrees, without mine vestibule. The first frame has an earth cover of 0.60 m. Tunnel length 17.0 m.

Tunnel 7. Mine vestibule 2.50 × 2.90 lateral clearance, then sunk shaft 1.25 × 1.25 lateral clearance, 9.0 m deep, from there a tunnel 1.0 × 1.25, 18.0 m long, then buried. The sunk shaft is used by us.

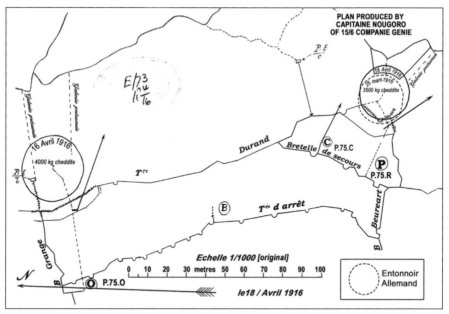

Plan produced by Captain Nourogo, *15/6 Companie Genie*, of French blows on 16 April 1916. This formed the original Grange crater.

In general, the mine vestibules are poorly carpentered and in some cases covered only with corrugated iron and two layers of sandbags. The carpentry of the shafts consists of hardwood and is very poorly executed, while the frames in general are not properly set up.

It should not be thought that the German engineers had everything their own way. Plans from the Munich *Kriegsarchiv* show many French counter-blows, mostly small and probably camouflets, but sometimes with heavy charges. On 16 April they blew two substantial mines to attack encroaching German tunnels, utilising 16,500 lbs of cheddite. The following is an extract of a report from Captain Nourogo, Commander of *15/6 Compagnie* (of Engineers), sent to the Chief of Mining Staff at HQ Tenth (French) Army and copied to Lieutenant Colonel Danford, Controller of Mines, Third (British) Army and accompanied by a plan (see above):

As a follow-up to the evening's report by Lieutenant Gauthier, I have the honour to advise the results of the crater explosions – the recce of same could only be carried out at daybreak.

1. Crater at the head of 'O' [tunnel P.75.O]. The 1st line trench was filled in to a length of 12m by the rim of the crater. Diameter of crater approximately 30m. Link between right and left sides of 1st line assured

by a trench. British infantry are digging a sap to occupy the west lip of the rim. The east side is occupied by the enemy.

2. Crater at the head of 'P' [tunnel P.75.P]. The explosion impacted on an old crater, moving the crater approximately 10 to 12m to the right. No damage to our 1st line trenches; no changes to the section occupied by the British infantry.

Our galleries behind the tamping were not damaged and the air is adequately breathable. I will give the order to check things out during the day so that any repairs can start when the troops are relieved at 7pm. [A side note advises that this order was subsequently countermanded – the galleries were probably full of lethal carbon monoxide.]

The crater at the head of the Grange communication trench formed the first of what was to become the Duffield/Grange Group. Specifically, it is the large crater on the southern side of the track between the 'conserved' trenches in the Canadian Memorial site. The P Crater absorbed a previous German blow in part of what became the Birkin Group, located in the Memorial site forested area.

The British miners who replaced the French on the Ridge (note that some French engineers stayed on in the sector after the French Tenth Army had been moved), although critical of their methods, paid tribute to their extraordinary courage. Let the reader try to envisage working deep underground in little more than crawl tunnels, with scarcely space enough even to turn around, often gasping for air and under the constant threat of entombment. They were most certainly brave, but not as efficient as their enemy. However, the Germans were about to face a new foe who brought speed, structure and state-of-the-art mining technology to the underground war.

172 Tunnelling Company in the La Folie Sector

On 22 May the French *15/6 Compagnie Genie* was replaced by 172 Tunnelling Company, commanded by Major G.A. Symes (who was to gain a DSO, an MC and four Mentions in Dispatches). Formed in February 1915, the company had engaged in intensive mine warfare in Flanders, at St Eloi, Armentières and the Bluff and had acquired a distinguished record. They needed all the experience they could bring to bear at Vimy, and it was an inauspicious moment to arrive. Two days before their arrival the Schleswig Holstein offensive (see page 76), immediately north of the La Folie Sector, had just

The 172 Tunnelling Company motif and a Royal Engineer cap badge.

Major Symes

Captain (later Major) G.A. Symes, Officer Commanding 172 Tunnelling Company.

driven 182 Company out of their tunnels and two of the 172 Company advance party had been killed and three wounded. Along the La Folie Sector the Germans were pressing forward underground in a score or more of tunnels.

At this stage British mining policy had undergone a radical change. Except in support of specific offensive objectives, or for local tactical reasons, it had been decided that mining was to be tactically defensive and where the enemy were not pressing underground they were not to be provoked into tit-for-tat explosions. In a letter of 11 August this was strongly emphasised by Brigadier General Harvey, the Inspector of Mines at GHQ, writing to Lieutenant Colonel J.G. Hyland, the Controller of Mines in Third Army:

Please inform all your Officers that the policy of pressing forward a defensive [*sic* – sap?] to close proximity with the enemy's works, when no Infantry offensive is contemplated, is forbidden without your authority. We do not want to stir the enemy into activity except at places where serious action is intended. This case may result in the interruption of more important work, as has happened elsewhere.

In March 1916 the Controller of Mines in Third Army analysed the German activity on his front. Of the La Folie sector he observed:

The enemy policy here is puzzling. There has never been any attempt at an attack on a big scale, and he seems content to blow short of our line every time. It is probable therefore that his object is, in the main, defensive, and that he wishes to form an obstacle in the form of a ravine of craters along the whole front.

From this he concluded: 'The best way of protecting the main line seems to me to make the enemy blow in front of the observation line by forcing his hand with the forward galleries'. It should be added that he went on to compliment the French tunnelling companies in the sector on their 'excellent work'.

Symes accordingly chose to bide his time and, by a skilfully directed process of guile, to generate alarm and force the German miners to show their hand. Between his arrival and the end of August 172 Company blew only three mines and one camouflet compared with seven mines and six camouflets blown by the Germans, none of which seriously affected the infantry and only one inflicted significant casualties on the company. A report by Symes on 3 July indicates something of the methods, the area in question being below the Grange Crater:

On 28-6-16 enemy was located below the chamber in the right gallery of P.75.O. at a distance of about 30 ft (by Western Electric Sound detector).

The French 15/6 Coy had reported having heard working near this point and suspected a charge to have been put in during April. Since then only distant sounds had been heard until 27th June when work again started.

Owing to the shallow depth of O galleries (39 ft) and the position of the crater in front, it was impossible for us to camouflet with any hope of destroying the enemy's gallery; hence it became necessary to make him blow to prevent him reaching our front trench.

On 29th we commenced putting down bore holes in the floor of the chamber, partly by auger, partly by 'jumping' owing to the presence of flints. The Germans were working actively at first, but during the afternoon picking ceased and only a scraping sound was audible.

On July 1st enemy became active again. At 10 a.m. talking could be heard plainly by geophone and picking recommenced. At 10:15 a.m. we blasted one hole. At 12:00 a.m. picking could again be heard, and we fired the second shot. At 1:00 p.m. he was quiet; we fired the third shot. At 3:00 p.m. faint picking (by geophone) and two blasts were heard. At 3:15 p.m. enemy blew a camouflet wrecking 60 ft from our chamber; listener being at Junction Y was unhurt.

In common, no doubt, with other officers whose civilian occupation was mineral mining, Symes was a competent explosives engineer and brought considerable care to the calculation of charges to produce a specific effect. The details are far too complex to set out here but involved elaborate formulae depending on the geology, depth of mine, explosive in use and intended effect, all worked out in hand, presumably with the benefit of logarithmic tables or a slide rule. An illustration of this is provided in a report by Symes on a camouflet blown at the head of P.73.U. on 10 June:

On 9-6-16 enemy could be heard very plainly talking, being quite clearly audible by geophone. Estimated distance of enemy gallery 25 ft. L.L.R [Line of Least Resistance] 60 ft. Charge 5,000 lb of ammonal.

The object of this camouflet was to produce maximum H.R.R. [Horizontal Radius of Rupture] at the same time not to crater but, if possible, to liberate all gases to the surface, so as to prevent mine being inaccessible for a long period.

Taking Ammonal = 3.8 times power of gunpowder and S* = 2, a common mine would have required 11,370 lb; the maximum camouflet would have been 2,274 lb. By formula 7 over 4 times the cube root of 10C* divided by 3 the H.R.R. would be 80 ft.

Hartkopf Trichter (Duffield Group Crater) photographed by Leutnant Olaf Grieben the day after it was blown by the Germans on 26 July 1916. The charge comprised 5,000kg of explosive at a depth of 21.5 metres. The crater measured 40 metres in diameter. Note the British piquet positions with steel loophole plates already in place. (*GPGR*)

The result was quite satisfactory. The surface was cracked and slight depression without lips formed. The gases broke through and burned on the surface. About 80 ft of our gallery was destroyed. The mine was entered within 2 hrs; practically no gas was found.

[*S is a Soil Factor depending on the geology, and C the charge to be employed calculated through one of a set of complex formulae depending on the type of crater intended or containment in the ground.]

Occasionally the enemy got hoist with their own petard. Of a German blow in front of P.75 on 19 June, 172 Company reported that their men nearby were thrown to the ground and had to be treated with oxygen for carbon monoxide poisoning but

a considerable column of whitish smoke also shot up from enemy trench at an angle of 45° as if in prolongation of the line of their incline. Shouts and cries were distinctly heard from the German trench. The only explanation of this blow seems that the Germans had a gallery close to B, where the face was cracked, and they blew from there; but that owing to insufficient tamping or an accident during loading, it blew back along their own gallery.

However, 172 Company also had its disasters. On 14 August the Germans blew a small camouflet in front of tunnel P.75.B. (a tunnel just inside the forest area that is still accessible and that has been investigated). Although there was no damage underground, a sudden inrush of gas killed all seven men in the gallery before the 'proto' rescue team could reach them. Lance Corporal L. Statham, Sappers H. Dyson, F. Russel, P. Shields, G.E. Sell and Privates T. Cufter and J. Oliver, from the 9th Loyal North Lancashires, rest together in III D of Ecoivres Military Cemetery (see Cemetery Tours).

Having forced the Germans' hand, in August the company concentrated resources on developing a lateral system at depths from 18 to 30 metres below the surface, connected in places by vertical shafts or stairways to the earlier shallow tunnels, and running forward listening tunnels and some fighting galleries. Around 1,100 metres in length, this lateral, completed in late October, made undetected penetration through to the British infantry lines effectively impossible. Seismomicrophones, placed in the forward galleries and connected to a central listening station, consolidated the defences. The company, which also took over the O Sector to their south from 175 Tunnelling Company in November, was then able to concentrate most of its resources on the construction of the Grange and Goodman infantry subways.

The rival miners still bickered underground and between the end of August and the opening of the Battle of Arras on 9 April 1917, 172 Company blew five mines and three camouflets, plus two Wombat mines in support of the Canadian Corps attack. The Germans blew five mines and seven camouflets; four of these mines were concentrated just to the north of the Duffield/Grange Group and were blown two weeks prior to the Canadian Corps attack, forming the Longfellow Craters, of which more later. None of these had a serious impact on the miners or the infantry in the line.

Defending La Folie and later O Sector between May 1916 and 12 April 1917 had its cost. The company suffered twenty fatal casualties and fifty-two wounded, or hospitalised from carbon monoxide poisoning. The last of the junior ranks killed in this sector was Sapper W. Arrowsmith, probably by shell fire or a sniper, on 6 April 1917; he is buried in Ecoivres Military Cemetery, V.F.23.

A particularly bitter blow was the death on 9 April 1917 of Captain Richard Brisco MC. He went forward with the advancing Canadian troops to clear the Prinz Arnulf Tunnel and was reporting back to HQ 7 (Cdn) Brigade in the Goodman Subway when a chance shell caught him at the entrance, only moments from safety. Brisco had a reputation as a particularly

The grave of Sapper Walter Arrowsmith, killed on 6 April 1917. Note the commemorative inscription to his brother, Guardsman H. Arrowsmith of the Welsh Guards, who was reported missing at Loos.

intrepid officer who had stamped his personality on the company. On several occasions at the Bluff (in the Ypres Salient) he accessed German tunnels and engaged the enemy miners in underground fights, seemingly impervious to the risks. In the nature of the time he was something of a *Boys' Own* character. Aged 20, he had served in the Boer War as a trooper in the Duke of Cambridge's Own. Afterwards he qualified as a solicitor, but never practised; instead he travelled widely, undertaking several exploratory expeditions, notably in the upper reaches of the Amazon. He became a successful big game hunter in British East Africa, moved to North America, having qualified somewhere along the line as a mining engineer, and was in San Francisco during the great earthquake in 1906. On the outbreak of war he hastened back from the Yukon to enlist as a trooper in the 2nd King Edward's Horse (the regiment formed by Norton-Griffiths); promoted to sergeant in August 1915, he was appointed a temporary second lieutenant in 172 Tunnelling Company in September 1915. Wounded in the arm by a rifle bullet in February 1916 and hospitalised in England, he returned to the company in May 1916 and was with it throughout its time at Vimy. He is buried in Ecoivres Military Cemetery, VI.E.1. In a letter to his family, Major Symes wrote, 'I cannot tell you how sorry I am about him and how irreplaceable is his loss to the

Richard Brisco, photographed some years before 1914. (*Courtesy the Brisco family*)

The memorial to Richard Brisco in Hayton churchyard near Brompton in Cumbria. The inscription reads: 'In Memory of Captain Richard Brown Brisco MC. Son of Richard and Jane Ann Brisco and Grandson of Richard and Margaret Brown, who was killed in action on the 9th of April 1917, aged 39 years. "To live in the hearts we leave behind is not to die."' (*Carol Nubbert*)

company. He was full of energy and keenness, and did not know what fear was; the work he has done has been magnificent.' The family subsequently erected a private memorial to him in the churchyard at Hayton, near Brampton, in Cumbria.

There were lighter moments. In a TOCA [Tunnellers Old Comrades' Association] bulletin, Captain B.D. Plummer MC of 185 Tunnelling Company related:

> One memory of La Targette was a visit to 172, when they lived there, on New Year's Eve 1917, by a bunch of 182 and 185 officers, accompanied by a full Canadian battalion band. Roads were slippery and drinks were free and there were many casualties on the great march from Ecurie to La Targette. There was a trench across the entrance of the 172 camp that engulfed the band, still playing gallantly, almost to a man. Last but not least there were no indoor sanitary arrangements in the 172 mess, and as drinks were free and bandsmen are only human, who could blame them if they mistook 172's little vestibule for something else?

A whole band being engulfed by a trench while still playing allows much scope for imagination: was there a last despairing wail from the pipes and a final 'bong' on the big drum as they all fell in?

The British La Folie Tunnels and the Residual Mines

An especial aspect of the La Folie mining sector is that almost all the British tunnels have been investigated in detail in recent times. The defensive and fighting system extends to almost 3,140 metres, incorporating seven access inclines, over thirty fighting galleries and defensive listening saps (excluding those blown in) and the connecting lateral. If the linked Pylones and Goodman Subways are included, the whole system amounted to about 6 kilometres of tunnels.

The system had long been closed to access, and its initial investigation arose by chance. In 1985 a Canadian historian gained access to the fighting tunnels and in the course of an impromptu exploration chanced upon and reported what he judged to be a mine charge. This was subsequently established as being the Durand Mine, a 6,000 lb charge laid for Fougasse effect, located at a depth of 23 metres, only 45 metres distant from what was then the guide kiosk and dangerously close to the Grange Subway. It was one of nine mines that were laid to support the Canadian Corps attack on 9 April but had not been employed. Only three common mines, all in the Carency Sector, and two bored Wombat mines, both in the southern part of La Folie, were actually used on 9 April 1917.

An attempt to investigate this find by the French *démineurs* was aborted because of concerns about possible toxic gas and roof stability in that area of the tunnels. This left the then manager of the Canadian Memorial site in something of a quandary and in 1988 he was only too willing to accept an offer from Phillip Robinson for a specialist team from the Royal Engineers to investigate the mine, and also to check through the tunnels for any other potential explosive hazards.

The 1988 investigation of the Durand Mine, including tests of the ammonal, indicated that, with the command wires cut away, the risk of an induced explosion was minimal. Meanwhile archival research determined that two other mines had been laid in the vicinity: another, similar sized, Fougasse mine under the Duffield Craters and a large 20,000 lb charge below the road junction by the Broadmarsh Crater. The investigation of the tunnels also revealed a sitting camouflet charge of about 800 lbs in tunnel G.3, near the southern extremity of the system. The search established that the Duffield mine had been salvaged, but attempts in 1989 to cut through a blockage into the Broadmarsh tunnel (P.77.D) failed.

From 1990 resolution of the issue of the mines remained in abeyance with the absence of Phillip Robinson on service abroad. The investigation was then resurrected in 1996 by Veterans Affairs Canada (VAC), which was concerned about the status of the Broadmarsh mine ahead of the Vimy 80th Anniversary commemorations. The mines may have lain dormant but the question was whether they could be activated through some misfortune – a lightning strike, for example. The risk was small but the consequences were potentially catastrophic. In October 1997 Robinson assembled a team to investigate the Broadmarsh mine. Direct access to the tunnel was obtained using an excavator.

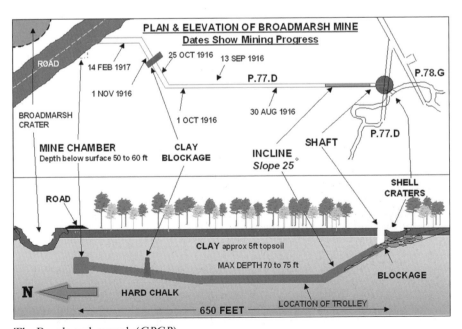

The Broadmarsh tunnel. (*GPGR*)

Despite problems with low oxygen levels and a clay ingress blocking part of the tunnel, the mine chamber was finally accessed. The team found that around half of the explosive had been removed as well as, crucially, the initiation system, thus rendering the charge safe. The Broadmarsh tunnel proved of especial interest, for salvage work had been abandoned in haste and the tunnel remained a time warp, complete with abandoned tools and every feature of mining at the time.

The Durand Group (an association of individuals with an interest in military mining) sprang from this operation. Working closely with VAC, its members resumed their investigation of the La Folie system. In early 1998 the Durand mine was neutralised by Lieutenant Colonel Mike Watkins MBE, a Royal Logistics Corps specialist in explosive ordnance disposal whose expertise was recognised internationally. In a 4 hour operation, alone in the mine chamber, he removed the detonators and primers, the former having degraded into a very sensitive condition. Mike Watkins, the driving force behind the forming of the Durand Group, was tragically killed six months later through the collapse of an excavation to access the O Sector tunnels to the south of La Folie. He is commemorated on a plaque, erected by Veterans Affairs Canada, close to the entrance to the Grange Subway, an exceptional tribute to an outstanding and heroic officer. The story of the work on the Broadmarsh and Durand mines is eloquently told in a documentary produced by Fougasse Films Ltd, entitled *One Of Our Mines Is Missing*.

The camouflet at G3, in the area of the Albany Craters, appears to have been in the nature of an underground ambush. The 172 Company Weekly Mining Report, dated 7 December 1916, notes 'Gallery working intermittently in front of P73G3. Talking very distinct; distant about 25ft.' On 6 January 172 blew an overcharged camouflet of 5,000 lbs from the head of G3, but (as established recently when the German tunnels in this area were accessed) it did no damage. The Germans continued working, getting ever closer. A break-in was feared, so

The Brisco 'patent' remote listening device. (*Durand Group*)

a small tunnel was hastily driven to one flank to confront the advancing German gallery and the 800 lb charge placed at the head of the tunnel. An improvised listening device, comprising a water pipe with a fuel funnel on the front end, was led back with the command wires, through the tamping, to a form of sentry point close to the lateral. An armed miner (clips of ammunition were found there) would have been in position, ear close to the hose, ready to fire the charge should the Germans break in. When in 2006 the Durand Group actually accessed the opposing tunnel, they found that the Germans had taken precautions against a British break-in, with grenades ready placed for instant use and careful camouflaging of the connection into other parts of their system. Although the German tunnel was about 3 metres lower, speech in one tunnel was clearly audible in the other, indicating that the precautions by both sides were well merited. The 172 Company War Diary notes a similar trap laid by Richard Brisco at the Bluff a year before, so there is a certain poignancy in reflecting that this may have been his handiwork. The camouflet was finally rendered harmless in 1999 by Lieutenant Colonel Mike Dolamore, also of the Royal Logistics Corps. Working alone in the confined space and in a chemically foetid atmosphere, he tenderly removed the detonators and primers.

An adequate written tour of the La Folie tunnels would necessitate a separate book in its own right. Just to traverse the lateral from one end to the other and return is an arduous journey, taking about 4 hours. For most of its length it is only 1.6 metres high, while after a period of wet weather there is one section that can involve a waist-deep wade. Wooden trolley rails ran along most of its length, along with a cat's cradle of wires for listening apparatus and

telephone and electrical links between the Grange and Goodman Subways. Periodically the remains of the gas doors that isolated each section are encountered. Fighting and listening galleries contain the detritus of the mining war. Rotting wooden boxes of explosives, rusty metal air pipes (including a chamber where pipes were stored), the remains of water hoses, digging and boring tools, winches and cables, numerous food and water cans and much else have been found. Timber supports remain in some galleries, although these were only employed where the chalk had been fragmented, usually by explosions, and at one point a mass of cables disappears up a bore hole to the surface,

Progressing along part of the La Folie lateral. (*GPGR*)

The Rt Hon. William Hague with Nick Pryor at point K2 in the La Folie lateral. (*Durand Group*)

probably to the dugout where the central listening station was situated. Graffiti abounds, most commonly names and dates written on the walls, using the then ubiquitous indelible pencils, but sometimes they are carved. At times these are poignant, in memory of a comrade; sometimes humorous, often poking fun at the rations or the sergeant major; occasionally religious – but very rarely vulgar.

Stairways or shafts ascend to higher-level tunnels and along the length there are seven entry inclines leading up to the trenches. Some galleries have their own especial characteristics, like the 'echo tunnel', which throws back the slightest sound, or another where the unwary can step into water so crystal clear it is not apparent. There is little that lives down there, but spiders have been encountered, along with a few insects, and, in one tunnel incline that has a tiny exit to the surface, several bats. Occasionally small burrowing animals find themselves in the system. Near the above-mentioned camouflet, over 24 metres below the surface, the skeleton of a rabbit was found by a burrow it had started into a clay fault. Presumably it had been happily creating a home for itself near the surface when it fell through into an incline. It must then have wandered the tunnels, going ever deeper, seeking a place where it could burrow out, but its efforts were of course in vain and it must have starved to death. There are, though, hazards for other than rabbits. While most of the tunnels are in solid chalk, there are faults and places where slabs are delicately poised, particularly in those fighting galleries where the chalk has been fragmented. Carbon monoxide may remain in pockets and there is potential for methane build-up. These are risks easily countered by those with experience and suitable equipment, but casual wanderings, as in 1985, are not to be recommended.

The German Tunnels

The German gains from the Rupprecht counter-offensives, their February attack in the La Folie Sector, and the Schleswig Holstein offensive in May 1916 gave them sufficient space below the ridge line to develop several defence lines, albeit they still lacked room for a convincing defence in depth system. Accordingly, after May 1916 their stance became predominantly defensive. The exception to this was in the Carency Sector, including the Pimple, where the protagonists continued to squabble over the crest line until it was finally taken by the 4th

(Cdn) Division on 13 April 1917. The German mining effort was therefore aimed primarily at creating obstacles and preventing the development of enemy offensive mines. (Had they simply consulted each other, both sides might have saved themselves a lot of trouble!) Until the build-up for the Arras offensive in early 1917, British mining policy likewise remained passive. However, without letting down their guard, this defensive posture allowed the Germans to divert mining resources to the construction of the Hindenburg Line.

As shown on the plans on pages 77 and 94, the Germans confronted 172 Company with a string of deep tunnels across the sector. With a couple of exceptions, most had a single entrance and then, at depths of 24 to 33 metres, reached right and left with two or more galleries. Surprisingly, they misjudged the depth of the water table and suffered serious flooding problems in many of their galleries.

German mining practice differed considerably from that of their British opponents. Inclines were usually steeper and in many cases entrances comprised a short stairway to a winch chamber with about 4.5 metres of head cover. A vertical shaft was then sunk to the required depth, from which ran horizontal galleries. These were generally close-timbered, even in firm chalk, possibly because it was supposed that the timbering would muffle sound, but it was a practice that involved considerable logistical effort and slowed the rate at which they could advance a gallery – a considerable disadvantage in chalk, where silent digging was rarely practical and speed was often of the essence. Much of this is encapsulated in a report from an Inspector of Mines circular on the examination of the German mine systems following the First Army's capture of the northern part of the Vimy Ridge in April 1917:

> The surveys and examination of the Enemy Mine Systems, captured on the First Army Front in the operations that commenced on April 9th, elicit the following facts:
>
> 1. The rate of progress is from 4 to 5 feet in 24 hours (in chalk). An instance of recovery of a blown gallery is worth recording, viz, 30 ft. recovered in 8 days.
> 2. The enemy's galleries were in many instances driven without reference to the permanent water level and, consequently, he lost much work by going too deep. This was also our experience, and points to the importance of obtaining accurate information on the subterranean water level before determining the depth of a mining system.
> 3. The size of the enemy galleries has been found to vary as under:-
> $5' \times 2'6''$; $4' \times 2'6''$; $5'5\frac{1}{2}'' \times 2'$ to $1'6''$; $5'3'' \times 2'8''$; $6' \times 2'8''$.
> The tendency in recent work is to increase the dimensions of galleries; this may be due to the fact that the work was done by Pioneers and not properly skilled Miners.

4. In the majority of cases the shafts were inclines 50° or 45° sunk in or close to the front line trenches. In one case the incline started from a communication trench 150 ft. back from the front line.

5. The following is a description of one of the few elaborate instances of enemy work:

<u>Shaft No. 20.</u> This shaft is of a more elaborate design than the others. It is approached from the support line by an inclined gallery, which enters a large heavily timbered compartment or shaft head, having a cover of about 15 ft. of chalk above the timber. The shaft is vertical for 100 ft below the floor of the shaft-head. It is of two compartments (haulage and ladder way) each 6 ft. × 4 ft. built of 9″ × 5″ timbers. The ladder way compartment has stagings, at 25 ft, 50 ft, and 75 ft, below the collar set, at each of which a chamber 12′ × 6′ × 4′ has been cut and close timbered. In the haulage compartment the truck runs on two 5/8″ steel guide ropes. There were no rails in the gallery below, which was close timbered with 9″ × 5″ timber sets 6′ × 3′4″ in the clear for a distance of 120 ft. on the level. Apparently the

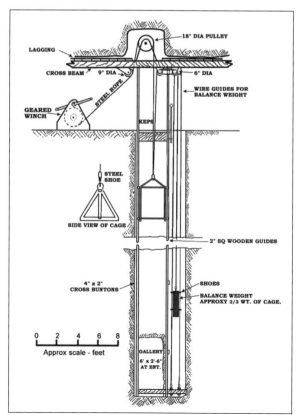

Diagram of a German shaft captured at Fricourt; it is very similar to the description of German shaft No. 20 at Vimy. (*GPGR*)

truck, which had wide wheels, was pushed by hand along the timbered floor of the gallery. Air was supplied, as in the case of the other galleries, through a 6″ diameter 22 gauge galvanised iron pipe from a hand blower in the shaft head. A geared winch was used for hauling the truck without balance weight. No dates were marked on the timbers but our listeners repeatedly reported sounds in the direction of this gallery, the last occasion being on 12.4.17. The timbering of this shaft is very good.

A German covered tramway for spoil disposal.

6. Disposal of Spoil. The enemy pays strict attention to this. No cases of large visible dumps are reported; it is extremely probable that this is one reason why his rate of progress underground is so much slower than ours – for unless large working-parties were provided, the mining shifts would have to clear the bags. In this respect the German work compares very favourably with ours, for as a rule the site of our underground work is betrayed by enormous accumulations of spoil.

7. Surveys of enemy systems transferred to our plans have proved that our listening reports were extremely accurate and reflect great credit on the training in this important adjunct to Military Mining.

This description of Shaft No. 20 is particularly fortuitous, for this is a part of the interconnected German system accessed and investigated by the Durand Group in 2005–2008. Entry was gained through a lengthy hand excavation of the T19 entrance (see the Arnulf Sector North plan). The excavation exposed a ragged and narrow incline, initially descending at 45° and levelling out at just over 30 metres below the surface. Oxygen levels were low, around 15% (the norm being 21%), so it was necessary to install a pumped air system before further investigation could proceed. This was the system that confronted the G3 camouflet and, as already described, it was apparent that the Germans had taken precautions against a breakthrough from the British tunnels. It was almost by chance that the investigating team found the concealed connection into the rest

Excavating the entrance to the T19 incline. (*Durand Group*)

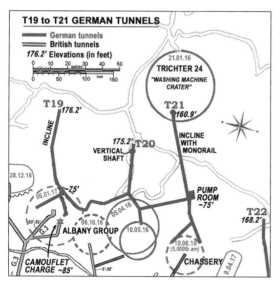

T19 to T21 GERMAN TUNNELS
▬▬ German tunnels
▬▬ British tunnels
176.2' Elevations (in feet)

TRICHTER 24
"WASHING MACHINE CRATER"
21.01.16

T19
■176.2'

T21
●160.9'

INCLINE

175.2' **T20**
VERTICAL SHAFT

INCLINE WITH MONORAIL

28.12.16

06.01.17 ■-75'

05.04.16

PUMP ROOM ~75'

T22
168.2'

60'-30'
06.10.16
G.3 **ALBANY GROUP** 10.05.16

10.06.16
(5,000lb am)

G.3 **CAMOUFLET CHARGE ~85'**
—0'-30'

CHASSERY
9.04.17

The T19 to T21 German tunnels showing their proximity to British tunnels. (*GPGR*)

of the system. Once opened up, this exposed a short lateral and several fighting galleries, well timbered, preserved by a combination of previous flooding and the low oxygen levels. The T20 shaft, described above, was totally blocked, a tribute perhaps to the efforts of the battlefield clearance teams who had poured in enough material to fill a 30 metre shaft. It remains a mystery as to where they got the material to block this and numerous other tunnel and dugout entrances.

Evidence of the problems the Germans faced in sinking below the water table is immediately apparent further along, at the bottom of the T21 shaft. A complete mechanical pumping station had been installed in a chamber. Much of the machinery remains in place, though not the pumping engine, which was presumably salvaged by the 172 Company miners. Still in place is an overhead gantry, which extends up a stepped incline to a point below the aforementioned Washing Machine Crater, where the incline is blocked by what was clearly a demolition charge that destroyed the entrance chamber. Curiously, the system is almost wholly devoid of personal graffiti, although there are periodic writings on the side walls giving depth and length of the tunnels.

The only other point in the La Folie System where a German tunnel has been accessed is within the conserved trenches area around the Duffield and Grange Craters. Stollen 3, on the North Arnulf plan, could for many years be

A hose line in a German gallery. (*Durand Group*)

The T21 pump room. (*Durand Group*)

viewed through a grill door. Sadly, as a consequence of frequent break-ins by vandals, this was finally blocked off with a concrete slab, but not before a motorised pump had been retrieved, which is now exhibited in the Grange Subway 'Water Chamber'.

On balance, 172 Company acquired the advantage in the mining war and was able to lay several offensive mines (albeit unused) ahead of the Canadian Corps' attack on 9 April 1917, but the German miners could be said to have conceded little, and responded with vigour in late March 1917 with the blowing of the Longfellow Craters, described below.

The Crater Line

For the visitor the most visible manifestation of the mining war is the crater line within the Canadian Memorial site. From the Broadmarsh Crater, through the publicly accessible conserved trenches and then into the forest area, where the La Folie Sector meets the O Sector at the Chassery Crater, the British and German plans indicate fifty-three mines and large camouflets that broke surface, many of them being within or extending previous craters. Of these, thirty-six were of German origin. The French and British expended slightly over 120,000 lbs of explosive. Extrapolating this figure suggests that the Germans would have employed roughly 240,000 lbs of explosives, making for an astonishing total of around 360,000 lbs along the 1,200 or so metres of the sector.

It is understood that the Canadian authorities have in mind the provision of additional viewing points on the crater line, but meanwhile the Duffield and Grange Group, in the area of the conserved trenches, are the most evident. About sixteen mines or large camouflets were fired to form the jumbled crater ravine that is interposed between the opposing trenches in this small area. The first such was the French 'blow' near the head of the Grange Trench on 16 April 1916, referred to on page 102. The Germans struck back with a mine just to the north on 24 April. On 4 May the French attacked underground with a camouflet at the head of the P.75.O. tunnel, followed on 8 May by an 8,800 lb

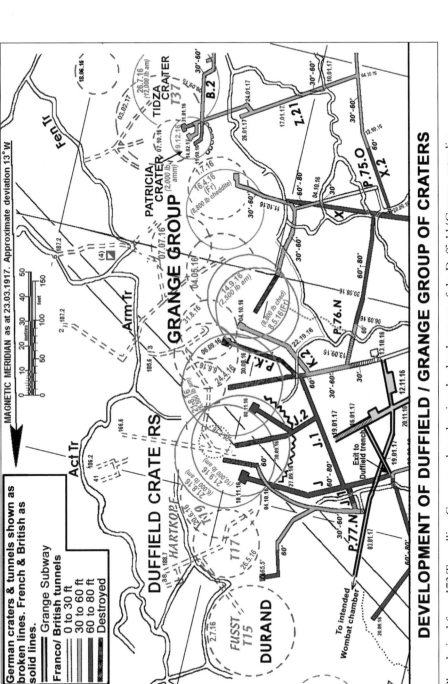

Plan derived from 172 Tunnelling Company plans showing the development of the Duffield/Grange crater line.

Trolley rails in the P.77.J incline. (*GPGR*)

The P.77.N fighting gallery. (*GPGR*)

An air pipe in the P.73.C incline. (*GPGR*)

The P.75.C fighting gallery with timbers still in place. (*GPGR*)

cheddite charge in the centre of what is now the Grange Group. On 26 May the Germans fired a mine just ahead of the P.77.N. tunnel (the tunnel later used to place the Durand Mine), forming the first of the Duffield Craters at the head of the Duffield communication trench. The fourth of the Grange Group craters was formed on 6 June, when the Germans attacked the P.76.K. gallery, without causing any damage. Nearly three weeks passed before the Germans struck again, firing a powerful mine alongside that of 26 May in the Duffield Group and forming the Hartkopf Crater (T18). On 1 July they again attacked the P.75.O. gallery, extending the 16 April crater; and on 2 July they fired a large mine to the immediate north of the Duffield Group, forming the Durand Crater (Trichter Fusst, or T15 on the German plans). On 26 July they fired another camouflet against P.77.N.

By now 172 Company was perhaps getting a touch irritated and on 27 July it exploded a 12,000 lb charge to the immediate south of the Grange Group, forming the first of the Tidsa (or Tidza) Group of craters. They followed this up on 21 August with two large mines, totalling 12,500 lbs, creating the craters that link the Duffield and Grange Groups and destroying part of the German forward line. There were only two further blows within the Duffield/Grange Group: a German camouflet on 31 August and a small British mine on 14 September. By then, as shown on the plan on page 119, the whole of this frontage now comprised what was effectively a ravine of craters. Saps had been run forward onto the rims by both sides to form a string of defensive posts, known as the Observation Line, each sap being equipped with steel loophole plates and manned by a section of infantry. Some of these positions are sufficiently close for a strong man to throw a grenade across, thus it is likely that the opposing infantry operated a tacit policy of live and let live. Nevertheless, raiding parties did cross the craters from time to time, harassing the outposts, seeking prisoners and endeavouring to destroy enemy dugout and tunnel entrances.

Mine fighting continued to the south of the Grange Group. To accompany a raid by the Princess Patricia's Canadian Light Infantry (PPCLI) on 19 December, three mines were fired by 172 Company within and on the flanks of the Tidsa Crater Group, the northernmost being designated Patricia Crater. The PPCLI War Diary for 19 December is fairly sanguine:

Between the hours of 1.30 and 1.45 a.m. three mines were blown in the vicinity of the GRANGE, BIRKIN, TIDZA groups. The near lips were consolidated with few casualties. Lieut Pearson was in charge of the operation in the front line. The new crater has been named PATRICIA. [The CO, Agar Adamson, sought and got permission for this from Controller Mines First Army.] The 42nd Bn relieved during the evening and the Regiment moved back to reserve at NEUVILLE ST VAAST.

The 172 Company War Diary for 19 December is a bit more explicit:

At 1.40 a.m. three mines were blown by us against enemy galleries.

(i)   In the face of P.75.B2. 4,000 lb of ammonal.
(ii) In the face of P.75.BII. 2,000 lb of ammonal.
(iii) In the face of P.75.BI. 3,000 lb of ammonal.
Result: (i)   PATRICIA crater formed. Enemy post on N. lip of TIDZA crater destroyed. New lip formed joining GRANGE and TIDZA craters.
(ii) Enemy post on S. lip of TIDZA crater destroyed. New high post created on our lip giving very good observation.
(iii) An overcharged camouflet against enemy gallery estimated 25 ft distant. New crater lip occupied and consolidated by PPCLI.

On 28 December 172 Company fired a 12,000 lb charge from P.73.G3. at a depth of 21 metres, destroying a German post and forming Edmonton Crater, joined on to the previous Devon Crater. The 49th Battalion CEF occupied and consolidated the new crater. Then on 3 January 1917 the Germans fired a camouflet against P.75.Z21. in the area of Patricia Crater, killing Sappers J. Reilly and W.M. Griffiths (both buried at Ecoivres Military Cemetery, IV.C.11 and 12) and fatally wounding Sapper M. Moyler (buried in Aubigny Communal Cemetery Extension, I.F.54). Perhaps in retaliation, on 6 January 172 Company fired an overcharged camouflet at the head of G3 – the site of the previously described ambush. Excepting a bored mine on 9 April 1917, this was the last of the mines to be fired in the sector by 172 Company. It was left to the Germans to have the final word. On 23 March 1917 they fired a series of four large mines between the Broadmarsh and Durand Craters to form what became known as the Longfellow Craters, situated today just uphill from the present Visitors Centre. Oberleutnant A.D. Brettner, commander of 5th Company *Reserve-Infanterie-Regiment Nr. 262*, wrote afterwards: 'Already during the first half of March our listening teams had established that the British had worked their way round our tunnels and had begun to approach our lines closely. As a result, the engineer commander ordered the mine galleries in Sector 1 to be charged and Galleries 35, 36, 37 and 38 to be blown.' The War Diary of the 2nd Battalion records a statement by the miners that this was one of the largest explosions on the Western Front, if not the largest, up until that date. The plan was to blow the galleries using 700 *Zentner* (35 tons or 77,000 lbs) of explosives! Brettner's report continues;

During the night 22/23 March charging of the four mine galleries was completed and the explosion took place at 4.10 a.m. Everything went according to plan. Our own lines were barely damaged and the rim of the easternmost crater, which was approximately four metres high, was occupied by us. The explosion took place in front of the 5th Company sector, which at the time was being commanded temporarily by Reserve Leutnant Mauer. The company was deployed on the right (northern flank) of the regiment (Zollern I). Altogether four craters were produced. Unfortunately during this operation two of our comrades, *Unteroffizier* Gürtler and *Grenadier* Bartel, were shot through the head and killed by British snipers. With the death of *Unteroffizier* Gürtler, a secondary school teacher by profession, 5th Company lost a man who would never be forgotten because of his exemplary soldierly bearing and unshakeable calmness. The extent of the explosion, during which Engineer (Mining) Company 293 especially distinguished itself, was underlined by the fact that during the previous nights a relay of 400 men of 1st Battalion Reserve Infantry Regiment 262 brought forward approximately 150 *Zentner* of explosives to the front line.

The 42nd Battalion CEF (Royal Highlanders of Canada) had come into the line the day before. Their reaction, as recounted by the Regimental History, was swift:

Events developed quickly with the beginning of the tour. The Battalion was disposed with B Company in the front line and A Company in close support. The relief was completed well before midnight on March 22nd and the garrison had just settled down in their places when, on the stroke of 3 o'clock on the morning of March 23rd, the enemy exploded a tremendous mine on the Battalion front. There was a rending blast and the whole area rocked for a moment. Lights in every dugout were extinguished, extra trench stores, dishes and other movable articles crashed to the floor, while smoke, dust and debris were everywhere. The Officer Commanding B Company (Captain C.B. Topp) had just returned to the Company Headquarters dugout in LaSalle Trench after a tour of inspection of the crater posts when the explosion occurred, and on reaching the entrance observed a tremendous wall of earth extending across the left of the front line for a distance which was afterwards found to be 250 yards. Proceeding forward immediately, he joined Lieutenant Small, who was on duty in the front line, and accompanied by Small and two Lewis gunners at once rushed out and occupied the highest point on the near lip of the crater. From here parties of the enemy were observed digging in on the far side of the crater and the Lewis gun was promptly brought into action with good effect while the officers used their revolvers. Several of the enemy were seen to be hit and the consolidation work in the immediate vicinity terminated abruptly. Shortly afterwards severe enfilade rifle fire was brought to bear on the B Company party, which was then withdrawn to a less exposed position after one of the Lewis gunners had been severely wounded, there being insufficient time to establish a post on the crater lip before daylight.

At daylight it was found that the enemy had evidently exploded a series of four large mines simultaneously. The new craters extended from Durand Crater in a northerly direction to a distance of 250 yards and consisted of a series of four separate craters merging into one. It was promptly christened 'Longfellow'. The German tunnellers had failed to drive their gallery far enough to extend beneath the British line, the near lip of the crater being well short of the observation line, though at one point thirty yards of the observation line trench was destroyed. The explosion of the mine itself caused no casualties but there were several shortly afterwards, including slight wounds sustained by Lieutenant L.C. Montgomery while making observations of the crater and by Lieutenant D.F. Small while reconnoitering the lip. The blowing of this mine completely changed the configuration of a large section of the front over which the Battalion was to advance in the attack on the Ridge and formed a most dangerous obstacle that would have to be overcome just as the attacking troops jumped off. Its immediate and effective consolidation was imperative and during the day careful plans were prepared for this work. At dusk consolidation was energetically pushed forward. Every available man from the front line and support Companies, in addition to 120 men who were brought up from C and D Companies in reserve, were put to work under the supervision of Captain Topp and Lieutenant H.B. Trout. On the first night 'Topp Sap' was dug, extending from the observation line to the lip of the new crater where a defended post was established. A post was also established at the southern end of the crater.

The following night men were again brought up from the reserve Companies and Longfellow Trench was commenced, extending across the front just under the lip of the crater. Four additional new posts were also commenced, together with a new communication trench. By this time the enemy had detected the new work and throughout the night heavy rifle fire was maintained from positions on Broadmarsh Crater to the left, from which point the site of the new work could be enfiladed in some degree. Covering parties with Lewis guns were able to keep down enemy machine gun fire, but could not stop the constant sniping by individuals from numerous points of vantage in the enemy line, with the result that work was carried on under most trying conditions. During the night three other ranks were killed; Lieutenant R.W. Stewart was mortally wounded [buried in Aubigny Communal Cemetery Extension, V.A.39] while carrying a wounded man to a place of safety and a number of other ranks were wounded. The men, however, did not pause in the work at any time and consolidation was well under way before dawn. On the night of the 25th the same procedure was followed and by this time the new positions were deep enough to provide a fair measure of protection for the working party and fewer casualties were sustained. Daylight on the 26th found a number of the new posts on Longfellow sufficiently near completion to enable them to be occupied and the Battalion was able to retaliate for its uncomfortable experience of the previous days by maintaining most active sniping. It was found that the near lip of the crater was considerably higher than that on the enemy's side, with the result that much German territory previously not under observation could be completely dominated. From one post the snipers were able to enfilade an enemy communication trench and in this one place alone seven hits were obtained the first morning.

By 23 March the Germans were well aware that an offensive was in the offing and it is thought that the blowing of the Longfellow Craters was aimed at pre-empting a mining attack. The German judgement was not too far out in that the Broadmarsh, Durand and Duffield mines had been laid nearby, but the only damage done to the British mines was the destruction of a Wombat boring chamber at the head of what is now termed the Black Watch Tunnel, a spur off the Grange Subway. The consequences were, though, more profound. It was judged that blowing further mines on this part of the front would seriously impede the planned attack on 9 April, in particular the firing of the Broadmarsh

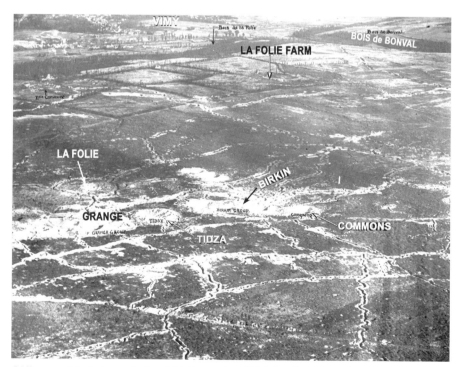

Oblique aerial photograph dated 26 September 1916 showing most of the La Folie Sector. (*Durand Group*)

Mine, which would effectively close the crater gap between the Longfellow and existing Broadmarsh Crater. Thus it was decided, whether at Divisional or Corps level is not known, to abort firing of the Broadmarsh, Durand and Duffield mines. With hindsight this proved a costly mistake. The German defences in and around the existing Broadmarsh Crater remained largely intact and on 9 April checked the advance of the 87th Battalion (Canadian Grenadier Guards) on the right flank of the 4th (Cdn) Division, whose main objective was Hill 145, the highest point of the Ridge (where the Canadian Vimy Memorial now stands). This in turn allowed Reserve Infantry Regiment 261, facing the 4th (Cdn) Division, to enfilade the advancing 3rd (Cdn) Division to the immediate south and to inflict disproportionate casualties. In the event Hill 145 was not taken until a fresh attack with heavy artillery support was mounted by the 12th (Cdn) Brigade on 10 April.

The Final Act: 9 April 1917

The War Diary for 172 Tunnelling Company on 9 April (by then also responsible for 'O' Sector) noted:

> 5:30½ a.m. [30 seconds after Z hour] Two bored mines blown in connection with the attack on VIMY RIDGE.
> 1. From the east end of GOODMAN Subway into German front line, forming trench across No–Man's-Land 170 ft long × 35 ft wide × 15 ft deep.
> 2. On south of CHASSERY Crater from Observation Line into German front line, forming trench across No–Man's-Land 150 ft long × 30 ft wide × 15 ft deep.

The following operations were also carried out in conjunction with the attack:–

(i)   Three mobile charges exploded in lip of LONGFELLOW crater in order to make passages for the infantry into the crater.

(ii) Two forward exits from GOODMAN subway opened up into No–Man's-Land and saps driven into communication trench formed by bored mine.

(iii) Forward exit from LICHFIELD subway opened for taking signal cables forward into captured trenches.

(iv) After assault, party went over with Capt BRISCO, located PRINZ ARNULF TUNNEL, investigated it for mines, and entrances that had been destroyed, reopened for use of infantry.

(v)   Similar party under Capt COOPER located VOLKER TUNNEL. Entered it, taking prisoner a number of Germans found inside, cut the leads of a charge found ready to destroy the tunnel, and cleared it of the enemy, then started work on reopening entrances.

(vi) Parties investigated all mine shafts (about 50) in 'O' & 'P' sectors, taking prisoners and making certain no mines left by the enemy.
Casualty. Temp Capt R.B. Brisco, killed in action.

Within a few days 172 Tunnelling Company moved on to the construction of roads and dugouts in the newly gained territory (apart from a few maintenance parties left in the subways and some salvage teams in the British and German tunnels). Apart from the attention of battlefield clearance organisations in the 1920s, the tunnels were left undisturbed until the investigation of the British La Folie system in the period 1988–2002, and subsequently of the German T19 to T21 galleries, revealed this extraordinary legacy of the mining war.

Lieutenant Colonel Mike Dolamore MBE, Royal Logistics Corps, about to work on neutralising the G3 camouflet. (*Durand Group*)

Graffiti in the La Folie tunnels: 'In memory of Pte Thomas Latham – Killed in action ? 2.5.1916 – Love by us all – gone but not forgotten by his mates – J.D. 28.3.17.

The nearest match on the CWG website is that of a T. Latham of the Worcestershire Regiment, killed on 12.5.16, buried in Aubigny Communal Cemetery, I.B.37. (*GPGR*)

Chapter 7

Neuville St Vaast to the River Scarpe

O to J Sectors, including the Labyrinth

The Front and the Labyrinth

The Carency, Berthonval and La Folie mining sectors, covered in the last two chapters, extend just 3½ kilometres along the northern part of Vimy Ridge. The seven 1916 mining sectors along the rest of the Ridge, from the Canadian Memorial site to the River Scarpe, cover a further 7½ kilometres in a direct line. Some of these sectors were also the scene of mine warfare at least as intensive as that in the Berthonval and La Folie sectors, though none as severe as that at the Pimple in the Carency sector at the northern extremity of the Vimy Ridge. 'Why', the discerning reader may ask, 'has so extensive a part of the mining war been relegated to just one chapter?'

The answer is that today there is little trace on the surface of the First World War, let alone the endeavours of the rival miners. Apart from that part of the O (Neuville St Vaast) Sector situated within the southern part of the Canadian Memorial site, the evocative calm of the two crater cemeteries, Lichfield and Zivy, and the sites of Cuthbert and Claude Craters in L Sector (see Tours), almost all traces of the fighting have been effectively erased by agriculture and urban and commercial development. For the visitor today it is difficult to envisage the total devastation wrought across this swathe of ground in the battles of 1914 and 1915, in the defence of the lines in 1916 and from the opening of the Battles of Arras on 9 April 1917.

The terrain to the west of the 1916 British lines between Neuville St Vaast and Roclincourt was so tangled with former French and German trenches and so devastated by shell and mine craters that it earned on both sides the title of 'the Labyrinth'. Captain Trounce of 181 Tunnelling Company wrote of their arrival in the N Sector in April 1916:

Some six months before my company reached the scene, in September 1915, the French and Germans had met in some terrible struggles. Nothing was left of the villages of Neuville-St-Vaast and La Targette but a heap of crumbling bricks here and there. The casualties were ghastly. The total casualties for the attacks in this region were estimated at about 150,000. The French had succeeded in capturing the German lines, but at a terrible cost. The trenches were so numerous and mazelike that the district is named 'The

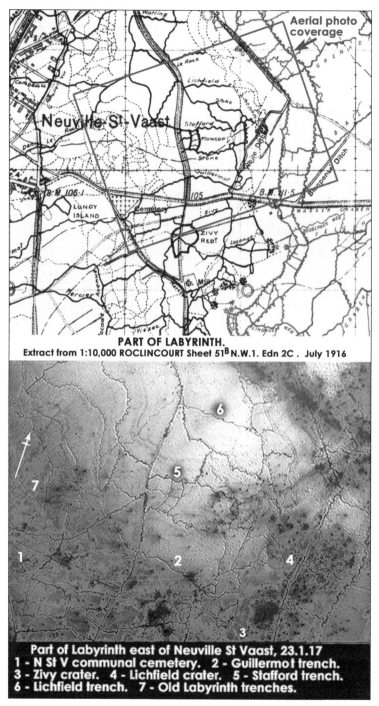

PART OF LABYRINTH.
Extract from 1:10,000 ROCLINCOURT Sheet 51^B N.W.1. Edn 2C . July 1916

Part of Labyrinth east of Neuville St Vaast, 23.1.17
1 - N St V communal cemetery. 2 - Guillermot trench.
3 - Zivy crater. 4 - Lichfield crater. 5 - Stafford trench.
6 - Lichfield trench. 7 - Old Labyrinth trenches.

N Sector trench map showing part of the Labyrinth trenches, with (below) an aerial photograph showing part of N Sector to the east of Neuville St Vaast. (*IWM 16A48b, dated 23-1-17*)

Labyrinth'. It was certainly a puzzle to get in and out. We would enter the communication trenches at a point near the crossroads at Aux-Rietz, where our billets were situated on the main Arras–Souchez road, and walk up the communication trenches as hard as we could go for three-quarters of an hour before we reached the front line. The trenches retained the names left them by the French: Boyau Zivy, Boyau Bentata, etc. It took us several days to get our bearings here. It is seldom a pleasant business taking over new trenches. Just about the time you get hopelessly lost, Fritz thinks it's the correct time to start a bad trench-mortar strafe, and your efforts to find any sort of cover always prove unavailing.

Captain Plummer MC, of 185 Tunnelling Company.

In similar vein Captain Plummer of 185 Tunnelling Company, writing of a visit to the battlefields in 1929, commented:

No trace remains of what used to be our headquarters camp near Ecurie from April to June 1918, except what might have been the road levelling at the entrance. What tales these cornfields could tell, if they were articulate, of the happening there! The old front lines in this area are now non-existent. Somehow, one thought that they would have lasted for ever, such a maze of trenches was The Labyrinth in the old days. When one realises that on our

French soldiers at a dugout entrance in a communication trench at Carency or in the Labyrinth. (*Fonds documentaries Alain Jacques*)

'Known Unto God.' Unburied casualties.

Company's front alone in that sector there were over 100 mine craters and that there were said to be something like 60,000 unburied dead – French and German – lying in No Man's Land, and in shell holes in and around the trenches of The Labyrinth, it will be realised that the change in that countryside is remarkable. The chalky outlines of mine craters are all that remain of the efforts of 1915–1917. Some day in the years to come someone who knew not Armageddon will find an underground entrance.

Today not even the 'chalky outlines' of the craters remain visible on the ground and the visitor needs a vivid imagination to visualise the many kilometres of French, British and German tunnels hidden deep below their feet and the subsurface fortresses that existed on both sides of the lines. These nevertheless manifest themselves fairly frequently through ground collapse, particularly into former dugouts or weapon pits, sometimes to the detriment of farm machinery, very occasionally with injurious or tragic consequences for the operators.

The BEF Takes Over

The mining situation facing Third Army as it progressively took over the front from the French Tenth Army in February and March 1916 was not encouraging. French mining policy appeared to be reactive, attempting to meet each crisis as it arose. They were, it should be noted, at a considerable disadvantage. Third Army Mining Reports indicated that over 4,500 German Pioneers were largely engaged in mining on the front, considerably outnumbering the French mining companies. Furthermore, the French were operating both in terrain totally devastated by the furious battles of 1915, with the consequent logistical complications, and under the eyes of the German guns and mortars.

The first of the British tunnelling companies to arrive was 185 Tunnelling Company, which at the end of February 1916 initially took over the quiet sector in Arras, south of the River Scarpe. Next to arrive was 184 Tunnelling Company, commanded by Major J.R. Gwyther, taking over K Sector (and extending into part of L Sector). Hard on its heels were the New Zealand Engineers Tunnelling Company (NZET), which relieved 7/1 French Territorial Engineers in L Sector (Lille Road). As related in Chapter 8, the New Zealanders had only arrived in France a couple of weeks before and were complete novices with no experience of mine warfare – but they soon made their presence felt.

At this point the Controller of Mines for Third Army made a plea for more mining companies and at the beginning of April 181 Tunnelling Company arrived to take over O Sector (Neuville St Vaast) from 15/3 French Engineer Company. The battle-hardened 175 Tunnelling Company, under Major T.H. Carlisle (later promoted to lieutenant colonel, and winner of a DSO and MC),

A group of 175 Tunnelling Company miners, probably in the early days. (*Peter Barton*)

moved down from Ypres on 2 May 1916 to relieve 181 Tunnelling Company and part of 182 Tunnelling Company in the O Sector. By that point there were five tunnelling companies deployed along the front, plus 176, 182 and 172 on the northern end of Vimy Ridge (see map on page 20), making eight tunnelling companies along the length of the Ridge.

There were various adjustments later, such as 181 Tunnelling Company moving to the Somme in mid-August 1916 and 175 Tunnelling Company, also to the Somme, in November 1916 (replaced for a short time by 256 Tunnelling Company), while the NZET was relieved by 184 Tunnelling Company in November 1916 so that the New Zealanders could focus on developing the Arras Caves. Periodically sections from other tunnelling companies were drafted in to assist with works ahead of the April 1917 offensive, such as sections from 179 Tunnelling Company to support the NZET. In modern parlance there was a certain dynamic: the mining company, with its semi-independent section structure, was a very flexible organisation.

The O (Neuville St Vaast) Sector
Although, as has been said, there is little to show today of the mining endeavour along the front from the La Folie Sector to the Scarpe, it is fortunate that a part is conserved within the southern forest area of the Canadian Vimy Memorial site, containing some of the most dramatic craters, while excavations by the Durand Group since 2000 have given access to the northern part of the O Sector tunnel system.

The largest of all the craters on the Ridge (B6 on British plans; Trichter 27 on the German Arnulf Sector plan) is here, shrouded by dense undergrowth and brambles. It was blown as part of the Rupprecht III German local offensive at the beginning of March 1916, and something of the Franco-German fighting around it has already been described in the chapter on the La Folie Sector.

The changeover in this particular area was complicated: 181 Tunnelling Company took over part of O Sector from the French, and between 2 and 5 May 175 Tunnelling Company took over that part held by 181 Tunnelling Company and the balance from the much battered 5/6th and M6 French Engineer Companies. At just this time the Germans blew a mine (the B4 crater group on British plans – not to be confused with a crater the Germans titled B4), which is still apparent in the extreme south of the Vimy Memorial site and visible, behind the site boundary fence, from the Neuville St Vaast to Thélus track.

Nevertheless 175 Tunnelling Company was fortunate in that the Germans miners had used their advanced tunnels to attack the French the previous month; except for a couple of defensive camouflets, 175 had time to start redeveloping the underground system for defence. There were no 'blows' by them of significance until 16 June when, at the head of the O.65.A. tunnel (see plan), they fired two Fougasse charges totalling 10 tons (22,400 lbs) of ammonal to create an overlapping pair of craters subsequently named The Twins. These were not aimed at the German lines or miners. The purpose was entirely tactical: to throw up high lips to screen off a German machine gun that had been enfilading the forward trenches, with dire consequences for the infantry in that area. To any visitors privileged enough to enter the Memorial site's forest area, these craters remain quite apparent from the main track running through the forest and demonstrate clearly the height of overcharged mine crater rims above the surrounding terrain.

As elsewhere along the front, 175 Tunnelling Company quickly initiated the excavation of a deep defensive system around 24 metres below the surface, protected initially by a screen of listening posts in the former, shallow, French tunnels. The comparison with the work of 172 Tunnelling Company immediately to their north is interesting. The defensive

Members of the Durand Group conferring in the O Sector lateral. (*Durand Group*)

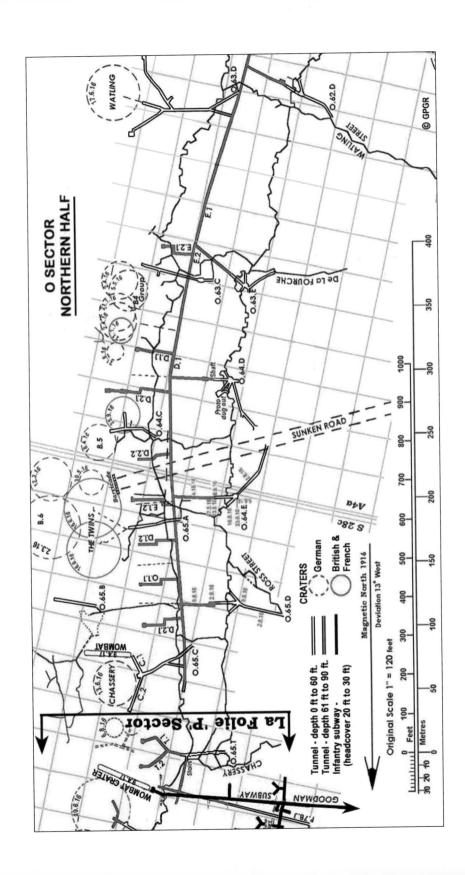

O SECTOR
NORTHERN HALF

La Folie 'P' Sector

CRATERS

German

British & French

Tunnel - depth 0 ft to 60 ft.
Tunnel - depth 61 ft to 90 ft.
Infantry subway -
(headcover 20 ft to 30 ft)

Magnetic North 1916
Deviation 13° West

Original Scale 1" = 120 feet

© GPGR

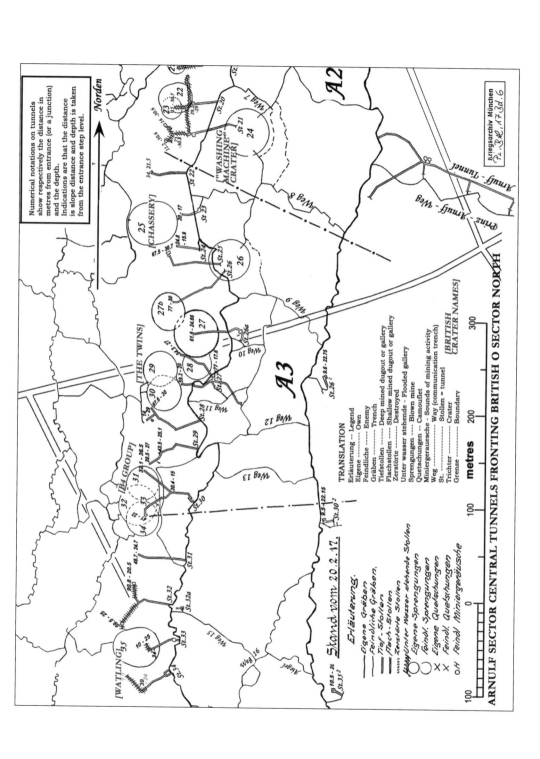

ARNULF SECTOR CENTRAL TUNNELS FRONTING BRITISH O SECTOR NORTH

lateral was developed in strict textbook format, with listening galleries wherever there was a threat every 55 metres or so off the lateral. The lateral itself is level, neatly squared off and low, between 1.5 and 1.65 metres. All inclines are angled at 45° down from a winch chamber, itself situated about 4.5 metres below the surface, much as was the case with many German tunnels and contrary to the more common British practice of sinking an incline at around 22½°. Though steep inclines had the merit of reducing the amount of spoil to be removed and speeding the process of gaining depth, they also had their hazards and could hamper rescue. This was tragically illustrated by a disaster on 21 August 1916:

REPORT TO INSPECTOR OF MINES 1st ARMY
GAS POISONING AT 175th COMPANY R.E. 21.8.16.

Six sappers were on duty at the face. At 4am they lit fuses for 2 shots, and the whole party cleared out of the mine. While waiting, they heard the first shot, then a shock, which they were not sure was a mine or a trench mortar, as it appeared to be at a considerable distance, then the second shot. The face which was being blasted was a dead-end, and anyway required a considerable time for the fumes to clear. These men waited for an hour before re-entering the mine.

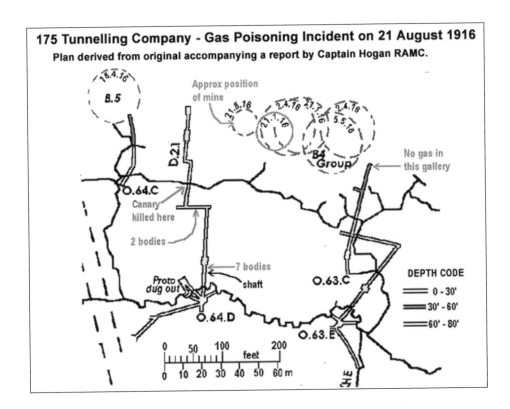

175 Tunnelling Company - Gas Poisoning Incident on 21 August 1916
Plan derived from original accompanying a report by Captain Hogan RAMC.

At 5am, Cpl Scothem and Sapper Walne went down and in a few minutes were followed by Sprs Harrison and Miller. At the shaft bottom, Harrison, seeing Miller collapse, and feeling the effects of the gas, called up the shaft, when the other two, taking this for a signal to resume work, came down. Keeling, one of these men, tried to get Miller out but failed, and feeling the effects of the gas made his way out, passing Sapper Cook and four Infantrymen [sic] (Dragoon Guards). He was so much affected by the gas that he didn't realise what was happening and did not warn these men. He went to the dugout, which was across the trench from the shaft head, and informed 2nd Lt Pyott. This Officer had not been disturbed by the mine, as he thought the shock was due to a trench mortar.

The grave of Second Lieutenant Basil Armitage Carver.

This was between 5:30 and 5:45. On going across to the shaft-head, he found Lieut. Carver (6th D.G.) there. With his help they managed to get Harrison out – this man was not far down the incline. After warning Carver of the danger, and telling him not to go down, Pyott went across to Proto dugout for the mine rescue man and apparatus. In the dug-out were 2 Proto,

'Proto' rescue men in training at a mine school. Note the training dummy in the background.

2 Salvus and 2 O.R.A. When Pyott returned with Smith (the Proto man), he found that Lieut. Carver had descended the mine and, evidently becoming gassed, had fallen to the bottom. While Pyott rendered first aid to Harrison (artificial respiration and administration of oxygen from an O.R.A.), the Protoman descended and found a heap of men at the shaft bottom, with Lieut. Carver lying on the top.

This was about 6am. Protoman disconnected the air pipe in order to allow air in at this point. While struggling with one of the Infantrymen, Smith's nose clip was knocked off and he had to return to the surface. Lieut. Carver and all the infantrymen were wearing their gas helmets.

Lieut. Pyott and Protoman Guy then went down and found six men lying in a heap. Lieut. Pyott commenced fastening a rope round one of the men, but his apparatus was not working properly, owing to having been put on hurriedly and excitement preventing him using it properly, and, feeling himself being overcome, he came to the surface. Realising how serious the position was, this Officer sent to the Sections on the right and left for Protomen and apparatus, and also to advanced Company Headquarters. At 0.65.D., about 700ft to the North, there were 2 Proto, 2 Salvus and 2 O.R.A. The Central Rescue station was at Warrington Road (0.61.E.), about 1,000 yds away.

By this time the air at the bottom of the shaft and in the incline must have improved, owing to the air pipe being disconnected at the shaft bottom, because a Sergt. of the D.G., wearing his gas helmet, was able to go down three times without being overcome, although he felt the effects of the gas. He failed to move any of the bodies. The Protoman Guy, who seemingly was in difficulties with his apparatus, took it off and went down with his smoke helmet on. He was only slightly affected by the gas.

It was not until 8 o'clock that three men were brought to the surface by the aid of other Protomen, who had now arrived. [Here Captain Logan makes a number of critical comments about Pyott and Guy and their failure to use the proto apparatus effectively.]

The work of bringing up the bodies was carried out by Lieut. Claiston, who also tried to restore animation to bodies by artificial respiration and administration of oxygen; by Sapper Cook, who again and again went down, using up 3 Proto Sets; and by Cpl. Macaulay & Sapper Johnstone.

The last bodies to be brought were those of Cpl. Scothem and Walne, which were found lying one on the other facing forwards at a point 20ft from the junction of main drive with lateral.

Four Sappers, Lieut. Carver, of 6th Dragoon Guards, and four Infantrymen [sic] (Dragoon Guards) were killed.

At 1pm, two officers explored the galleries, carrying a canary with them – the canary was knocked out at point (see plan).

At 8:30am next day the mine was apparently entirely free of gas, as a canary carried into enemy part was quite unaffected.

REMARKS

Had proper use been made of the Rescue Apparatus, no difficulty should have been experienced in getting up the bodies. The incline is a very easy one (45°), there is plenty of headroom and a hand rope runs along the right side. Ventilation at the top is very good.

There must have been a dangerous percentage of CO present to have so quickly knocked out the men, and unless rescue had been carried out immediately with little delay, there was little chance of getting these men out alive. Every man was underground and gassed before the Officer was warned by Keeling.

The accident was caused by the men presuming that the shock was due to a mine fired at a distance or to trench mortars. A listening patrol, which was in the face 0.63.C., feeling the shock, came out, but in M.O.63.E., where two faces were being worked, although the men felt a slight shock, which they believed to be a mine exploded some distance away, they continued working.

It cannot be too strongly impressed on Officers and men that gas after a blow may percolate long distances through the disturbed strata, more especially in the vicinity of blown ground, and appear in galleries at a considerable distance from the blow. All working underground should be warned to come to the surface immediately a shock is felt, even at a distance, and no one is to descend until the mine has been proved free of gas. In this case, the mine probably liberated a large collection of gas that had been formed by previous camouflets and enclosed in the neighbourhood of this gallery.

Sgd. D. Dale Logan. Capt: R.A.M.C. G.H.Q.

[All of the nine men killed are buried in Ecoivres Military Cemetery in III Row E. One of these is no. 158596 Sapper L. Cook, who is not the same person as no. 15272 Sapper Cook, whose valiant attempts at rescue were subsequently commended.]

Access was gained to the O Sector tunnels by the Durand Group in December 2001 following extensive preparatory excavations over the previous year, entailing the removal of around 45 tons of in-fill. It was expected that the tunnels would have lain undisturbed since the battlefield clearances of the 1920s; to their chagrin the Group discovered that during the construction of the A26 péage one of the interlinking high-level tunnels had been breached and the road engineers had been in and surveyed the system. Frustratingly, at the point where the lateral, here 21 metres below the surface, passes below the line of the péage, the engineers had filled the tunnel with concrete grout, denying access to the southern half of the system. It was also clear that the tunnellers had been assiduous with salvage, although one well-stocked explosives store was found, inside which remained a legible copy of *The Toronto Sunday World*,

Excavation into the 0.64.E
incline employing miniveyors.
(Left) Major Andy Hawkins,
QMG, RLC, and (right)
Colonel John Swanston RAMC
(retd). (*Durand Group*)

dated 11 March 1917, well conserved by the ammonal. A rich crop of
tunnellers' graffiti was also harvested from the listening post tunnels.

The engineering techniques revealed were impressive. In digging the incline,
the 45° angle was often maintained by first cutting horizontally into the roof
followed by a vertical cut of the same measure (for example, dig horizontally
1 metre and then down vertically 1 metre, giving the appropriate angle),
resulting in the roof having a stepped appearance. Clearly much thought had
also gone into the efficient moving of the spoil. At the top of the incline the
winch had been mounted on a wooden platform 1.8 metres above the floor. The
trolleys when winched up could then be passed under the platform into an
unloading bay, where the spoil was transferred into a light railway or trench
trolley. In turn that would have been manhandled back along a nearly
horizontal tunnel into a sunken road about 45 metres to the rear and thence
taken for dumping.

Durand Group member Chris
Martin makes his way to the
top of the now fully cleared
incline and into the winch
chamber. (*Durand Group*)

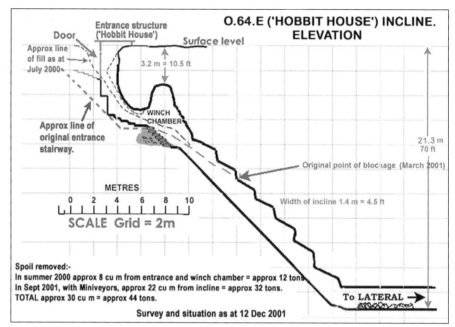

The O.64.E incline. (*Durand Group*)

O Sector was also to turn up a surprise later on. In the course of examining the 175 Tunnelling Company War Diary, Nick Pryor, one of the Durand Group members, drew attention to a drama at the beginning of July 1916. The entry for 2 July reads:

950 lb of Ammonal being charged in O.65.C. During this work enemy heavily shelled the SAPHEAD and completely wrecked same. 2Lt R Horsley and 2 O.R. wounded and 3 O.R. (RE) and 5 O.R. (carrying party of

Lieutenant Colonel Mike Dolamore MBE, RLC, with trolley wheels recovered in the O.64.E incline. (*Durand Group*)

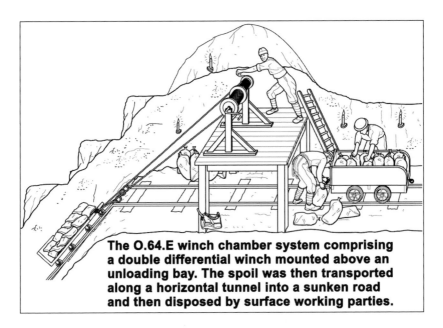

The O.64.E winch chamber system comprising a double differential winch mounted above an unloading bay. The spoil was then transported along a horizontal tunnel into a sunken road and then disposed by surface working parties.

INFANTRY) killed. 2 Lt R Horsley continued to discharge his duties for 2 hours after being wounded. [Horsley survived the war to return to work at Tiverton Park Colliery, near Sheffield.]

The infantry working party referred to came from 2/13th London Regiment (2nd Bn Kensingtons) who had only just arrived in France as part of the 60th (2/2 London) Division. Their regimental history noted the incident:

… It also fronted Vimy Ridge, where the RE were engaged in vast tunnelling operations underneath the front line, and it was carrying parties for this work that the Kensingtons were called upon to provide. It was eerie work down there, far under the ground, watching the white-faced miners picking away at the chalky soil, which was filled into sandbags as it fell and carried away, especially when it was known that the German engineers were engaged in similar work only a few yards through the chalk! The working parties were fascinated by the listening apparatus used by the miners, through which the faint thud of the German picks could be plainly heard, and by which means their progress could be judged to a foot. The work was extremely hard and unhealthy.

On July 1st [sic], when the never-ceasing gun flashes lit up the sky like a great bonfire, telling of the opening of the holocaust in the south, the 2/13th suffered its first casualties. Fatal luck seemed to dog new drafts and a shell struck one of the carrying parties, killing five men and wounding several more, most of whom were just out from home. The bodies were brought back by the light railway which brought up the rations and buried at Bray [Ecoivres Military Cemetery], near the transport lines. The long toll had at last commenced for the Second Kensingtons.

Durand Group drilling into O.65.C. (*Durand Group*)

The 0.65.C tunnel approach to sitting camouflet. (*Durand Group*)

The O.65.C camouflet exposed. (*Durand Group*)

A German 'Listener'. (*Fonds documentaries Alain Jacques*)

There are no further entries in the War Diary referring to the charge in gallery 0.65.C., so the question arose as to whether the camouflet might still be in place and viable. The gallery, which fronts Chassery Crater, had previously been accessed up a very steep and somewhat perilous chalk stairway from the lateral. Most of the passage was blocked with chalk cuttings; could this be tamping? In 2005 the Durand Group mounted a project to clear the passage, an arduous task requiring a bore hole from the surface to feed down an airline, electrical power and a telephone link, then manhandling in a trolley and supports. Several days of underground labour finally breached the mine chamber, to reveal the charge still in place. Major Andrew Hawkins QGM, an Ammunition Technical Officer of the Royal Logistics Corps, working on his own over several hours, rendered the charge harmless by removing the detonators and primers. (The story of the accessing and investigation of O Sector, and the disarming of the mine, is told in detail in a DVD resource pack produced by Fougasse Films.)

It is worthy of note that an extended Wombat crater exists on the south side of Chassery Crater, blown, along with the similar Wombat crater at the head of the Goodman Subway, in support of the 3rd (Cdn) Division assault on 9 April 1917. These, we believe, are unique features, the only two examples of their kind left on the Western Front.

Shortly before the southern extremity of the Canadian Memorial site the O Sector lateral runs due south and under the A26 péage, then for a further 460 metres almost exactly parallels the péage on its western side. Given the existence of listening and fighting tunnels coming off towards the German lines, on the other side of the péage alignment, the road engineers' anxieties may be appreciated. The poignant Lichfield Crater Cemetery is situated about halfway along that part of O Sector, on the eastern side of the péage. This mine was fired by the Germans on 29 April 1916 during 181 Tunnelling Company's occupation of this part of the line, killing three infantrymen and destroying a listening shaft.

The Labyrinth (N and M Sectors)

The Labyrinth encompasses the four sectors N to K (working from the north) and until mining activity on both sides died down in August 1916 primarily involved 181, 185 and 184 Tunnelling Companies, mostly confronting the 14th Bavarian Pioneer Company. The mine and counter-mine fighting was initially as fierce as that further north on Vimy Ridge, and by August 1916 stretches of the line were rent with overlapping craters, much as may be seen today in the Grange area of the Canadian Memorial site. Yet the only surface manifestation left today is Zivy Crater, which, like Lichfield Crater, has been sculpted by the CWGC into a small and beautiful cemetery.

Zivy Crater was formed by a 3,000 lb overcharged camouflet fired by 181 Tunnelling Company on 12 June 1916, although there is no apparent evidence of enemy offensive tunnels in the immediate vicinity. However, the tunnelling plans for this sector show a large *souterraine* immediately to the east of the crater, extending under No Man's Land into the German lines and today presumably situated underneath the péage. Anxiety was expressed about the Germans working from several such caves and it is probable that the camouflet was intended to pre-empt German occupation of the cave.

For 181 Tunnelling Company, as was the case with the other tunnelling companies, April to June 1916 was a period of intense activity as they sought to wrest the initiative back from the enemy. Captain Trounce wrote of this period:

> When we started our operations, his [the German] tunnels in many places were right underneath us, and these he would work intermittently, firing some and holding others to fire later when he thought he could take us by surprise and do the most damage. It was always a great relief when he finally exploded these delayed mines; after investigating matters we would

immediately hike along to a near-by dugout and celebrate. This state of affairs continued for about three weeks, at the end of which time we had pretty well figured out, by listening carefully everywhere, just where his tunnels were.

We had been welcomed with open arms by the British infantry. The poor fellows had been having a bad time, especially in the advanced posts. The old Fifty-first (Highland) Division were then holding the trenches there. These Scotchmen were great fighters, and liked nothing better than meeting the Hun on anything like equal terms, and would positively revel in any attempt of the enemy to raid our lines. The latter would only occasionally try this, however, and never outstayed their welcome ...

It was a different matter, however, when it came to mines. They would fight anything they could see, but were admittedly not pleased with the prospect of mines going up under their feet every night. The poor fellows who had to hold the most advanced posts, mostly bombing sentries and Lewis gunners, did not at all relish the alarming regularity with which the Germans blew their big mines. The poor infantryman gets hell on the surface and from the air without adding troubles from below.

Twice in May 1916 181 Tunnelling Company broke into German tunnels without the enemy being aware of the fact. The first occasion was from tunnel N.42.J., situated about 450 metres immediately south of Zivy Crater. According to Trounce:

At 7:30 pm (on 17 May) the sapper working on the face pushed his grafting tool into one of the enemy underground workings. He at once plugged the hole, extinguished all lights and reported to 2Lt Brown at the shaft head. Lt Brown reopened the hole and looked in. The enemy's work consisted of a flight of steps, probably a mine shaft. The depth below ground was twenty feet.

Brown watched for a time and saw a group of German miners taking over the shift and descending. He decided that it would be appropriate to lay a larger charge than the portable one available to him. He plugged the hole and reported back to the duty mining officer, Captain Beasley. He in turn reported to HQ of 153 Brigade and arrangements were put in hand to blow two camouflets in conjunction with a raid. By 12.30 am on 18 May, 1,200 lbs of ammonal was in place and tamped, along with another charge of 3,700 lbs, previously laid, in a neighbouring gallery.

At 12:34 a.m. both mines were fired. A bombing party of the 7th Black Watch went as far as C [in the German firing line] and brought back one wounded German. They reported signs of several of the enemy having been killed, and heard groans and shrieks.

In the same locality 181 Tunnelling Company again holed into a German gallery on 31 May. This time it was decided to maintain a listening watch while preparations for four mine charges were completed. An interpreter was acquired who, according to Trounce, was a most reluctant volunteer. This attitude is certainly understandable when it is realised that at 1.15 am on 2 June the Germans fired a nearby camouflet that partly buried three of the miners, although they were safely dug out. A transcript of the listening report made immediately after this event is provided below:

Date & time	Listening, etc.	Remarks
2nd June 2:30 a.m.	German conversation 'Well Baner, have you found anything?' 'No Sir, nothing at all so far, but they have come further in this direction than I would have thought. We must wait.'	Enemy trying to ascertain result of his blow. He may have found an old untamped gallery of ours.
2:45 a.m.	Intermittent conversation in low tones.	
4:15 a.m.	German conversation – 2 men at winch: 'Karl, have you heard from your wife lately?' 'No she has not written in two weeks.' 'We shall not get any leave now.' 'Why?' 'I have heard it said.'	Enemy is satisfied with his blows, but less cheerful than before. During this morning 93rd Regt ask 64th if they have been working on the trenches, as something has been heard above the shaft.
5 a.m.	Working and talking – not understood. Tamping continued [by 181 Coy]. Nothing heard.	
9 p.m.	Talking & walking about. Nothing understood. Timber is being carried in.	German shift comes on.
10:30 p.m.	Officer or NCO comes down. All work and talking stopped.	Listening period [by the Germans].
3rd June 12:30 a.m.– 6 a.m.	Work continues as usual.	End of night shift.
7:45 a.m.	Nothing heard through tamping.	Listening pipe stopped & tamping finished.
8:55 p.m.		Mines fired.

Four mines were fired at 8:55 pm, two from branch galleries of N.41.J. and one each from the head of galleries N.40.H. and N.39.F. Major J. Cash, the Officer Commanding, reported:

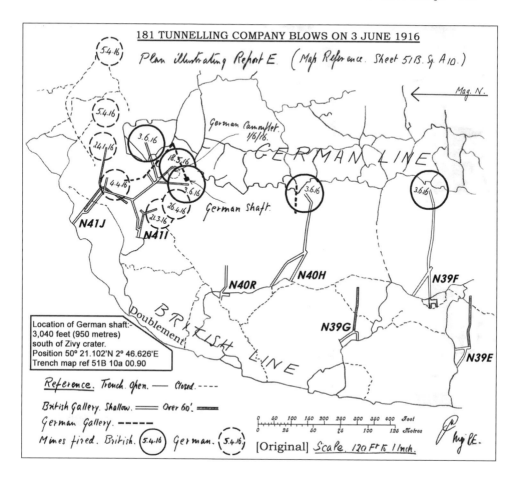

All charges were the same, 3,000 lbs Ammonal in guncotton bags. Fired with two exploders & separate circuits, 3 detonators & primers in series on each. L.L.R. [Line of Least Resistance] uncertain, 15' to 20'.

Results – The detonation appears to have been unusually violent, men being struck with large clods at a distance of 100 yards. Considerable damage was done to the enemy front line. No trench mortars or machine guns fired from this part of the line during the subsequent raid, or during the night. 2 mineshafts & a considerable extent of clay workings are thought to have been destroyed.

Our workings were undamaged & could be entered within half an hour of the explosions. There was no trace of gas.

For 181 Tunnelling Company this marked the turning point at which they seized the initiative. This attack was followed up in July with several more heavy camouflets and mines, drawing only a limited response from the Germans and enabling 181 to work on a deep defensive lateral similar in nature to the La Folie system. On 19 August 1916 the company moved to Foncquevillers on the Somme and was temporarily replaced by 256 Tunnelling Company, commanded by Captain W.T. Wilson. During 181's period in the N and M Sectors they had suffered nineteen ORs killed and two officers and thirteen ORs wounded or gassed. Four of the company sappers remain entombed in tunnel N.37.B.

256 Tunnelling Company was only briefly in the sector, from 15 August until 29 October, at which date they handed over to 175 Tunnelling Company. On their very first shift the 256 men had the misfortune to lose, through carbon monoxide gas poisoning, a newly joined officer, Second Lieutenant S.L. Faithfull and two sappers, Lance Corporals H.G. Hinton and A.G. West (buried in Maroeuil British Cemetery III.D.6–8). It was not a propitious start, but apart from Sapper W. Gregory, killed by an aerial torpedo on 7 October and 2nd Corporal J. Elliott, killed by shrapnel on 17 October (also buried in Maroeuil, III.G.15 and III.H.16 respectively), they did not suffer any serious losses. Indeed, their period was without major incident excepting a sudden burst of aggression from the enemy on the night of 6/7 September, when the Germans blew a mine and a camouflet – an act they may well have regretted when 256 retaliated later the same day with a 6,000 lb charge.

The Labyrinth (L Sector)

L Sector, immediately east of Ecurie, was initially taken over from 7/1 (French) Territorial Engineers in mid–March 1916 by the NZET (see Chapter 8) but this unit was in turn replaced on 1 May by 185 Tunnelling Company, which remained on this front until the advances of 1918. 185 Tunnelling Company was relocated from La Boisselle on the Somme to Arras at the end of February

Men of No. 2 Sub-section of No. 1 Section, 185 Tunnelling Company. Most of the men were ex-coal miners.

185 Tunnelling Company officers. Major Euan Tulloch is seated in the centre, and Captain H.W. Graham (then a second lieutenant) is on the extreme right.

1916. The men badly needed the break on a quiet front. Just three weeks before, their much-respected OC, Captain T.C. Richardson, had been killed as a result of a German camouflet, along with Second Lieutenant A.J. Latham (both buried in Albert Communal Cemetery Extension) and no fewer than sixteen other sappers; in addition they lost another officer and several men gassed. Morale had suffered. In the words of Second Lieutenant H.W. Graham (later to be promoted to captain and to win the MC), who joined them a week later:

> Our Company was still more or less disorganised by depleted numbers in officers and men. There had been much internal friction in the Company for this want of a recognised leader and the appointment was delayed too long. In the middle of March Captain Tulloch MC, now to receive his majority, duly took over and sorted out the sixes and sevens.

The company's temporary commander, a Canadian, Lieutenant Wilson (later Major Wilson DSO MC) was posted to the command of 256 Tunnelling Company and Tulloch (who was subsequently awarded a DSO and four Mentions in Dispatches) swiftly revitalised the company. He had inherited something of a poisoned chalice. As Arras continued slowly to disintegrate under the attention of the German guns, the company saw no wrong in salvaging from crumbling dwellings; before long the officers' and sergeants' messes were furnished in a palatial style, as also were some dugouts. But Tulloch's calm disposition was severely tested in early June when 185 Company suddenly found itself in serious trouble with the authorities. The Provost

Major Tulloch DSO, MC.

MAJOR E. TULLOCH, D.S.O., M.C.,
O.C., 185TH TUNNELLING COMPANY, ROYAL ENGINEERS,
1916-1919.

Marshal had been investigating looting charges said to involve men from the company.

The story went back to early February, during Wilson's temporary command and while the company was based in Albert. The officers' quarters there had been uncomfortable. Yet a nearby shop, abandoned by its owner, had many carpets visible through the windows. It had been a tantalising situation for long enough. Soon after Wilson took command, he sent five subalterns out late one night with a service wagon and wire cutters on what he described as a salvaging job. They cut their way in through a fanlight and almost cleared the store of everything useful. The haul transformed the mess and sleeping quarters and within a day or so there was cosy comfort in all the rooms while outside it snowed. Then came orders to move to Arras.

Wilson went ahead of the unit and found that 185 Company was to be almost the first British unit to move in to the sector. He consequently had almost a free choice of billets and chose two rows of good houses for his officers and men. All were very well furnished. By now the company had so many home comforts in its hands that off-duty hours were passed in extraordinary luxury. Even the dugout up in the line was furnished and carpeted. The officers were living 'like eastern potentates', as one of them later confessed.

Then, towards the end of May, came another change of address. Arras, now under heavy German fire, had become an unnecessarily dangerous HQ zone and the company moved to a hamlet further back, Haute Avesnes. It took its ever-growing cornucopia of comforts. But this time, while the long labour of loading up the wagons went on, a group of French civilians watched, braving a bombardment to do so.

A few weeks later two gendarmes and some non-uniformed Frenchmen called unexpectedly at the camp and looked round. Some officers noticed with unease that they showed a most unusual interest in all the furnishings on view. Next came a party from the Provost Marshal's office to interrogate Tulloch (probably the least guilty officer of all) and the adjutant, Percy Shute, a cheery, knock-about, practical-joking lieutenant. Asked about a piano in the NCOs' mess, Shute explained that under the stress of the bombardment it had accidentally been loaded in place of a canary cage. To explain a night commode found in an officer's hut, Shute told a rambling story about the officer having come from the Gold Coast with a bad dose of dysentery and the commode. The explanations grew less and less likely. Then, before the Provost Marshal's men left, a chilling development took place: Tulloch, as OC, was put under open arrest pending the setting up of a Court of Inquiry. Frantic efforts now began to dispose of everything that could possibly be claimed by civilians as theirs. When the excitement was at its peak, Wilson telephoned Tulloch. In his unflurried Canadian drawl, he offered to take away all the evidence to his own, newly formed, 256 Company for storing until the trouble blew over. Gratefully Tulloch accepted and 185 Company's luxurious lifestyle soon disappeared in Wilson's lorries.

The Court of Inquiry sat and acquitted the company on all charges. But the victory had its price. When Wilson was asked to return the furniture he regretted he was unable to do so; it was such incriminating material he had had it all burned! It was many months until 185 Company was able to recreate an atmosphere of comfort in its quarters – and when it finally did so everything was promptly lost again in a disastrous fire.

Captain Graham encapsulates the situation facing 185 Tunnelling Company upon moving from Arras into L Sector where they were pitted against the 1st Bavarian Reserve Pioneer Company:

> After just a month [i.e. in Arras] we took over the New Zealand Tunnellers' 'pitch' on Vimy Ridge. It seemed that they had some difficulty in organising their mining dispositions, probably due to lack of experience, as they had only recently arrived from overseas. On taking over our 'going concern' at Arras they soon got into their stride and were at a later date one of the most efficient units among Tunnelling Companies. Our new sector extended from Roclincourt, astride the Arras–Lens Road, to Ariane, on the Arras–Bethune Road, an area held by the 51st (Highland) Division. It was on this front that our Company did its best work, and we were to remain here for the greater part of the War, gaining much distinction. On our right we had the 184th Tunnelling Company and on our left 181.
>
> We soon got wise to the new sector and our Division and, with the advice of our Section Commanders, we arranged our listening parties and selected sites for the new shafts at such points where we would expect to intercept enemy galleries. Our work was fully cut out, and it had to be carried on night and day without break. An

An example of the cigarette cases given by the officers of 185 Tunnelling Company to their soldiers at Christmas 1916. (*Stephen Chambers*)

officer fully trained with the use of the geophone paid frequent visits to all the posts, especially at such places where the sounds of picking were heard, and very soon enough information was collected to show that the front line was threatened in several places. Our desperate straits needed desperate energy in counter-mining in order to force the enemy to blow prematurely to save our troops. The suggestion of evacuating those small portions of the line that were in immediate peril, as advised by our OC, was viewed with displeasure.

Thus our position in the middle of April was unenviable. On the one hand we were forcing the pace and knew that, sooner or later, the subtle Hun was bound to put up his mines, with dire losses to ourselves and the troops in the line. Furthermore, he was starting mining operations in several fresh places in the same sector, and how to meet these new dangers caused us a certain amount of anxiety. We felt, in any case, that, unless we were particularly fortunate, our prestige as a mining unit was bound to suffer, itself a cruel blow. Moreover, we had strict injunctions from headquarters to allow no knowledge of advanced enemy mines to leak out to the infantry. Their lot of ordinary trench warfare was bad enough and the rumour of mines underneath them would hardly tend to improve matters. Many can still recall that unpleasant feeling, one of the most uncanny I know of, and one that sticks persistently behind one's mind, of the possibility of being blown to eternity at any moment.

We had to exercise some tact and ready wit to meet all and sundry enquiries of a mining nature and to squash at once any rumours. On one occasion I remember meeting a Jock major in the front line as I was watching my men dumping the spoil carried out in sandbags from the mine.

'Good morning. Things quite quiet down below?' he enquired.

I replied, 'Yes, sir; not a pick heard during the night.'

'But,' said the Major, 'my fellows report enemy picking at M.33 post.'

'Oh, yes,' I answered, 'that's our miners working below. The Hun is still some way off yet.'

Indeed, we knew only too well that the Hun had undermined that part, and, although we were making desperate efforts to check him, we felt that the men in that area were doomed, save for a withdrawal of the garrison. The longer the enemy delayed touching off his mines, so did our danger increase by approaching too close in counter-mining. With the enemy working quietly, we could only know his position within rather wide limits. We would therefore go out of our way to examine all reported rumours and do our best to convince those about us that what were heard were just ordinary trench noises. A very large number of these rumours were purely fanciful; they could be easily detected and explained away by some simple cause, such as rats among empty tins, chopping wood, revetting in trenches and such like. Our prestige was high and explanations were readily accepted.

Owing to losses from sickness and casualties, the Company was woefully under strength in men and so, in April, the OC applied to Division for reinforcements. Volunteers were called for from the 51st Division and we soon got some 150 sturdy Scots miners to supplement our ranks and two officers, Spence and Forrest. These North Countrymen were at first only temporarily attached to us and might at any time have been withdrawn, but they became so indispensable that they remained with us to the end of the war, some as permanently attached infantry and some transferred to the RE. Being trained soldiers, they added a new lustre and spirit to the company, and as civilian miners they were used to mining work, were glad to get free from the irksome duties of the infantryman and to live, as we did, in good billets, with settled hours of work and rest.

I have dwelt on the subject of listening because, at this time, it was foremost in our minds and mining activity was at its height. Not only were listening posts established in the mines, but also in various dugouts in the fire and observation trenches, and in some cases in outlying posts two-thirds out in No Man's Land. These outlying posts were extremely difficult to reach in daylight, as the trenches to them were seldom more than thigh deep and often less, in which case one had to crawl along them; moreover the infantry never kept their posts out so far, but frequently, if we so desired, they would send out a couple of men with us as a covering party whilst we descended the dugout to listen. At night these errands were no great pleasure, in view of the possibility of meeting a hostile patrol. Plummer had a close shave on one such occasion when loading an old French mine in No Man's Land and was nearly nabbed. Fortunately he did not hear the noise and when he finished his job and came out all was quiet, but his covering party had been taken prisoner! I may appear to exaggerate our difficulties, but at this stage of which I am writing they were very real trials, and other tunnelling units experienced much the same sort of thing. Our men responded to the strain in fine spirit and no task was too heavy, no trial too great. If they were poor soldiers in the sense of military carriage, they had grit and a desire to come to grips with the enemy.

The infantry experience is encapsulated in the following extract from Bewsher's *History of the 51st (Highland) Division*:

On first taking over, the mining situation was obscure. The French tunnellers had been withdrawn, leaving only old French Territorials to man the listening galleries. These veterans considered this duty 'très dangereux', as indeed it was.

In consequence, the period was marked by a constant state of anxiety as to what portions of the line were safe from the possibility of being blown up at any moment. However, on the arrival of the British tunnelling companies, which were again largely reinforced by the coal miners in the Division, accurate information was soon obtained as regards the enemy's underground activity. The defensive galleries were first perfected, so that timely warning could be given of any mine that was likely to explode. By this means camouflets could be used to hinder his progress. Subsequently it became possible to take the offensive and mines were blown to destroy his crater positions and trenches.

It became evident that the ground in the forward area was far too thickly held. Orders were in consequence issued for the line to be thinned immediately. Small sectors of disused trenches were dug out to accommodate the surplus men temporarily while a more detailed scheme of defence could be formulated.

The advisability of this measure was soon proved, as from 24th March mines were continually being exploded under or in close proximity to the front line. A typical case occurred on 26th March, when at 2.30 am the enemy fired two mines simultaneously, one on the left of the 152nd Brigade, the other on the right of the 153rd. These explosions were followed by a heavy bombardment of our front and support trenches with shrapnel, all types of trench-mortar bombs, and rifle and machine-gun fire. A party of about eight Germans then advanced towards the crater in the 153rd Brigade area, but were driven back by two officers and a party of grenadiers. Our losses were severe: four officers (one killed, two wounded, and one missing) and seventy-four other ranks (fourteen killed, twenty-four wounded, and thirty-six missing). In addition, there were twenty-four other ranks suffering from shock. Of these, one company of the 6th Argyll and Sutherland Highlanders lost Second Lieutenant MacNeill [buried in Maroeuil British Cemetery] and four men killed, five wounded, and fifteen missing. The missing were those unfortunate men who were buried by the falling earth. Of these two craters, the one on the right proved to be seventy yards in length.

On 31st March another mine was fired by the Germans on the front of the 153rd Brigade, with the loss of one officer wounded, six other ranks killed and three wounded. The explosion of this mine was also followed by an intense bombardment by weapons of all natures. A party of Germans then entered a sap. Of these one approached a Jock who had survived the explosion and, pointing his rifle at him, said, 'Hands up, Englishman!' The infuriated Jock threw a Mills bomb at the German, having failed to remove the safety-pin, and shouted, 'Scotsman, you fucking bastard'. The bomb struck the German full on the forehead and felled him. He was captured, and subsequently died in the Casualty Clearing Station from a fractured skull.

The 6th Argyll and Sutherland Highlanders were particularly unfortunate as regards mines, and by the 10th April had already experienced six mines on their front. On 28th April four mines were exploded in front of the 6th Seaforth Highlanders and 8th Argyll and Sutherland Highlanders. The resultant casualties to these two battalions were six officers wounded, twelve other ranks killed, seventy-five wounded, and thirty missing, believed buried. The explosions of these mines were followed by a forty-five minutes' intense bombardment. The Divisional artillery, however, opened a barrage on the enemy's lines opposite the newly formed craters with such rapidity that he was unable to employ his infantry. Throughout the whole period the manner in which the artillery supported the infantry in this form of warfare was admirable, and gave the latter great encouragement.

The explosion of mines became of such frequent occurrence that the troops became very expert in rapidly seizing and consolidating craters. Dumps were made at frequent intervals along the front containing all the materials required for consolidation. In a short time the troops could be relied on to establish themselves on the near lip, however unexpectedly a crater might be blown. This was largely due to the gallantry and initiative of the junior officers, on whose skill and leadership success in these enterprises was dependent.

Demonstrations were given in consolidation and a platoon for each front-line battalion was earmarked for the consolidation of any mine crater that might be blown on that battalion's front.

The tunnelling companies' policy of forcing the pace bore fruit when on 28 April the Germans blew thirteen mines astride the line where the Arras–Lens road crosses what was then the front line, approximately 55 metres south of the present turn-off on to the A26 péage. Accompanied by an artillery and mortar bombardment and raiding parties, they wrought havoc among the Scots defenders, killing and wounding over 120 all ranks, of whom thirty were missing, believed to be buried. 185 Tunnelling Company, which surprisingly suffered only slightly, turned their hand to rescue:

The scene in the morning was indescribable. Dead British and German bodies were lying about here and there waiting to be picked up by the stretcher bearers. One poor wretch, whom I examined, was evidently carrying hand grenades in an apron when they exploded – he belonged to a Bavarian Regiment. I next came across a Jock being dug out of his living grave. He was buried to the shoulders and it was said that two Germans were disturbed digging him out to take him prisoner. Robbed of their prey, they rapped him over the head in his defenceless position, intending to kill him, and in evidence of the story he had a nasty gash over his head and there was a German shovel lying nearby. Our labours were given over to releasing men buried in their dugouts and cleaning up the general debris.

For 185, though, this was the turning point. The men redoubled their efforts in the following days to gain ground and at least equalise or better the German advantage, and began putting in a deep defensive system. In May they also hit back with several mines, one on 19 May being a Fougasse charge of 3,500 lbs of ammonal, which formed a crater 55 metres across and 9 metres deep at the head of Argyll Street Trench (trench map reference 16a.70.00, GPS 50° 20.608′N 2° 46.567′E – see plan in Tour 2 section). In Graham's words, the enemy never seriously endangered our line again. It did not spell the end of the subterranean fighting but over the next two months German efforts were directed at hindering any prospective British offensive mines rather than attacking the infantry. Apart from one mine to support a raid on 1 July 1916, in sympathy with the opening of the battle of the Somme, 185 concentrated on underground defences. The monthly footage excavated was impressive: in June, 3,937 feet (1,199 metres); in July 3,305 feet (1,007 metres); in August 3,054 feet (930 metres). The company excavated almost 10 kilometres of tunnels over the whole period to the opening of the battle of Arras in April 1917.

From October 1916 the main effort was directed to the construction of four infantry subways, Douai, Zivy, Bentata and Barricade, along with dugouts and some specialist requirements; for example in October a shallow gallery above the chalk strata was dug to put in place a telephone listening station close to the German lines.

The personal accounts of the time do demonstrate a certain insouciance among the tunnellers and their officers, but, after all, most of them were civilians in uniform, and the officers often came from quite senior managerial backgrounds in the mining industries. Certainly they sought some relief from front-line stress with boyish pranks and humour. Graham recounts an episode when he and Captain Plummer, returning from a listening patrol in No Man's Land, were challenged by a sentry who had not been adequately briefed. The suspicious sentry called for an officer:

A major in command of the company garrisoning that sector came forward and peered into our faces and asked our business. We explained matters but it left some doubt in his mind and he replied, 'Ah, yes. The sentry told me that. Will you please step this way to my dugout and we might discuss the mining situation over a cup of cocoa?' And he saw to it that there was an adequate guard with his sergeant to bring up the rear.

The whole position tickled us and we looked forward to the expected refreshment. When we got to his dugout he did not dismiss his sergeant, which seemed strange, and I began to suspect that the Major really had thought he had artfully trapped two spies. I looked at Plummer and saw a twinkle in his eye.

'Now, gentlemen,' asked the Major, 'will you kindly tell me about the mining?', pushing over a bottle of whisky and pressing us to help ourselves, hoping, I expect, to loosen our tongues. We did so – liberally, and we partly evaded his questions to get more time to finish his bottle of whisky. The bottle being only half full we soon managed that and also the cocoa, which his batman brought in.

The joke having gone far enough, we suggested that the Major send for one of our corporals to identify us, or ring up the Battalion, the Adjutant of which knew us personally, and so matters were cleared up.

It may be remarked that the apparent paranoia about spies was not as absurd as it may seem. German records show that on the Somme German officers actually entered and measured up some of the Russian saps that were under construction. Trounce also remarks on exchanging words with a very pukka 'British' officer in the firing line who was later arrested, found to be a German and shot as a spy. One does have to admire the courage of those fluent English-speaking Germans who engaged in this deception.

Notwithstanding the occasional light-hearted episode, the period after August 1916 was not without its perils, mostly from trench mortars and artillery. On 8 January 1917 Lieutenant Jack Benjamin Joseph was killed by a trench mortar just by Zivy Crater. Such as could be found of him was buried at Haute Avesnes British Cemetery (A7); the rest, poignantly remarked by Captain Plummer, remains in the crater. By background a Russian Jew who was brought up in South Africa, Joseph was a most popular officer, always cheerful under the most adverse circumstances. Two weeks later Second Lieutenant R. Thomson was seriously wounded, dying later at the base hospital at Étaples (buried at Le Tréport Military Cemetery, II.O.4). The company officers were

Lieutenant Joseph and his grave at Haute Avesnes British Cemetery.

apprehensive for, as the French were wont to say, *jamais deux sans trois* and, sure enough, six weeks later, in mid-March, Captain W.F. Tomlinson was severely wounded; losing a leg and with thirty other wounds, he was fortunate to survive. Another officer who was with Tomlinson at the time escaped unscathed.

The opening of the Battle of Arras carried the Third Army's lines forward 8 kilometres in places and 185 Tunnelling Company, like the other tunnelling companies, was mostly redeployed to the repair and construction of roads, a critical factor in trying to maintain the momentum of the attack and move forward the artillery. Then, as the initial impetus was lost, they engaged in salvage of material from the British and German tunnels, construction of mined dugouts in the new front line and the investigation and outfitting of *souterraines*. One of the sections was attached to 170 Tunnelling Company near Loos to work on subways and a scheme to discharge huge quantities of gas from tunnels – this was eventually aborted because of concern for the French civilian population, but that is another story.

Remaining in the Arras area, the company went through several further changes of role. In early 1918, like the NZET, it was committed to urgent improvement of the defences in anticipation of the German *Kaiserschlacht* offensive of March 1918, then demolition work ahead of the German advance and deployment as infantry to help stem the offensive. It is interesting to observe the quiet confidence of the company officers as the battle raging on their front came closer. The officers were poised to take up position but meanwhile passed the time playing poker with Canadian officers. In the event the German advance was halted before they had to test their mettle in the infantry role. However, German shelling did somewhat disturb the calm of the new camp at Ecurie when some of the wine glasses were broken; this obviously proved the dangers of the place and they shifted to a fresh site at Mingoval, near Aubigny.

There is something indefatigable about the attitude of the company in this period from late 1917 through to mid-1918, which perhaps epitomises the BEF's confidence in the final outcome. War Diaries and personal accounts give some emphasis to sports days, to polo and to rugger matches. Priorities were certainly rather explicit, as Captain Plummer shows in talking of some ground that lies between Maison Blanche and Ecurie:

It was on this ground that one of our officers, a golf enthusiast, laid out a rough, nine hole golf course, a few disused trenches making excellent natural bunkers. It was late in March 1918, when the war was grim and our own front was beginning to be affected by German attacks, that the authorities had the temerity to send some tanks across this ground. This was too much for our golf enthusiast, who straightway complained to the tank officer in charge that they were damaging the fairways. This was just before the famous Hughes Brigade came into existence, 185 forming part of the battalion of death for a few weeks.

The summer of 1918 is described in almost halcyon terms. 185 Tunnelling Company moved from Mingoval camp to La Targette, occupying what were described as luxurious quarters, with electric light in all the Nissen huts. Nos 1 and 2 Sections were working at Petit Vimy, mostly on the construction of machine-gun dugouts. No. 3 Section was working in similar fashion at Avion and No. 4 Section at Liévin, driving a long tunnel for observation purposes. As Graham observes:

All the work was 'cushy', and the front was as quiet as could be. We had forward billets in some old German concrete gun pits in the woods below La Folie Farm. The weather was good and life was healthy and the work went on without our interference. We strolled round it more for exercise and a talk with the men than for any other purpose. Hollingshead, my batman, used to scout the woods for blackberries and turned them into jam for me. Sometimes in the early morning I'd take pot shots at partridges, of which there were many, and I often brought in the mangled remains of a brace, but they were none the worse for it when stewed.

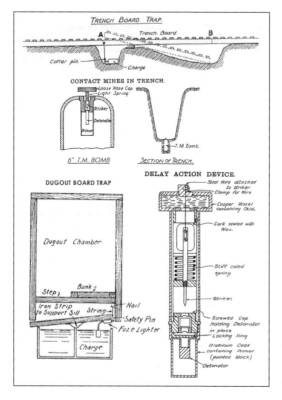

It was not all peace and joy, however. One officer, Lieutenant Douglas, had a near-miraculous escape when a shell passed him at the entrance to an empty dugout, bursting inside. Aerial bombing raids became frequent, with a number of near-misses but, it seems, no casualties. There were other more unlikely hazards, too. One afternoon, in the course of rifle practice on a range, the men from 185 suddenly came under heavy fire; the range had been double-booked and they were in the path of a tactical exercise with live ammunition! It says something for the speed with which all took cover that no one was injured.

Common German booby traps.

It was not until the end of September 1918 that the company left the now thoroughly familiar area of Vimy Ridge as it followed up the retreating Germans, tasked with lifting or neutralising booby traps, delayed action demolitions and improvised land mines. For the record, in one week at the beginning of October 1918 Captain Graham's section alone dealt with ninety-five booby traps and more than forty-four anti-tank charges.

K Sector

The first of the tunnelling companies to be deployed to the Labyrinth was 184, commanded by Major J. Richard Gwyther, who took over from a French Territorial Mining Company in K Sector (in front of Roclincourt) at the beginning of March 1916. As elsewhere it was immediately evident that the Germans were advancing galleries along most of the front. However, most were not yet in position below the Allied lines, giving the company an advantage denied to the tunnelling companies who arrived later in the sectors to their north. 184 Tunnelling Company immediately set about seizing the initiative with an intensive listening programme to identify the threats and develop counter-galleries. They fired their first camouflet within a week of arriving, followed up on 15 and 27 March with more heavy camouflets. It was not until

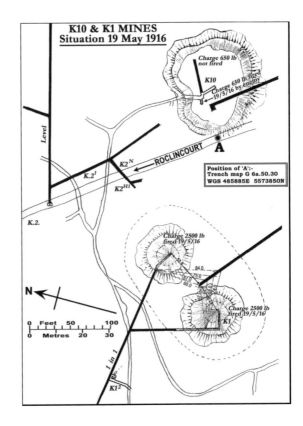

11 April that the enemy struck their first blow. After that, until mid-July, blows and counter-blows from both sides followed rapidly, with 184 firing at least eleven mines and the Germans about thirteen.

Some of the most intensive fighting was just a kilometre out from the centre of Roclincourt, either side of the Thélus road. On 1 May 184 Tunnelling Company fired here a 1,200 lb charge, the K10 mine, against a German working party only 1.5 metres or so away from the chamber. In another flurry of underground exchanges on 19 May, 2 kilometres to the south (just short of where the present D60 road from Roclincourt joins the D919 to Bailleul) a German camouflet, aimed at the K13 tunnels, triggered a pre-prepared charge; the resulting explosion must have come as something of a surprise! Then, within a few hours and only 90 metres west of this event, 184 fired two 2,500 lb mines, bracketing a German tunnel in work.

There was a certain amount of satisfaction at having apparently dealt with the enemy efforts at these points, so an unexpected German response four days later came as a painful surprise. Evidently the enemy recovered their damaged gallery at K10 and on 23 May blew a heavy camouflet, killing eight miners attached from 14 Brigade of the 5th Division. Only one body was recovered, that of Private A. Wood, the winch man at the top of the shaft. The company's War Diary states that he was from 1 East Surreys, but curiously, on his gravestone in the Faubourg D'Amiens Cemetery (I.C.3), he is shown as a Royal Engineer. This suggests that some of those who were in infantry battalions permanently attached to the tunnellers were also considered as Royal Engineers; this rather underlines the difficulty of trying to establish to any great degree of accuracy how many tunnellers were killed in the war. All the other seven attached infantry – Privates S.A. Tebutt, T. Williams, C.H. Tyler, E.W. Weaver, C.G. Hopwood (all from 1 East Surreys), E.A. Farrington of the Middlesex Regiment and H. Jones of the Queen's Own Royal West Kents – are commemorated on the appropriate regimental bay on the Arras Memorial to the Missing.

Mine crater on the Roclincourt road, from a German perspective. This is probably the K1 or K10 crater. (*Bayer. Haupstaatsarchive München / Jean-Luc Letho Duclos*)

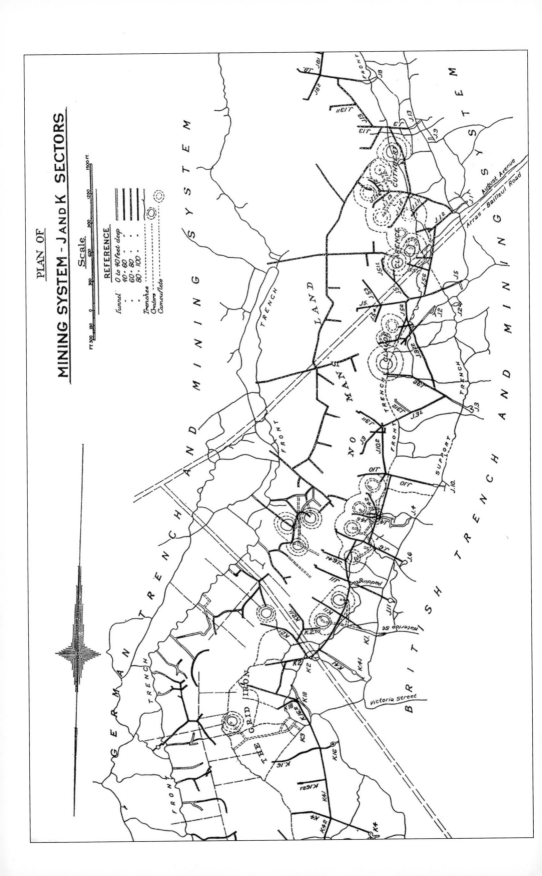

PLAN OF

MINING SYSTEM - J AND K SECTORS

Scale

REFERENCE

Funnel 0 to 40 feet deep
40 - 60
60 - 80
80 - 100
Trenches
Craters
Camouflets

A German portable charge.

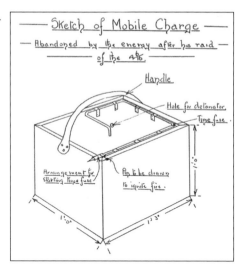

Sketch of Mobile Charge

Abandoned by the enemy after his raid of the 4/6.

Handle

Hole for detonator.
Time fuse.

Arrangement for starting time fuse.

Pin to be drawn to ignite fuse.

Raids by both sides were common enough events along the Vimy–Arras front but at the beginning of June the Germans made what appears to have been a major effort to destroy tunnel entrances in an area known as the Grid Iron, a small British salient located today at approximately the southern end of the Aérodrome d'Arras–Roclincourt. The 184 War Diary for 4 June succinctly describes what was an eventful day:

Having been able to obtain definitive listening in K12–2, the enemy gallery is located as being only 12 ft 70° from this gallery, about our level and heading directly towards us. This mine has consequently been charged with 800 lbs ammonal and tamping commenced.

This morning enemy shelling has been slightly more active than usual and seems to be on an increase.

4 p.m. Hostile shelling is now acute and increasing in intensity. There was a lull between 6:30 and 9 p.m. when the enemy started a second bombardment and at 9:10 fired three big mines opposite K19, K6 and K7, doing very little damage to our mines, with the exception of K19, which was completely lost.

The two bombardments completely flattened out the trenches and closed all the entrances with the exception of K4.

Immediately after the mines the enemy raiding party came over opposite our Trenches 105 and 106 with the apparent intention of disorganising our mining operations. They could only find K4, however, and in the entrance to this mine they left a large bomb which did not explode.

Owing to the splendid work of the officers and NCOs on duty at the shafts (especially 2Lt Birt, 2Lt Galloway, 2Lt Malcolm-Sim and 2Lt Unwin, No. 13931 Cpl Allen, No. 102873 Cpl Taphouse), who went round collecting their men, the Company only suffered two casualties, No. 121856 Sapper Hall, who sustained a broken leg through a fall of roof in K22; and No. 154988 Spr James, who is missing, having been probably buried in the trenches by a shell burst.

No. 79215 Sapper Thomas and Sapper Lowe succeeded in capturing a prisoner near K21.

Sapper James's body was found later. He is buried in Faubourg d'Amiens Cemetery, I.D.13. An appendix to the War Diary contains a lengthy report about the raid, along with a sketch of the German 'bomb'. Some of the company had very close shaves: 2nd Lt Malcolm-Sim and the Proto men were in the Proto dugout during the second bombardment and the raid and heard running about above them. All the men kept quiet and sentries were placed over the damaged entrance. No attempt to enter was made except by one of their dogs. The dugout was severely shaken and the dog escaped.

Inevitably the infantry suffered and quite a lot of men were trapped in dugouts where the entrances had collapsed under what must have been a very accurate bombardment. The miners were much occupied for a time in locating these and rescuing men who might otherwise have been entombed. They were mostly from the Warwicks and West Kents.

The 184 Tunnelling Company War Diary is something of a treasure house because of its detailed reports and appendices; the war diaries of other tunnelling companies, as for many other units, vary greatly in their detail. Space here does not allow for more than a bare selection of these entries, but a copy of their Standing Orders, concerning action following a 'blow', is included: see Appendix II.

Not found in the War Diary, however, is the anonymous tale of the 'Comatose Sergeant', an event thought to have occurred during their tenure with the 5th Division, though its exact provenance has not been determined:

Did you ever hear the story of the best sergeant the ??? Company had getting a slight dose of gas on top of an extra rum ration he had scrounged somewhere during a very hellish night? Mud and strafe outside, and a collapsed gallery with two men caught in a blow underground, B— was a tiger that night, if ever there was one! Towards nine o'clock in the morning, he collapsed, but not altogether. He kept coming round to consciousness and giving vent to snatches of ribald song and language usually quite foreign to him. The Company was working in a part of the line held by a very posh brigade, all spit and polish and discipline and fight. Tunnellers had already fallen very low in the estimation of the Brigadier and his colonels, who had tried to strafe them into decent shape, so as to have nobody in their trenches who did not look like a soldier. Of course, they had no direct authority, and, the Brigadier having been short-changed in an encounter with the powers that be regarding the discipline displayed, his officers could only pass rude remarks about the dress and deportment of Tunnellers and class them with those who were the caretakers of underground lavatories.

In such a high-class trench environment, B—'s fits of song, though due to the effects of mine-gas, would surely be coupled with the undeniable aroma of rum that hung about him, rather than with the after-effects of the strenuous and gallant efforts of the night's work. So, when he calmed down into sleep, he was hoisted on to a stretcher, covered with a blanket and, when the shift was relieved, the party staggered off, a weary, dirty, bedraggled outfit, apparently following a corpse.

As fortune would have it, the doings of the previous night, both above and below ground, had brought the Divisional Commander up first thing in the morning to have a look see. He was one who believed in the personal touch with the troops, and the weary Tunnellers met him.

With the Brigadier and two or three other brass hats, he lined up tightly against the back of the trench to let the little procession pass, and all came smartly to the salute as the 'corpse' came abreast of them. The GOC said something about the gallant dead, and at that moment B— took it into his head to wake up, and, throwing back a corner of the blanket, called in his hoarse, fighting voice, 'You silly bastard, I'm not dead, I'm just making these buggers carry me.' It may have been astonishment, plus the fact that B— at once pulled the blanket back over his face, that left the Staff wondering if they had really seen and heard aright, that saved the Company from further trouble.

From July 1916 onwards 184's experience is generally similar to the other tunnelling companies. The underground fighting died down, although both sides occasionally exchanged explosive greetings. The company focused on putting in a defensive lateral, though its depth was limited by the water table, sitting only 15 metres or so below the surface. They experimented with monorail haulage systems, deeming them considerably superior to the usual trolleys on wooden rails, and rendered detailed engineering diagrams and analysis of the different methods. There was a bit of shuttling to and fro in the sectors with 185 Tunnelling Company and the NZET. Then in November they took over the whole of J Sector and part of I Sector from the New Zealanders, freeing up the latter to work on the cellars, tunnels and *souterraines* of the Ronville system in Arras. That brought them into St Sauveur and the opening up and development of the tunnels through the *souterraines* in that area, handed over for completion to the New Zealanders in late January 1917. At the same time they worked on the extensive Fish Subway, with its brigade and battalion headquarters and expanded the L21 mine tunnel for infantry use, driving it forward just below the surface almost to the German lines. In addition there was tunnelling work to lay signals cables underneath roads and to construct numerous dugouts in preparation for the opening of the battle on 9 April.

With the withdrawal of most of the company at the beginning of April for training in their respective roles in the forthcoming attack, they took the opportunity to hold a company sports day on the 5th, apparently a day of fine spring weather, in contrast to the weather that followed. Perhaps they were too exuberant, for there was a fire in the lines, which destroyed the officers' accommodation and office buildings. While subsequently locked in battle, there was nevertheless much haggling over compensation.

A facet of the 184 War Diary is that Major Gwyther, the OC, was disposed to comment on the course of operations in his vicinity, which has the advantage of representing well-informed, authentic opinion at the time. Regarding the opening of the Battles of Arras on 9 April (First Battle of the Scarpe) the War Diary records:

> Our attack started at 5:30 this morning. The three investigating parties followed up the Infantry, keeping in touch with the 51st, 34th and 9th Divisions. The remainder of the road [construction] parties left HABARCQ at 5 a.m. arriving at ST NICOLAS in time for the second shift on the BAILLEUL and ST LAURENT BLANGY roads.
>
> Company Headquarters moved up to ST NICOLAS same night.
>
> Our attack has been successful. The Railway Embankment was taken by midday and the work of consolidation begun.
>
> By 6 p.m. 56 German officer prisoners and 2,460 OR had passed through the XVII Corps cage. Many others are on the road and it is estimated that the number captured is about 3,000. The right Division [9th (Scottish) Division] secured all its objectives and passed through it to capture FAMPOUX. The centre and left Divisions [34th and 51st] having captured the black line were delayed by machine gun fire. Their wings reached the final objective. The Corps on their left [Canadian Corps] and the Corps on our right [VI Corps] have equally succeeded. Our artillery barrage was most effective. Hostile artillery fire was feeble. No. 11660 Pte Sweeney 6/KOYLI was wounded by a bomb thrown by the enemy from a dugout whilst assisting wounded and admitted to hospital.

In following the battle, Gwyther reports on 12 April that 3,472 enemy and 59 guns were captured by XVII Corps, in parallel with the achievement of the Canadian Corps on the northern end of Vimy Ridge, possibly a BEF record at that stage of the war. On the down side the company orderly room in 9 Rue de Lille, Arras, was hit by a shell, destroying a lot of paperwork and delaying reports. (One feels that the powers that be had probably heard that excuse before!)

As with the other tunnelling companies, 184's endeavours now switched to a combination of work on communications, investigation of German tunnels, salvage – including German explosives, construction of dugouts and investigation of *souterraines*, including those at Roeux. Three large sitting mine charges in J Sector, each of 6,000 lbs, were disposed of by the simple expedient of firing them!

On 28 June 184 handed over all their works to their compatriots in the NZET and moved to Ypres. 184's casualties had been surprisingly light, given the intensity of some of the mine fighting and raiding. For the statistically minded, figures derived from their War Diary over the period from the beginning of March 1916 to June 1917, they lost one officer and twenty-one soldiers killed, and three officers and twenty soldiers wounded. One of the fatalities was a soldier accidentally bayoneted (perhaps by a stressed sentry) and another was from a motor accident. Of the wounded, one officer and one soldier were shot by accident and there was one case of a self-inflicted wound. Only about a third of the casualties were a consequence of mining. Most of the remainder resulted from shell or mortar fire.

So 184 Tunnelling Company passed out of central Artois, leaving the New Zealand Tunnellers and 185 Company to provide the main underground support into mid-1918.

Graffiti – artwork in the O Sector tunnels.

Chapter 8

Arras – Cellars, Subways and Caves

Arras and the Early Days of the First World War

On 6 September 1914 light German forces entered the city but withdrew after three days, having requisitioned a large quantity of stores and dipped their hands into the town's treasury. However, at the beginning of October 1914, as the Germans attempted to outflank the Allies to the north following the Battle of the Marne, their IV Corps and I Bavarian (Reserve) Corps closed in on the Artois. Just ahead of them the French 77th Division (consisting mainly of mountain infantry, *chasseurs alpins*), commanded by General Barbot, detrained on 30 September in Arras. In a series of epic actions, the thinly spread 77th Division delayed the German advance until the arrival of the bulk of the Tenth Army (General de Maud'huy). After heavy fighting the Germans were held in the St Sauveur and Beaurains suburbs of the city. To the north, however, the Germans took the eastern heights of Notre Dame de Lorette and to the south advanced to Gommecourt. When the 77th Division was relieved in late October 1914 it had been reduced to a quarter of its original strength. Arras had been

Artist's impression of German artillery firing on Arras. Note the belfry still standing.

saved from occupation but lay in a pronounced salient under the German guns. Its long martyrdom had begun. Of the 4,521 houses forming the heart of the city, only 292 had escaped damage by the time of the armistice in 1918.

In the course of further unsuccessful attacks in late October and November 1914 the German heavy artillery pounded the city, destroying the cathedral and the Hotel de Ville with its beautiful belfry, at the time the highest in France. Thereafter both sides developed almost impenetrable defences and, although the city was rarely free from shellfire, the Arras front, in the immediate vicinity of the town, became largely a 'live and let live' quiet sector. However, fighting in 1915, only a few kilometres to the north, was extremely fierce. It was during this fighting that the pressure on Arras itself was partially relieved in May 1915 when the French Tenth Army (now commanded by General Fayolle) forced the Germans off almost all the Notre Dame de Lorette spur in the Second Battle of Artois. The pressure on the town was lessened further when, in the Third Battle of Artois in September 1915, the Germans were pushed back on to the crest of Vimy Ridge. As a southern subsidiary to Third Artois, regiments of the French 33rd Division attacked the German positions from Beaurains to Bois de Blairville but suffered catastrophic casualties for no gain.

The Arras Sector under British Control

In early March 1916 Arras was again invaded, but this time by forces welcomed by the residual civilian population of the city. The British Third Army replaced the troops of the French Tenth Army in Artois, thus creating an unbroken BEF front from Ypres to the area of the River Somme. For the remainder of the war Arras remained under British administrative control, with (generally) comfortable relations between the military and the civilian authorities and people.

British transport at the Baudimont gate.

The Germans were rather less satisfied with their new enemy: *Somewhere on the Western Front – Arras 1914–1918* notes:

> The British takeover took place without incident, confirming the quiet reputation of this sector. There had existed a tacitly agreed suspension of hostilities between the Germans and the French. Small arms fire and shelling were unusual; a strange peace extended over the battlefield. Protected by thick barbed wire entanglements the Germans seemed to have set up a system of 'live and let live' … The German troops

A French boy delivering newspapers to troops in Arras. (*Fonds documentaries Alain Jacques*)

who had recently been pulled out of the heavy fighting on the Somme had come to man this sector of the line to have a quieter time and a moment of rest. However, the British were combative. They mounted raids constantly …

In addition to the small-scale raiding, and there were few nights when a British raiding party or patrol did not discomfit the enemy (and vice versa), there were occasional big-scale raids. For example, on 18 April the 14th (Light) Division mounted an attack, supported with gas, on the 10th Bavarian Jäeger (Reserve) Battalion at Tilloy-les-Mofflaines, to the southeast of the town. This was repelled but on 27 June a large gas discharge inflicted heavy casualties on the

Troops resting by the ruins of the Hotel de Ville in La Petite Place.

10th Bavarians. The 14th Division was replaced in mid-July by the 11th Division and it in turn, in August, by the 12th (Eastern) Division, which set out to dominate No Man's Land. As the pace of trench warfare became more intense, the Germans were not slow to retaliate, so Arras was subjected to increasing artillery harassment. The British thus actively began to seek better protection for troops and facilities in Arras.

The Development of Underground Arras

Since very early times, perhaps extending back in some cases to the Romans, one of the chief curiosities of Arras has been the *boves*, these being cellars under the older houses, often 'subimposed' to a depth of three storeys below ground level. The first sub-basement, frequently fitted out as a tavern, a workshop or for dwelling, was usually vaulted and often supported by decorated stone columns. But below these the inhabitants quarried the chalk for building stone, and in the process created caves for storage and refuge. The Italian historian Guichardin (1483–1540), in his description of the Low Countries, wrote: 'In all the houses there are finely vaulted caves and cellars. These were purposely built wide and deep, so that in time of war whole families might find shelter there from the fury of the enemy's cannon.'

Certainly the civilians who had remained in Arras and the French troops had taken advantage of the protection offered by the *boves*. The French had also sought the deep medieval *carrières* (quarries) known to exist in the Arras area and a plan for the defence of Arras, drawn up by Lieutenant Colonel Lespagnol of the *27th Régiment d'Infanterie Territorial*, revealed deep cellars, particularly under the brewery and the sawmill on the Bapaume road. It does not appear that the potential of these workings was systematically developed until late 1916, when the *boves* were interconnected so that it became possible to move freely beneath Arras, from one part to another, without being exposed to shelling. The plan overleaf shows just one part of the system at the northwest side of the Grand' Place. These deep quarries have today been restructured into the underground car park. (Details about public access to systems in the city centre, and to the Wellington Caves in Beaurains, are given in the Arras part of the Tours Section.)

Arras also possessed other subterranean features that, along with the *boves*, facilitated the development of what effectively became an underground military canton. A small river, the Crinchon,

Boves below the Hotel de Ville.

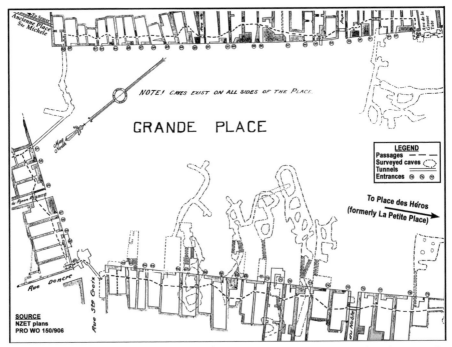

Plan of La Grande Place in 1916, showing the caves and the interconnections between the *boves* (cellars).

which fed the moat around the citadel and flowed through the centre of the old city, was progressively covered over during the eighteenth and nineteenth centuries, becoming a sewer debouching into the River Scarpe (it makes a guest appearance in Victor Hugo's *Les Misérables*). Between 1890 and 1900, when the city walls were demolished, a purpose-built sewer was constructed in the ditch and covered in. Connecting on the southern side with the Crinchon, it parallels the former city wall on the eastern side and flows, via a processing plant, into the Scarpe. With walkways along the sides, this provided a ready-made tunnel that was immune to all but the heaviest artillery. Furthermore, around the city, under what are now the suburbs of St Catherine, St Laurent-Blangy, St Sauveur, Beaurains and Achicourt, numerous long disused *carrières* were discovered.

It is unclear from the various War Diaries examined as to who first proposed developing these caverns on the eastern side of Arras. It was probably a case of serendipity, as their potential would probably have been apparent to a number of officers. The first reference we have found is one in the New Zealand Engineers Tunnelling Company (NZET) War Diary of 28 September 1916, which states 'today we abandoned the cave hunting project'. But as the company at that time was mostly operating in J Sector, north of Arras, it may have referred to their work in that area. On 28 October the War Diary remarks,

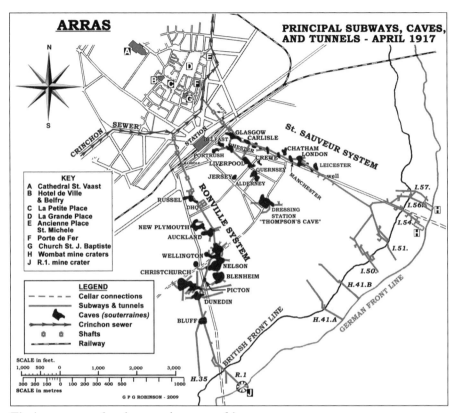

The interconnected underground systems of Arras.

'Mining very slack. Considering a deep level scheme for blowing up Beaurains. Got out details for Controller of Mines today. We go south unless a deep level scheme under Beaurains is adopted.'

It would appear that the initial intention was to develop a mining attack from one of the forward caves. By 16 November the tone had changed and the War Diary records, 'A start made on connecting underground quarries between Ronville and St Sauveur.' On 20 November it notes, 'Footage increasing as the work on opening up the caves advances. 212 ft today' (see above).

Almost simultaneously, 184 Tunnelling Company's War Diary of November 1916 was recording:

21-11-16   Caves at St Sauveur examined and roughly surveyed and a scheme got out to connect them by an underground tunnel up to the trenches.

22-11-16   St Sauveur tunnel scheme put before VI Corps and approved.

23-11-16   One relief from Nos II and IV Sections moved to St Sauveur and employed on cleaning up & repairing cellars and old houses as advanced billets.

24-11-16   Actual work on connecting the caves by galleries & galleries up to the support trench commenced at 4 pm today. This to be completed in 60 days. Length of drive 5,000 feet. Size of gallery 6' 6" × 4' 0" [2m × 1.2m]. Nos II and IV Sections under Capt. A.E. Eaton, DSO, RE and Capt. G.B. White have this in hand.

25-11-16   A theodolite survey of St Sauveur is in progress – the caves being surveyed below ground with the compass. The progress has been very satisfactory although the ground in several caves has been bad and treacherous.

Entries in 184 Tunnelling Company's War Diary relating to the works on St Sauveur continue almost daily with reports of more caves being found, some of them unsuitable for development. There is much lamentation at the shortage of available timber, a constant problem for all tunnelling companies. Something of the importance attached to this work and that by then under way with the NZET in the Ronville caves, is reflected in a diary entry of 18 December, noting that 'General Harvey, Inspector of Mines GHQ, went over our system in St Sauveur', while an entry on 21 December reported that, 'The tunnel at St Sauveur was visited by the Chief Engineer III Army and by the General Staff of VI Corps.'

Disentangling exactly which tunnelling company was doing what at any point of time is difficult, as sections were freely interchanged and within the army area mining sectors were adjusted between companies as the threat and the requirements altered. Today there is a touch of xenophobia over who did what, but at the time all the BEF contingents regarded themselves as British, worked to a common purpose in accordance with GHQ directives, and duly engaged in the friendly rivalry that has always existed – and still exists – between units and formations. The only really serious competition was on the sports field.

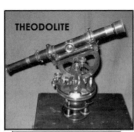

The Third Army Inspector of Mines report on the situation on taking over from the French in March 1916 states that, 'South of the River Scarpe there was no enemy mining'. North of the river the situation was, however, dire, with the Germans offensively mining along most of the front up to and including Vimy Ridge (later taken over by First Army). Both 184

A selection of surveying instruments used by the tunnellers.

and 185 Tunnelling Companies and the newly formed NZET were hastily drafted into the area immediately north of the Scarpe (J, K and L Sectors, the latter being within the notorious Labyrinth) and, on replacing the French engineers, found themselves engaged in a deadly cat-and-mouse battle underground. It was, though, in Third Army's interest to avoid stirring up the quiet sector south of the Scarpe, and the only activity there was the laying out of a system of defensive galleries, interestingly by a section from the 4th Division (presumably of miners drawn from the infantry and Royal Engineer Field Companies) under the supervision of the NZET.

The New Zealand Engineers Tunnelling Company (NZET)

Each of the thirty-two BEF tunnelling companies had its especial characteristics and personalities. In this respect, perhaps, the New Zealanders were not that much different to any other tunnelling company, but they brought their own innovative style and claimed to drive their tunnels faster than anyone else. The recruits to the company were first assembled in October 1915 at Avondale in New Zealand. Almost all were mature men and tough miners, many of them too old for service with the infantry. Their officers were drawn from the engineering staff of the Public Works Department and mineral mining managers. Imparting the essence of military discipline and a respect for King's Regulations on around 400 unruly miners was something of a triumph of leadership, which may also be said of most other tunnelling companies. Perhaps the essence was a sense of 'brotherhood', and an officer who was not up to the job was quickly moved elsewhere. These often elderly civilians in

A shift of New Zealand tunnellers at Arras. (*J.C. Neill*)

uniform were not only admired for their mining skills and resolution, but for a time in 1918 performed capably as infantry. Under the command of Major J.E. Duigan of the New Zealand Service Corps, with a strength of seventeen officers (less their padre, who was left behind) and 429 other ranks, they arrived in France on 10 March 1916, the first formed New Zealand unit to arrive on the Western Front. Their inexperience as soldiers is perhaps reflected by a comment in the company history that they turned up for training at the 'Bull Ring' in Étaples with live ammunition – 'fortunately without incident'.

On 16 March the new arrivals replaced the 7/1 French (Territorial) Engineers in the Labyrinth, 3 kilometres north of Arras, without any prior instruction in mine warfare. The company history notes,

> … the company had to work out its own destiny, for here it was thrown into the line without the slightest knowledge or training in the methods of underground warfare or even elementary trench routine – the French mines were mere rabbit burrows with Hun galleries below and amongst them …

The New Zealanders learned quickly and applied their own techniques. A particular preference was to cut their galleries 1.8 metres high, rather than the more common practice of cutting low fighting galleries around 1.3 metres high. Although this resulted in much more spoil, it allowed the miners room to swing a pick and advance the face faster. When digging in chalk, speed was of the

**Lieutenant W M Durant
N Z Engineers
14th September 1916**

Lieutenant W.M. Durant of the New Zealand engineers, and his grave in Point du Jour cemetery. He was killed on 14 September 1916.

essence and they soon had the enemy on the back foot. A typical NZET company footage in a week might be around 600 feet (180 metres) or more. The company was also judged a lucky one, for despite numerous close shaves, mostly while moving into or out of the line, it was not until 22 June that they suffered their first fatal casualty, Sergeant S. Vernon, who died of wounds sustained in the trenches and is buried in Faubourg d'Amiens Cemetery, I.D.59. On 14 September 1916 they suffered their first officer fatality:

> Lieutenant Durant, with Sergeant Pownceby, along with eight of our men, volunteered to accompany a night raid of the Cheshires. Their job was to blow a passage for the raiding party through the enemy wire by means of a loaded pipe, and afterwards to investigate and if possible destroy any German mine entrances. The raid proved a failure, only Lieutenant Durant, Sergeant Pownceby and a sergeant of the Cheshires apparently reaching the German trenches … In the darkness and confusion of the abortive raid no one had seen the three go forward and many of Durant's men spent the whole night searching no-man's-land, in spite of heavy enemy fire.

Initially posted as 'missing', the fate of the three men was not definitively established until April the next year. A War Diary entry of 22 April 1917 states,

> Lieut. Durant's grave found at St Laurent-Blangy. Grave well kept and nicely set up, cross over grave and tiles around the sides. Pounceby [sic] evidently buried in the same grave, as the enemy had put on the cross: 'Here lies four brave Englishmen [sic], Lieut. Durant, 2 NCOs and 1 man.'

Whatever happened in the German trenches that night, it is evident that it evoked the admiration of the enemy. Lieutenant William Durant was reburied at Point du Jour Military Cemetery (I.A.6) as part of the postwar concentration of isolated graves. The body of Sergeant Pownceby, who was 39 years old and with parents and a wife in England, was not identified and his name is inscribed on the Arras Memorial to the Missing (Bay 10).

The Tunnellers in Arras

By November 1916 the rival miners on the Artois front had fought themselves virtually to a stalemate. It is to the credit of the staffs of Third and First Armies that they then opted to redirect the mining efforts primarily to the protection of the infantry, with the construction of subterranean accommodation and subways giving safe passage to the front, albeit some offensive mining was initiated in great secrecy. This led to a considerable readjustment along the front. 185 Tunnelling Company moved north on to Vimy Ridge, 175 Tunnelling Company took over some of their sector and 184 Tunnelling Company became responsible for the sector astride the River Scarpe, including initially the

St Sauveur tunnels. In November the NZET moved entirely into Arras to work on developing the Ronville caves and tunnels, then took over the almost-complete St Sauveur tunnels and the J mining sector from 184 Tunnelling Company on 22 January 1917. It was an unfortunate day for 184 Company as 'No. 132044 Lcpl [sic] Poole, RE, was accidentally bayoneted and killed by a man of 27th Infantry Brigade'. That incident alone is worthy of some investigation. Poole is buried in Faubourg D'Amiens Cemetery, II.C.2. Hereafter the NZET was mainly responsible for the development and maintenance of the Arras underground systems, although 179 Tunnelling Company took over work on the forward part of the Ronville system on 10 February 1917.

For the New Zealanders the switch to developing the underground communications and caves came as a considerable relief from the stress, discomforts and perils of front-line mining. They could concentrate on what they knew best and threw themselves into the task with enthusiasm. Some of the caverns were immense, hundreds of metres in diameter and 6 to 12 metres high. Between the supporting pillars of chalk, falls had gradually formed bell-shaped domes, so high that the roof was barely discernible in candle light. To make these caverns safe and habitable was no easy matter, for as soon as they were opened to the air the chalk began to swell and crack and slabs weighing

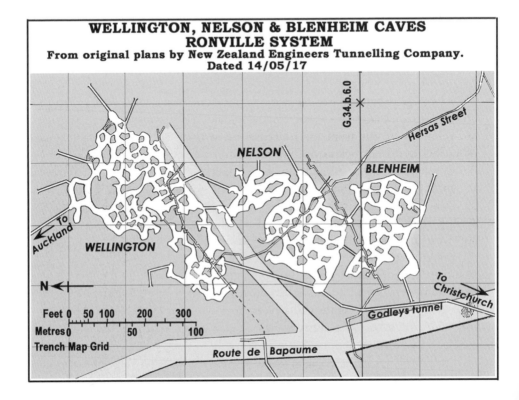

WELLINGTON, NELSON & BLENHEIM CAVES
RONVILLE SYSTEM
From original plans by New Zealand Engineers Tunnelling Company.
Dated 14/05/17

The connecting tunnel from Wellington to Nelson and Blenheim caves in 2003.

many tons could come crashing down with not even an instant's warning. To timber up to the heights of these roofs was out of the question, so instead the floor was raised by dumping the chalk cut from the galleries and dugouts until the roof was close enough for clear observation and support. The amount of wood needed was enormous and entailed purchasing and cutting trees from the woods at Le Cauroy, transporting them to a sawmill at Frévent, which operated around the clock, and thence to a workshop at Louez for finishing.

In both the Ronville and St Sauveur systems a main connecting gallery, some 2 metres high by 1.4 metres wide, was driven as far as the support trenches, where it branched into several galleries, spreading out fanwise into No Man's Land, in some cases within a few metres of the German front line trench. The Arras ends of the two systems were connected to the Crinchon sewer, while several gently graded approaches gave entrance to the sewer from the cellars in the Grand' Place and other points in the town. One such was from the Ancienne Place St Michel, at the northeast exit from the Grand' Place, where a chute was fitted for sliding ammunition boxes down to a connecting tramway. The main entry was through *La Porte de Fer* ('The Iron Door'), situated at the northeast corner of the Rue du Saumon, close to the present-day Place d'Ipswich. Troops could debouch from trains or lorries in the Grand' Place then, via the cellars and sewer, move into front-line positions along the galleries, or rest in reserve in the caves. The entire system was lit

Blenheim cave in 2003, prior to development. (*Durand Group*)

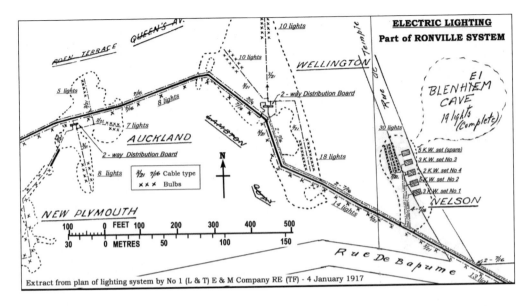

ELECTRIC LIGHTING
Part of RONVILLE SYSTEM

Extract from plan of lighting system by No 1 (L & T) E & M Company RE (TF) - 4 January 1917

throughout by two electric generating stations, designed, erected and worked by No. 1 (L&T) E&M Company, Royal Engineers, in conjunction with the NZET Company. The main galleries were also provided with a 2-foot gauge iron tram line, with numerous lay-bys to permit up and down traffic. Along the galleries also went 4-inch water mains, while scores of telephone wires were prepared that would come to the surface well across No Man's Land to follow the advance.

Well before Zero Day (finally fixed for 9 April 1917), all the arrangements were completed. The caves had all been levelled and made safe, the lighting completed, bunks, cook-houses, washing places and latrines installed, gas-tight doors fitted to all entrances and routes, galleries and exits signposted. In all, safe accommodation was provided underground for some 20,000 troops, while many times that number passed through the systems. Considering the fragmentation over the centuries and the difficulty of obtaining timber, it is a great tribute to the skills of the tunnellers that, beyond one or two small knocks, not a single man of these thousands was hurt by falling chalk.

The Porte de Fer (Iron Door), the original entrance to the Crinchon sewer. (See also page 234.)

A kitchen in the Arras caves. (*Arras Tourist Office*)

The immense work of developing this subterranean military town involved a substantial labour force daily of 500 or more men, mostly drawn from the infantry divisions in reserve, along with technical support by Royal Engineer Field Companies. It is evident from the

Soldiers relaxing in one of the caves.

records that the Scots from the 9th and 15th (Scottish) Divisions enjoyed a special place in the esteem of the tunnellers. But those who imposed their personality most were a small detachment of forty-three Maori Pioneers, who seemed to have developed an especial rapport with the Jocks and with them devised subtle means of 'liberating' temporarily abandoned wine cellars, leading to some very jovial parties – much to the chagrin of the military police. The Pioneers were said to be great favourites with everybody, splendid toilers, always willing and cheerful; they supplied an inexhaustible fund of drollery and laughter that was sadly missed when they were recalled at the end of February. The Maori Pioneers also developed effective means of raiding Royal Engineer dumps for timber and, if caught in the act, affected ignorance of the English language. There are many other stories attributed to them.

On one occasion a party of these Maori Pioneers was working in the main St Sauveur tunnel when a sergeant of the Gordons came down in charge of a miserable little Bosche kept 'as a sample' from a daylight Gordon raid. The Maoris had never seen a real live Bosche before and were immensely interested. They crowded round with many gestures and haka attitudes, finally all going on their knees to the Gordon sergeant with a fervent prayer to give them the prisoner to take home to their billets as a pet and fatten him up. There wasn't a more abject little object on earth just then than that Hun under his iron helmet – and no wonder, for in the uncertain light of the electrics in that underground place, the rolling eyeballs, protruding tongues and wild gestures of the Maoris would shake the stoutest nerve. It may or may not have had some connection with this that a German communiqué shortly afterwards accused the British of employing New Zealand cannibals on the Western Front.

In the course of the works in the Ronville and St Sauveur systems another large cave was found midway between the two and only 730 metres from the forward trenches. On the initiative of Lieutenant Colonel A.G. Thompson of the Royal Army Medical Corps, Thompson's Cave – as it became known – was developed into a Casualty Clearing Station (effectively a forward hospital). It could accommodate up to 700 wounded, along with the logistic services and medical staff, was equipped with electric lighting and water, and fitted out with operating and treatment bays. However, on 12 April, three days into the battle, a heavy shell led to the collapse of two bays and the hospital was redeployed to two new sites in the town. Closed off after the war, it was rediscovered in October 1999 in the course of repair work on a gas main under the pavement of the Rue St Quentin, and has since been examined in detail by the *Service Archéologique d'Arras* under its director, Alain Jacques.

On 4 April 1917 the NZET War Diary noted:

As the preliminary bombardment was to start at 6:30 a.m. on the 4th and all our construction work being finished, the majority of our men in the saps proceeded to our back billets at AGNEZ–LES-DUISANS. A number of men who had been sent back about a week previous for a rest proceeded at the same time to the saps and took up battle positions. The Company's advanced headquarters was moved from the ARRAS Post Office to cellars under the Chateau at G.30.c.2.1 [WGS 31N 485780E 557005N], these cellars being connected to the branch tunnel to India Lane Trench. The duties allotted to the Company during the battle were as follows – patrolling, inspecting and

Nick Pryor of the Durand Group struggling to squeeze into the manhole entrance to Thompson's Cave, watched by Duncan Allen, Chris Martin and on the extreme right Alain Jacques.

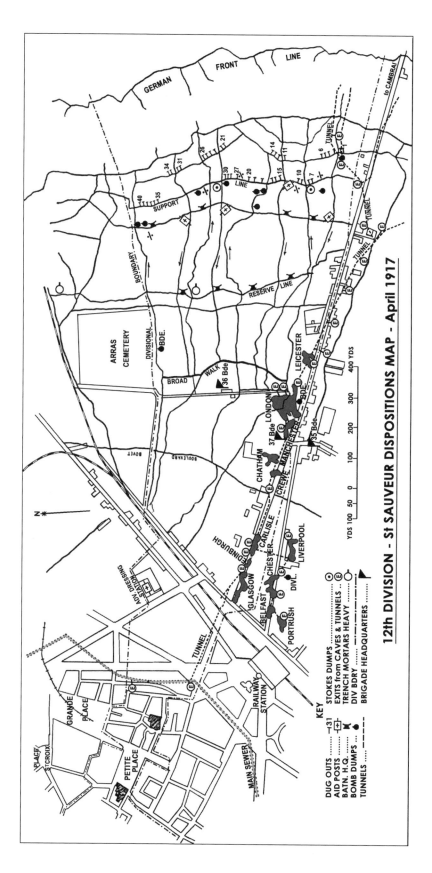

12th DIVISION - St SAUVEUR DISPOSITIONS MAP - April 1917

KEY

DUG OUTS .... ⌐31
AID POSTS .... ⊞
BATN. H.Q. .... ✕
BOMB DUMPS .... ●
TUNNELS .... ·····

STOKES DUMPS .... ⊙
EXITS from CAVES & TUNNELS .. Ⓔ
TRENCH MORTARS HEAVY ...... ○
DIV BDRY .... —·—
BRIGADE HEADQUARTERS ..... ▲

repairing the galleries, cave roofs, exits, gas-doors, sewer, and cellars in the VI Corps area; running and maintaining the electric light systems and emergency oil-lights in the complete RONVILLE, ST SAUVEUR and SEWER systems, also in the Casualty Clearing Station Cave, blowing communication trenches from the ends of I.56 and I.54 at zero and removing cover and debris afterwards; opening up the end of I.57 and the machine gun emplacements; blowing the mine at I.70.a.1; opening a way into the Hun gallery from there to his trenches.

It may be observed that the NZET tasks included the blowing of two Wombat mines to create 'instant' trenches across No Man's Land, and a shallow mine with a 2,000 lb (900 kg) charge (see the map on page 173). The War Diary contains a lengthy entry concerning events immediately following zero hour at 5.30 am on 9 April. The blowing of the mines was the signal for the waiting infantry to attack. In the vicinity of the mine the enemy hotly contested possession of the crater for an hour but the resistance was successfully overcome. By this time the main attack was so far forward that no more work was done to the (German) trench or the galleries (captured from the Germans). From the Wombat craters and from galleries opened elsewhere into No Man's Land, communication trenches were swiftly dug connecting to the German line but were never used as the attack was so successful that about a 7-kilometre advance was made in the first day. The majority of the tunnellers were withdrawn, leaving only those concerned with inspecting German tunnels and dugouts and the maintenance parties in the caves.

The initial success of the First and Third Armies' attack at the opening of the Battles of Arras, with advances of up to 8 kilometres, took Arras out of range of all but long-range artillery and freed the city from direct enemy observation. The extensive systems of interconnected cellars and caves had served their purpose. By late May 1917 the NZET had started stripping out the electrics, other fittings and fixtures and in particular the timber needed for new dugouts and defences. However, less than a year later, and with the so-called *Kaiserschlacht* offensive of March 1918 looming, the NZET (still in that sector) hastily started to restore the Ronville and St Sauveur systems, along with extensive defensive works and road, bridge and other demolitions. In April 1918 the town again found itself within range of German medium artillery, but it was not as closely invested as formerly. The long siege was finally lifted in August 1918 as the Allies began the series of offensives generally known as The Hundred Days. The NZET, at this stage united for the first time with the New Zealand Division, advanced eastwards, primarily in the engineering role, constructing bridges and hunting down German booby traps and delayed demolitions.

In the last few years the civic authorities have taken the bold and imaginative step of opening up a section of the work of the tunnellers under Arras and now visitors can tour a part of Wellington Cave; full details of this can be found in the Arras part of the Tours Section.

Chapter 9

The Tours

Tour 1: Zouave Valley to Maison Blanche
Tour 2: Neuville St Vaast to the Bailleul Road (extension to Roeux)
Tour 3: The Pimple (east) and the Canadian Memorial Site
Tour 4: Arras
Tour 5: Cemeteries: Maroeuil British, Ecoivres, Haute Avesnes, Aubigny Communal Extension and Faubourg d'Amiens CWGCs; and the French National Cemetery and Memorial, Notre Dame de Lorette

The tours require a combination of transport and walking; none of the walking is difficult but it can be muddy. As advised in the introduction, stout footwear should be worn and possibly have wellington boots available as well. The tracks have been found to be passable in a saloon car but where there might be some difficulty (on the basis of our touring, carried out in 2009 and 2010), this is indicated and relevant advice given.

Please be aware of other road and track users when parking your vehicle, especially if you will be moving some distance away from it. Do not block routes and bear in mind that there might be heavy (and large) agricultural machinery that needs to get past. At all times be respectful of private property and do not wander over the fields, especially when there are crops growing.

Larger vehicles will have some difficulties. We have done many of these tours in a minibus but most are not practicable in a coach. It is strongly recommended that a coach leader makes a reconnaissance of the routes before committing a coach to any one of them.

Distances are given in either metric or imperial units; in part this is because all the original British documentation is in the latter and in part because of the somewhat eccentric usage of both systems in the UK. Since guide touring is not an exact science, the difference between a yard and a metre in this case is something we have not worried about over much.

The French National Cemetery and Basilica at Notre Dame de Lorette are briefly mentioned in Tour 5. We would strongly urge you to visit this imposing site as soon as you can, picking a good day; however, it would probably be best (if a sunny day) to do this in the afternoon, so that you do not have the sun in your face. There is a good view from here over the great majority of the ground covered in this book.

Tour 1: Souchez – The Pimple (West) – Zouave Valley – possible extension to Au Rietz and Maison Blanche caves

For this tour, Chapter 4 on Subways, Chapter 5 on the Pimple to Broadmarsh and Chapter 6 on the La Folie Sector are particularly useful. For the extension part of the tour, see also Chapter 3 on the caves and *souterraines* of Artois.

This tour (bar the extension) can be done entirely on foot or by a series of stops in a car. The advantage of doing the tour on foot is that it is often easier to stop and look around – there are places where it is not easy to park a car – and there are plenty of interesting panoramic views, which help to put the various parts of the battlefield into context. Much, if not all, of this tour is not practicable in a coach.

Start Point: Souchez Church, about 13 kilometres north of Arras (50° 23.51'N 02° 44.62'E)

Souchez Church (1) is mentioned here merely as a point from which you can get your bearings; to reach it, coming from Arras, take the D937 towards Bethune. Dropping down into Souchez, note on your left the prominent statue of General Barbot, commander of the 77th Division, clad in greatcoat and beret. His division temporarily gained the Pimple and Hill 119 in its attack on 9 and 10 May, and Barbot was fatally wounded in the course of the fighting. He and his *chasseurs alpins* were also notable for the part they played in halting the German advance north of Arras in the autumn of 1914. Before you completely pass the main square on the left, take a right turn into Rue Raoul Briquet, which will bring you to the church. Continue past the church, keeping it on your left and follow the winding road (ignore the cul de sac and Zouave Valley Cemetery signs) until it comes to an open turning area with a number of seemingly unpromising tracks leading off it. Take the one on the right, heading almost due south; although narrow, the surface is quite reasonable. After less than 100 metres you will observe open ground on your right – note the use of salvaged light railway tracks and screw piquets in the fencing. At the end of the open area, shortly before the track bends to the right, and before the beginning of the wooded area on the right, find a suitable place to stop. Near here was one of the entrances to Souchez Subway (2); another came out further back along the track.

Souchez Subway was dug by 176 Tunnelling Company (as were the next two that we shall visit) and had 520 metres of excavated tunnel. On 9 April it was in the 24th (Imperial) Division's sector, but was taken over by the Canadian 4th Division for the final part of the assault of Vimy Ridge, the capture of the Pimple, which was achieved on the 12th. 'HQ was in the tunnel, a subterranean sewer but all was ankle deep and sometimes knee deep in water instead of sewerage. The Battalion Orderly Room was a fair sized chamber raised above the water level, but as it had to serve the four battalions of the 10th Brigade, there was only standing room for our HQ staff [10 Brigade], who were neither welcomed nor needed.' There is no evident sign of the subway today, though the lie of the land is suggestive of entrance sites.

Continue along the track (another one shortly comes in at an angle from the left) until you reach a T-junction – the road to the right goes into Souchez; continue straight on and head up the road, which bends quite sharply to the left, towards the crest of the Ridge. On the left (3) (there is space to stop the car here; there is a large cattle water trough in the field a few metres from the road) was an entrance to **Coburg Subway,**

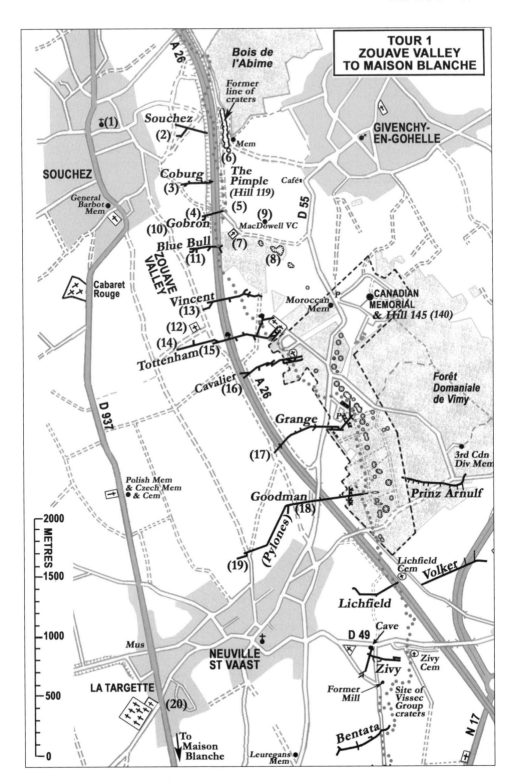

TOUR 1
ZOUAVE VALLEY
TO MAISON BLANCHE

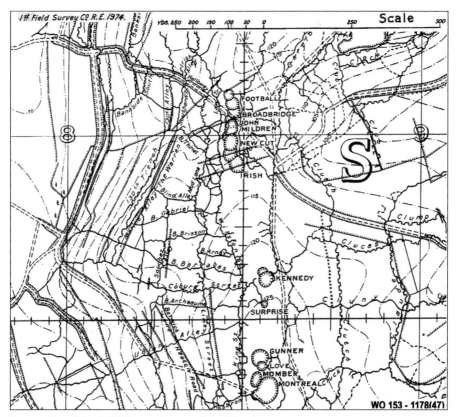

Extract from March 1917 trench map of the Pimple area.

which had about 310 metres of tunnel and which came up behind the support trenches. It was connected to the 'advanced HQ of the Company's officers [176 Tunnelling Company], which, just prior to the operations, was handed over to the Infantry and was used ultimately as a battalion and, later, as a brigade Battle HQ. The Subway also contained the Company's explosives magazine, an electric power station, forward bomb reserve store, water tanks chamber and urinal recesses. Lighting, as in the case of Gobron Subway, was by means of protected hurricane oil lamps. The average depth of cover was about 50 ft.'

Before going under the A26 there is a turning to the right; although space is restricted, it is possible to turn around at the top of this short spur road. There was an entrance to Gobron Subway at the back of a small copse at (**4**). This was a short subway, only 264 metres long and emerging just the other side of the péage, slightly to the west of Montreal Crater. There was a signals station in each of these three subways, with wires running between them in the deep defensive lateral; communications were, therefore, very secure. Two battalions, one in each, were in occupation of Gobron and Coburg Subways; they moved in during the night of the 8th, moving out into position at about 5 am on the 9th. Before you leave, note the prominent mast, painted red and white. This is a very useful marker in placing the area of the Pimple when viewing the

Ridge from a distance. If you have time you might like to walk along the track that parallels the motorway – there are excellent views to the west and several key features, such as Mont St Eloi and Notre Dame de Lorette are clearly visible.

Turn right and go under the A26 and then turn immediately left, heading along a fairly good but narrow road. Almost as soon as you turn up this road, over on the right was Montreal Crater (**5**). Go either as far as you can (normally the road is blocked) or stop at a point where the road widens and there are entrances to two fields on the right, one gated and one not; the road continues towards Souchez, but deteriorates further and is not open for public vehicular access. Until several years ago there used to be the remains of a memorial to the 44th (Manitoba – though renamed New Brunswick in August 1918) Battalion CEF nearby (**6**), but access to the site is now blocked. At the time of the construction of the national memorial on Hill 145 this was partially dismantled and the plaque taken to the battalion's home base in Winnipeg, leaving a simple concrete structure with 44 CEF impressed on it.

In 1917 the whole ridge line from (**5**) to a couple of hundred metres north of (**6**) was scarred with a chain of craters – see Chapter 5. The terrain in this area has been substantially changed by the construction of the péage and it seems that all of the large number of craters that were here have been filled in, possibly in part with surplus spoil from the péage construction.

About 200 metres south of point (**6**) was Kennedy Crater. It was intended to fire a mine behind the crater as part of the attack on 9 April, to remove any German defenders who might have survived the barrage. It was not used. About 200 metres south of that were Love and Momber Craters – all fired at 4.45 pm on 3 May 1916 (a fourth mine failed to break the surface). These mines were fired in reaction to the considerable activity of the Germans underground – they were believed to have eleven active galleries in this area. The only solution was to counter-mine as fast as possible, and the following extract gives a good example of the co-operation between tunnellers and infantry:

> The work was pushed on with all possible speed. Increased shifts of miners worked all night 2/3 May, burrowing forward from old French listening galleries: large parties of 141 Brigade brought up timber, and every available man from the trenches carried soil from the mine shafts.

Momber Crater was to mark the right-hand flank of the German attack on 21 May 1916.

It is usually possible to enter the right (or more southerly) field, which has a good tractor track. Keeping to the left, walk about 50 metres and you will be just about able to see the top of the Vimy Memorial off to the southeast. (We will be visiting the other end of this track during Tour 3.) In this area the Germans were planning an attack of their own in early April 1917, Operation Munich, with the intention of expelling the Canadians from their forward positions here and capturing the mine and subway entrances, and thus making their own defences more secure as well as dominating the head of Zouave Valley. It is far from clear whether the mine charges laid as part of these attacks were ever cleared or defused.

Return to the main track and turn left, stopping before you get to Givenchy en Gohelle Canadian Cemetery (**7**), which was just inside the German sector Fischer.

There is no space to turn around here, but there is adequate parking for a saloon car in front of a field gate about 20 metres back on the north (left) side of the approach road, or leave the car further back. It can also be quite muddy; you might prefer to leave the car on the road 100 or so metres further back. The track beyond is just about driveable up to the Canadian Memorial site, but it is very narrow and rutted, with barbed wire fences, brambles and low overhanging branches, and a new sign has recently appeared banning access to motorised vehicles. Southwest of the cemetery **Blue Bull Subway** emerged, now in the area of the A26; it had exits prepared for entry into No Man's Land, not for use by the infantry but for communications, notably signals and runners, as the line moved forward. This subway also enjoyed electrical lighting. These northerly subways might all have fallen into German hands if the putative Operation Munich had taken place.

The **Montreal** (location at 50° 23.17'N 2° 45.42'E), **Momber**, **Love** and **Gunner Craters** at (5) were about 110 metres northwest of the cemetery. Look over the field gate mentioned above, and you will see a wooded area at the bottom left of the field; this marks the area of their location. Montreal (the work of 176 Tunnelling Company) was fired at 9.50 pm on 27 November 1916 – that is, after the scale of mine attacks had reduced from the peaks reached in June. It was the job of the Royal Montreal Regiment (14th Battalion CEF) to consolidate the new crater. It is of interest to note the planning

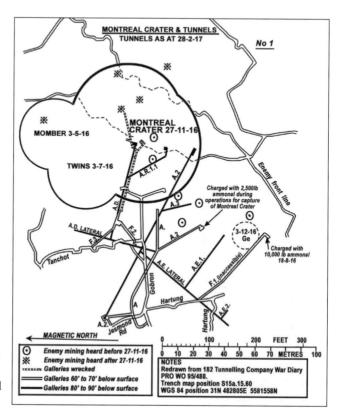

182 Tunnelling Company plan of the Montreal Group craters and related tunnels and charges.

Memorial to General Bardot in Souchez and grave at Notre Dame de Lorette.

Position of southern entrance to SOUCHEZ subway.

Northern entrance to Souchez subway to the left of camera position.

Souchez subway. South entrance approx at position of car.

Site of Montreal, Momber, Love & Gunner craters

Approx site of Kennedy Crater

N

View NNW from close to Givenchy-en-Gohelle Canadian Cemetery showing original locations of Montreal, Love, Gunner and Kennedy craters.

for the infantry side of this type of operation, the execution of which had become increasingly more sophisticated as the war progressed. Its history also records the front-line strength of the battalion at this time: twenty-six officers, 430 bayonets, seventy machine gunners, five bombers, twenty-four signallers, seventeen stretcher bearers and eighteen intelligence men (basically scouts). These were divided into: No. 1 Company, five officers and 109 ORs; No. 2 Company, five officers and 110 ORs; No. 3 Company, four officers and 114 ORs; No. 4 Company, four officers and 151 ORs; HQ, eight officers and eighty ORs. One can safely assume that there would be at least 200 men in the rear and transport lines, as well as others who were sick or lightly wounded, on training courses, leave and so forth.

The job of the battalion was to consolidate the near lip of the crater; besides its own men, it had a company of the 13th Battalion as a reserve. There were three storming parties, each commanded by a lieutenant, and a reserve party, the right and left parties having just over twenty men and the centre seventeen. The left and right parties had three sappers (from the 1st (Canadian) Field Company), two NCOs and eight soldiers, two stretcher bearers, two Lewis gunners and four bombers. On either flank wiring parties would be sent out. Men in the front-line trenches were to be withdrawn to a safe distance (this clearly designated) and then, immediately after the blow, were to move immediately back into position and carry out any repairs necessary. Two runners were attached to each of the storming parties and were to wear distinguishing marks. A sizeable array of trench mortars was allocated to the operation, while the seven rifle-grenade stands were to concentrate their fire on the flanks. Sixteen pieces of artillery were in support, including four howitzers, while the brigade machine guns were to lay down a heavy barrage behind the enemy lines, but were not to open fire before the mine was fired. In addition, there were three digging parties, each of a dozen men, who were to connect the crater to the front line, the new communication trenches to be dug 'zig-zag fashion'.

The participants in the attack were withdrawn to Villers au Bois to rehearse the attack – even the probable topography of the new crater was indicated in the taped-out practice area. When the blast came, there was far less debris than had been anticipated. Eight minutes after the blast the Germans reacted, with a barrage laid on the crater area and numbers of 'fish-tailed trench mortar torpedoes'. By 10 minutes after zero the storming parties were in position and consolidating the lip, suffering losses from shell fire, though the barrage died away after about 50 minutes. At this point a bombing post was pushed into the right of the old German line, but was withdrawn because of an attack by about 100 Germans at 11.30 pm; these were halted and dispersed from the new crater positions and two new bombing parties were sent forward. By 2 am wiring parties had already managed to string up a basic defence, while the Germans consolidated their side of the crater. By 5 am all front line and communications trenches had been made passable by day and at 6 am the consolidating parties were relieved. These operations did not come cheap – it was estimated that the battalion had inflicted seventy-five casualties on the Germans, but in turn had lost eleven killed and twenty-eight wounded. It is hardly a surprise that the new crater was named 'Montreal'. Its physical traces, alas, have now completely disappeared.

There is a poignant sequel to the consolidation of Montreal Crater.

Previous to relief, troops occupying the crater made every effort to locate and rescue a number of Germans who, from tapping noises heard repeatedly, were buried somewhere, probably in an old dugout, under the tons of mud and debris which the explosion had cast up. Parties strove to place the sounds and had traced them to a certain small area when enemy fire forced all attempt at rescue to be abandoned. Gradually the tapping grew fainter and finally ceased. Doubtless the imprisoned Germans died of thirst, starvation and want of air.

In preparing for the battle of Arras, staff officers were sent to the old Somme battlefields to look into the issue of moving men through this heavily cratered landscape. For example, Montreal Crater was compared with Y Sap Crater at La Boisselle. The opinion of the staff officers was that two or three small parties of six to eight men could get through this (Montreal) group of craters, but only slowly.

If you walk along the track past the cemetery for some 200 metres and can find a gap in the scrub and woodland on your right – no easy task – you are looking into an area where the Crosbie Craters (8) still lie, fired on 16 May 1916 by 182 Tunnelling Company. The nearest is about 50 metres off the track.

As explained in Chapter 5, the situation facing the British tunnellers on their arrival on the Vimy front was not good; of course, it was far from comfortable for the infantry as well! The Crosbie mines were laid with the intention of securing a strong line of observation in an area where the German craters dominated and gave good observation; five mines were laid. The supporting infantry included 11/Lancashire Fusiliers, who had already suffered at the hands of mines (see the first part of Tour 3, the Pimple). The men were as well prepared as possible, with rehearsals in the rear areas down to the blowing of a mine, so that the men had a clear idea of what was involved in seizing a mine crater. The men were to seize six craters, including an old one fired by the Germans as part of Rupprecht IV on 28 January, which was to be 'improved' by the explosions. At 8.30 pm on 15 May three of the mines were fired; two others followed ten seconds later. There having been a couple of days' rain previously, one soldier

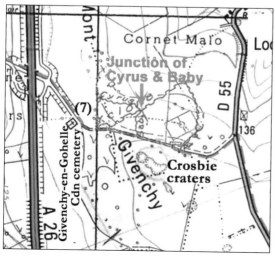

Location of Captain Thain MacDowell's VC action at the junction of Cyrus and Baby trenches, overlain on an extract from the Carte Bleu map. (See overleaf and Chapter 4.)

The rear entrance to Coburg Subway. The view is north-west over Souchez to Notre Dame de Lorette.

(4)

commented, 'Blimey, Bill, its raining Germans now!' On the left things went well, but on the right (i.e. nearest to the track) all but three members of an attacking group were buried by the explosion, having come too close to the blast area. Although the actual securing of the lips might have cost relatively few casualties, German attacks took their toll and by the time the battalion withdrew from the new positions four officers and thirty other ranks had been killed and forty wounded. The dead officers were buried at Ecoivres: Second Lieutenants A.K. McFarlan (I.N.26); W.F. Baker (I.N.12); E.L. Jewell (I.M.11); and R. Barrett (I.N.15). Interestingly, communications had been kept open largely by the use of the signallers' torches. The new group of craters was named after the temporary commander of 74 Brigade, Lieutenant Colonel Crosbie. British mining successes such as this provided one of the chief reasons for the limited but highly effective German assault on 21 May, which resulted in the loss of the hard-won Crosbie Craters, which remained behind the German lines until 9 April 1917.

A spot near the hedgerow in a field 100 metres north of the track (**9**) is the location of the VC action of Captain Thain MacDowell, 38th Battalion CEF, during the fighting for Vimy Ridge in April 1917; this action is fully described in Chapter 4. The Germans had a number of these lagers, or very large and deep dugouts. Inclines into them have been known to open up, the last instance of which we know being during the renovation of the Canadian Memorial in 2005/2006.

View south along Zouave Valley from just above point (3).

A trench light railway trolley, used today for a floral display.

Return to your vehicle and go back down the road, under the A26, and head towards Souchez; more or less at right angles to (4) you will find a space to pull the vehicle off the road. This spot provides good views of Zouave Valley, Notre Dame de Lorette, the rear entrance to Gobron and, below, the rear entrance of Coburg (3). Walk down the road about 50 metres and you will see on your left, heading down the side of the valley, clear outlines of old trenches, including what remains of Uhlan Alley. As you come into Souchez, take the first left, a very sharp turn. As you turn you should see the CWGC sign for Zouave Valley Cemetery, which is on the Givenchy side of the new road. Although not exactly buzzing, this road can be surprisingly busy; please pay especial attention to priority from the right – we have had a couple of close calls here, one with a child on a bicycle. Just as the road begins to deteriorate there is a normal road coming in from the right; at the junction between the two is a trench trolley, reincarnated to hold a floral display. After about 400 metres stop at (**10**); there is a house on the right and a bit of space on the left to get off the road, with a small track heading out into a field and barn-like constructions further along the road on the left. From here there is a good view up the east side of the northern end of Zouave Valley; again, you can see trench outlines and the ground under which Coburg, Gobron and Blue Bull Subways ran. **Blue Bull** was just a little further down the track (**11**), after a slight right and then left twist in the track. On the right there is a field track – or at least a definite field

The entrances to Blue Bull Subway, looking towards the Pimple and Tunnellers Ridge.

division – and on the left a small wood. There were a couple of entrances and many dugouts in the very evident embankment at the edge of the wood, which is fenced off. A trackway carried a small train from supply dumps in the rear, bringing up provisions, trench stores and other necessary equipment; this is said (although we have our doubts about this) to have actually entered into the subway, where everything could be offloaded and the wounded and dead then loaded up for the return journey: this in part explains the almost chronological system of burials in, for example, Ecoivres Cemetery. There seem to be indications of where the track ran on the ground today, though these may be of another track, now obliterated, which ran parallel to the track on which you are standing. For most of the run at the base of Zouave Valley the rail trackway ran to the west (right) of the track that you are now on, crossing over to the east side for only the last few metres.

Returning to your car, continue down towards **Zouave Valley Cemetery (12)** and find a place to park off the track leading up to it. About 50 metres back down this track towards Souchez, there is a scrubby area off to the right **(13)**; this is in the area of the entrance to **Vincent Subway**. This subway had many of the characteristics of Blue Bull and had a number of exits into No Man's Land (these exits were, of course, concealed; they had relatively little ground cover so that they could be quickly opened up once the battle began). Walk back up and spend some moments visiting Zouave Valley Cemetery; if you plan to eat on the hoof, as it were, this might be a good area to stop for refreshments. Albeit with a motorway only metres away from you, this is a pleasant, reflective spot: Notre Dame de Lorette may be seen, and there is an excellent view of the valley, so tranquil now, so full of tragedy then. Above the cemetery, on the west side of the valley, is the Chemin des Pylones, which the French army reached during the fighting in May 1915 and which became the second line after the advance on to Vimy Ridge that September.

Zouave Valley Cemetery has no direct connection with the tunnellers. It was started in May 1916 and many of the early burials were a result of the limited – but very effective – German attack in May 1916 (see Chapter 5). It is a battlefield cemetery for the most part; only forty-two isolated graves were relocated here after the war ended.

Drive to the top of the valley and find a convenient place to stop; you will be passing two rear entrances to the Tottenham Subway as you do so, e.g. at **(14)**. There are excellent views up to the Ridge, even better if you go a few hundred metres down the track towards Neuville St Vaast. However, this track is very rough in parts and is not recommended for someone in a saloon car; we have done it (and in February, too), but it was with clenched teeth and one can never be sure that a tractor might not tear out even deeper ruts. We recommend that you park up and walk along the track; another one comes up to meet it from the left, and from this point there are excellent views of the Vimy Memorial. Retrace your route back past Zouave Valley Cemetery. The track to the right is passable in a saloon car in our experience, and has a solid, if rough, surface.

Drive past the original Z1 rear entrances to Tottenham Subway **(15)** (50° 22.63′N 2° 24.3′E). Because this entrance was under observation and there was frequent German harassing fire, the subway was extended and new entrances were created on the western slope, near point **(14)**. This subway was the second longest of the group on the Ridge and, along with its neighbour, Cavalier, was more extensively equipped with

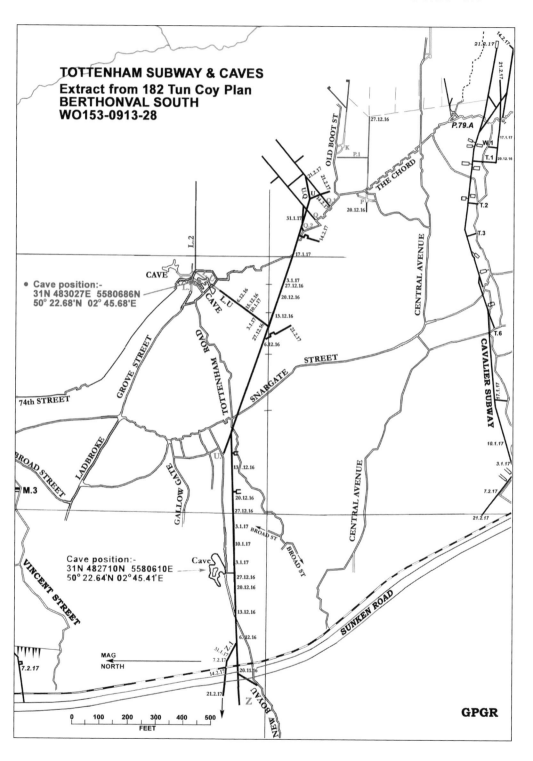

TOTTENHAM SUBWAY & CAVES
Extract from 182 Tun Coy Plan
BERTHONVAL SOUTH
WO153-0913-28

Cave position:-
31N 483027E 5580686N
50° 22.68'N 02° 45.68'E

Cave position:-
31N 482710N 5580610E
50° 22.64'N 02° 45.41'E

GPGR

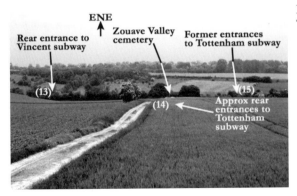

Rear entrances to Vincent and Tottenham Subways.

accommodation and other facilities than the others on the Ridge. This was probably because they were completed so relatively early and therefore there was time to develop them. Cavalier's rear entrance was located near **(16)**, now almost certainly buried under the A26, which the track closely parallels. It also had some exits emerging into No Man's Land. Considerable use was made of both Tottenham and Cavalier in the major raid by the 4th (Cdn) Division on 28 February/1 March, most particularly for the evacuation of the wounded. Finally, the last subway along this stretch of road running along by the motorway, Grange Subway – part of which is open to the public – had its rear entrance near **(17)** (50° 22.14′N 2° 45.78′E).

The road bends sharply right; keep to the good surface, heading sharply left – the track straight ahead becomes poor and we would not risk a saloon car on it. In the fields at **(18)** members of the Durand Group, at the time working in the Goodman Subway, discovered a collapse that had created a large cavity in the field above. At the time there was a full stand of crops and the farmer was unaware of the hole's existence; this was potentially dangerous, as it could have led to a nasty accident during harvesting. This incident highlights one of the risks today associated with the underground war: over time there is the increasing possibility of sudden collapses, such as this one, and there is no scientific way of being able to predict these events accurately. The authors have spent the last few years working with Veterans Affairs Canada over this matter of subsidence and in that time have come across several instances of sudden collapses,

Point (19), the location of the rear entrances to the Goodman (Pylones) Subway(s).

though none of them was in a publicly accessible area. One does not need to get paranoid about such events, but there needs to be an awareness of the possibility. Continue along the road, which will bring you out at the northern end of Neuville St Vaast.

Should you want to see the rear entrances of Goodman/Pylones, head for (**19**); the access road from Neuville St Vaast is fine for vehicles. At the point where the road meets a Y-junction, you are in the area of the rear entrances to Pylones; these emerged in the fields to the left and right of the junction and there was an exit in the triangle of ground formed by the two tracks. The Goodman, with its connection into Pylones, is the longest subway on the Ridge, extending to over 1,700 metres of tunnel. Return to Neuville St Vaast. This concludes this tour unless you decide to take in the next three points, situated along the D937. These could be covered separately or incorporated into another tour.

Tour 1 Extension

Proceed along the road to the D937 and go straight across the road, noting the CWGC cemetery on the right, dwarfed by the huge French military cemetery just beyond it. On the left, opposite, there is good parking. Walk back to the main road, noting the Le Relais restaurant on your right, which we have found serves excellent and reasonably priced meals. Opposite (**20**) is an entrance to the Au Rietz Cave, which some years ago was open to the public. For further information on this significant feature, see Chapter 3. It is hard to believe that this area – and the cave itself – witnessed such ferocious fighting in 1915, nor that the entrance to this system could have been such a hive of activity in 1916 and 1917, with at times literally hundreds of troops safely housed over 15 metres underground in what were originally medieval quarries.

Exactly a kilometre from Le Relais on the left of the D937 as you head for Arras is the very extensive Neuville St Vaast German Cemetery, sometimes popularly (but inaccurately) known as Maison Blanche or La Targette German Cemetery. The cemetery was in a part of the Labyrinth and the scene of desperate fighting in 1915. For many years after the war it was believed that there were just under 37,000 men buried here, beneath a seemingly endless procession of crosses (originally two to a wooden cross, now usually four to a metal cross); when the wooden crosses were replaced, getting on for forty years ago, an ossuary was constructed, and the number known to be buried here was raised to over 44,000. The very starkness of the cemetery, with black crosses seemingly stretching to the horizon, serves to underline the hideous cost of war. A rectangular stone memorial in the cemetery was brought here from a German cemetery south of Arras when many of the German graves were concentrated into a number of very large cemeteries such as this.

Opposite the southern end of the cemetery is the solitary Maison Blanche farmhouse and its associated buildings. Underneath these buildings and the nearby ground is a notable *souterraine* (see Chapter 3 for a full description). There is usually no public access to this *souterraine* and the farmer will certainly not grant access, so there is no point in asking him. However, 'subject to conditions' it may occasionally be possible to arrange a strictly regulated visit for a small group by contacting the Durand Group, www.durandgroup.org.uk. This would inevitably involve charges to cover expenses, which could be quite considerable if group members had to come over from the UK especially to accompany the tour.

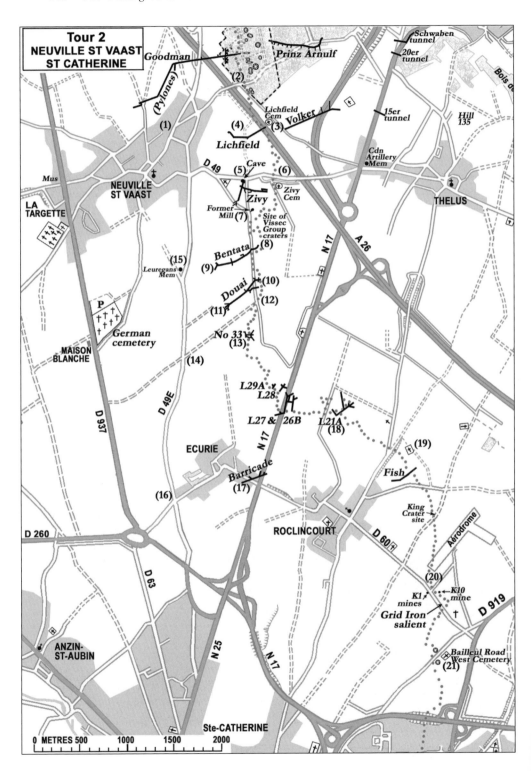

Tour 2
NEUVILLE ST VAAST
ST CATHERINE

Tour 2: Neuville St Vaast to Roclincourt (extension to Roeux)

For this tour, see in particular Chapter 4 on Subways and Chapter 7, Neuville St Vaast to the Scarpe.

This tour, for the most part, takes in the most featureless part of the Ridge and there are, essentially, no vestiges of the tunnellers' war, with the exception of two most unusual CWGC cemeteries and the infilled but very apparent sites of Cuthbert and Clarence Craters in L Sector. An optional extension to the tour takes visitors to the area of the Roeux Caves.

This tour starts in Neuville St Vaast, on the road leading towards the Canadian Memorial site at (**1**). Take the turning on the right (east); there is a CWGC sign for Lichfield Crater Cemetery. Cross over the A26 and very soon afterwards there is a turning to the right, with a rough track leading straight on; park in the area of the junction (**2**). Almost immediately, in the wooded area on the left, you can see the overgrown remnants of the main trench line in the Canadian front-line system. Walk up the track straight ahead; you are in the British O Sector. You will find that you are walking between fenced-off areas: the ground either side of the track forms part of the forestry area of the Canadian Memorial site, which is closed to public access. After 50 metres or so you will see a gate on the left in an area relatively clear of trees, and also a gate on the right leading into the southern extremity of the Memorial site. This is more or less in what was No Man's Land before 9 April 1917. The track running into the forestry area on the left roughly marks the forward edge of the Canadian line. In this immediate area there are a number of large craters; the Twins (British), the German

Point (3), view looking north towards the Canadian Vimy Memorial Site and the location of the former Watling Crater.

Trichter 27 (the largest surviving crater on the Ridge) and Trichter 24 (the Washing Machine Crater), and two Wombat mines; in addition, the area contains the German T19 to T21 tunnels, and an access to the British O Sector tunnels and associated features, described more fully in Chapter 7. On the other side of the track, in the other fenced area, there are also significant vestiges of the war, including the British B4 crater group. Do **not** be tempted to go into these areas. Besides being private and closed to the public, they are dangerous, not so much from remaining munitions (though there are plenty of those around) but also from the presence of very nasty caltrops – long, sharp metal spikes set into the ground; designed to cripple soldiers who might step on or crawl into them, they remain practically undetectable in the dense undergrowth. When a very small part of the forestry area was cleared in 2005 by demineurs, almost 100 of these items were removed in the process.

From (2) drive southeast along the narrow road towards Thélus (the western part of this village, straddling the N17, was known during the war as Les Tilleuls). After 300 metres on the right, just where the fencing of the Canadian Memorial site ends, is the site of the Watling Crater, now in-filled and used as a dump for farming material. A further 200 metres along on the right is a grass track leading to **Lichfield Crater Cemetery (3)**. Parking off the track here can be difficult, especially in wet weather, and it may be preferable to walk down from the area of the Watling Crater, where there is space off the road. Lichfield is one of two unusual CWGC cemeteries in the area; it is a mass grave (with one exception), and all of those in the mass grave were killed on 9 or 10 April 1917. Their names are engraved on the wall below the Cross of Sacrifice; they include a Canadian posthumous VC winner, Lance Sergeant E. Sifton, and an unknown Russian – how did he get there? This mine was fired by the Germans on 29 April 1916, killing three infantrymen and destroying a listening shaft. The forward entrance to the German **Volker Tunnel** abutted the track a further 150 metres along. As the battle moved over the ground on 9 April, 172 Tunnelling Company investigated the tunnel and with the 'aid' of German prisoners defused several demolition charges and reopened several entrances for use by the advancing Canadians. There have been rumours that it was connected to the Lichfield Subway, but there is no documentary evidence for this. Lichfield extended back just under 500 metres west from the crater (to which it was connected).

Retrace your route over the A26; almost immediately after the flyover take the narrow track bending very sharply to the left. After another sharp bend this runs parallel to the A26; after 400 metres the track makes a sharp right and then left turn (4), crossing the Lichfield Subway almost immediately after. The rear entrance was approximately 150 metres to the west of (4).

The track connects with the D49 from Neuville St Vaast, where the Zivy cave was located on the other side of the road (5). Turn left and almost immediately take the slip road signed **Zivy Crater Cemetery (6)**. The crater, which, like Lichfield, has been transformed into a poignant mass grave cemetery, was formed by an overcharged camouflet fired on 12 June 1916, probably to deter German tunnelling operations from a nearby *souterraine*, which extended from under No Man's Land to the German positions and now has the A26 over it. The cemetery holds the remains of fifty-three men killed in April and May 1917, forty-six of whom were identified and whose names are engraved on the wall below the Cross of Sacrifice. These two crater cemeteries are particularly evocative for those following tunnelling operations in this part of the Ridge

Point (6), Zivy Crater Cemetery. Neuville St Vaast is in the background.

south of Neuville St Vaast, as they are among the only surface indicators of the fierce mine warfare fought there (see (**21**) for the others), all other craters having been filled in over the years. **Zivy Subway** is the longest in the area covered by this tour, with just under 800 metres of tunnelling; it was connected to the *souterraine* located at (**5**). For descriptions connected to the crater and subway, see Chapter 7.

Return on the D49 towards Neuville St Vaast and take the first turning on the left, signposted to Arras Road and Nine Elms CWGC cemeteries. Within 100 metres you will pass over Zivy Subway. At a junction with a road coming from the right (**7**), the site of the Mill, stop and walk 100 metres back towards Neuville St Vaast in the direction of the local cemetery. The cemetery here has an interesting war memorial, and stone

View over Zivy rear entrance, photographed from near Point (7). in the background can be seen Neuville St Vaast church (left); the local cemetery (centre); and the site of Zivy cave (right) – see page 58.

tablets list – fairly accurately – the various formations involved in the battles fought near the village, indicating the sector where they fought, though regrettably the 5th (British) Division that formed part of the Canadian Corps in April 1917 is omitted. There were a number of entrances to the rear part of Zivy Subway here, protected to some extent by the fact that it was in an at least partially sunken road. Returning to the car, look into the field to the east; at about 60 metres from the road is the site of the Vissec group of craters.

Continue directly south along the road, which at this stage runs more or less along the former British/Canadian front line, with occasional salients to the left (east) of it. In one of these, 400 metres from (**7**), is **Bentata Subway** (**8**), currently marked by a prominent, solitary, elderflower bush (50° 20.92′N, 2° 46.48′E); this subway had some 680 metres of tunnelling and a number of exits, the rear entrances being at about (**9**), around 350 metres west of the track. The 14th Battalion CEF had its HQ in this subway for the attack on 9 April, having previously been in the rear at Maison Blanche. After another 150 metres or so (**10**) **Douai Subway** ran under the road, going into another salient, in part of which was Paris Redoubt. In No Man's Land here lay the Paris group of craters. Douai Subway was used by the 15th Battalion (the 48th Highlanders of Canada) CEF for the attack on 9 April 1917. Graffiti relating to this battalion is to be found in the Maison Blanche *souterraine*, including a particularly fine representation of the regimental badge. Both it and the 14th Battalion CEF (as well as the 16th Battalion CEF, on the left flank) formed the attacking front of 3 (Cdn) Brigade on 9 April, the left-hand brigade of Currie's 1st (Cdn) Division. The rear entrances of the subway (**11**) were situated in what are now arable fields, about 350 metres west-southwest of (**10**).

A short distance beyond turn right on to a narrow road at the junction (**12**) (50° 20.16′N, 2° 46.51′E). Just to the left of the road on which you have been travelling, on 19 May 1916 185 Tunnelling Company fired a Fougasse charge at the head of Argyll Trench, creating a significant crater 55 metres across and about 10 deep. This marked a turning point in 185's mining war in the sector, which in the preceding weeks had been dominated by German blasts (see Chapter 7 for more details and descriptions);

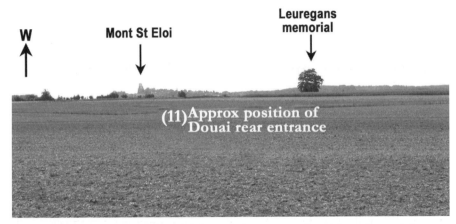

The approximate position of Douai Subway rear entrance, viewed from the track between points (12) and (14). Note Mont St Eloi in the background.

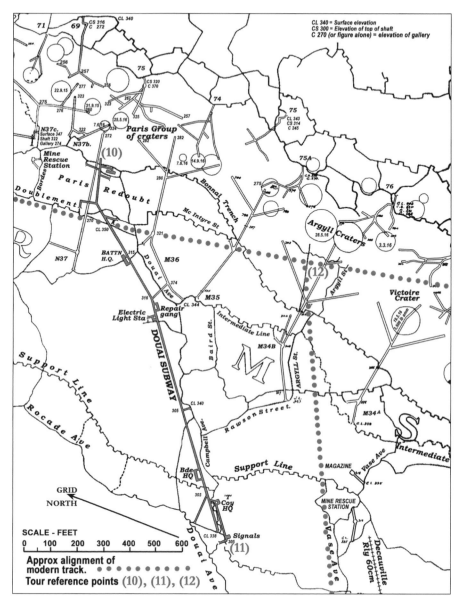

Tunnel and trench map of the Labyrinth area from Paris Redoubt to Victoire Crater, with modern track and tour references added.

with the firing of this mine, the company now felt that it could gain the upper hand in the sector.

There were a number of craters around here, which were known collectively as the Argyll Group. These craters and the nearby Victoire Crater (over to the right (south) of the group) formed a considerable challenge to the advance of the 10th Battalion CEF on 9 April, with only a narrow passage of sound ground between Argyll 1 (the

View from point (12) across the rear entrance to No. 33 Subway, with Ecurie and the location of Barricade Subway in the background.

northernmost and closest to **12**) and Argyll 2. Argyll 2 and 3 overlapped, leaving only about 60 metres of firm ground between 3 and Victoire. Sending soldiers across the craters was not a realistic option, as the walls of the craters were so steep and unstable that progress over them was extremely difficult – and in any case it was not clear what might await them at the bottom of the craters.

Take the turning on the right and after 100 metres or so look into the fields on the left to (**13**), under which area ran No. 33 Subway, about which little is known by the authors. However, a bored mine (i.e. a wombat mine) was laid from the end of No. 33, with the intention of destroying a German strongpoint. No. 33 Subway was almost at the southern extremity of the Canadian Corps front on 9 April 1917, and marked the southern boundary of First Army. The 51st (Highland) Division, the northernmost of XVII Corps' and Third Army's divisions, occupied and attacked from the ground immediately to the south.

Divert right (towards Neuville St Vaast) at the junction with the D49E (**14**) and proceed along this good example of a sunken road (even if it is, doubtless, considerably less deep than it was in the war, due to the practice of simply adding thick layers of tarmac as a means of road maintenance); its banks would have been used for a variety of shelters for all sorts of units and for forward headquarters. Lots of fast vehicles use this route as a 'rat run' to avoid traffic on the main roads, so drive carefully. As you come to the top of a rise you will see a prominent memorial on the left-hand side (**15**); park (carefully!) by it. There is a track on the left-hand side of the memorial, offering good views, particularly over the Canadian lines to the east and west – in the case of the latter, to the nearby German cemetery and Mont St Eloi in the distance; in 1917 this area was the site of Fort Redoubt. The memorial is to a young French officer cadet, Aspirant Augustin Leuregans of the 236th Infantry Regiment, a victim of the struggle for the Labyrinth in 1915. It and the accompanying trees also serve as a useful marker point in this otherwise largely featureless part of the battlefield.

Turn your vehicle around (again, carefully!) and proceed south towards Ecurie. At the junction with the D60 (**16**) turn left and drive through the village, which in 1916 was just behind the British lines. **Barricade Subway** (**17**) passed under the road leading southeast out of Ecurie and the main Arras to Lens road (now the N17). Its exact purpose is not entirely clear but it seems probable that this important junction was subject to persistent harassing artillery fire and the subway was intended to allow reasonably safe passage.

The British line crossed what is now the N17 about 800 metres to the north and a kilometre south of the turn-off on to the A26 péage. A number of short subways were located in this area, the **L29A**, the **L28**, the **L27** and the **L26B**. The N17 is, though, both busy and fast, and it would be most imprudent (and probably illegal) to attempt to stop on it. Instead continue into Roclincourt and, just after a sharp left-hand bend, continue straight ahead instead of going on into the centre of the village. After a kilometre, and some 200 metres beyond a right-hand bend, you will arrive at the location of the rear entrances to the **L21 Subway**, just to the right of the road (**18**). The ground between (**18**) and the N17 was the scene of a major mining attack directed at the 51st (Highland) Division. On 28 April the Germans blew thirteen mines astride the area where the Arras–Lens road crosses what was then the front line, approximately 825 metres south of the present turn-off on to the A26 péage. Accompanied by an artillery and mortar bombardment and raiding parties, they wrought havoc among the Scots defenders, killing and wounding over 120 all ranks, of whom thirty were missing, believed to be buried (see Chapter 7).

There is nothing now to give witness to the extensive cratering, but should you choose to walk the ground anyway, respect any privacy notices and the crops. Continue down the road and after a couple of hundred metres take the track on the right – we have found this to be quite passable. Within a few metres of the junction there were a number of exits from L21A. In the distance, to the east, you should be able to make out the woods before the village of Farbus, which more or less mark the limit of the first day's advance by the Canadian Corps on 9 April.

At the junction with the Roclincourt–Thélus road turn right, passing almost immediately a private memorial, sited close to the old front line, to a French officer killed in June 1915; an added plaque commemorates all those from the Allied nations and different parts of France that fought in this area. Find a convenient place to stop when you come to a junction with a track coming from the left. You might care to walk up to **Highland Cemetery** (**19**), the approach track to which is really very poor. Some 150 metres south of this was the forward exit from **Fish Subway**. Although short, Fish contained brigade and battalion HQ complexes and associated facilities. So far as is known, there were no other subways south of Fish until the **St Sauveur** system in Arras, south of the River Scarpe (see Chapter 8 and the Arras Tour).

Enter Roclincourt, passing the church on your right, and take the third exit on the roundabout, the D60, which will take you towards a grassed airfield. Some metres beyond the communal cemetery on the left is a track that leads up to the site of **King Crater**. An incident there on 26 November 1916 led to the execution of three NCOs; the episode is well described in a short, well illustrated book by Julian Putkowski, the French translation of which is still (2010) in print.

Continue to (**20**); straddling the road immediately south of the runway of the Aérodrome d'Arras-Roclincourt were the K1 and K10 mines where the Germans, retaliating against heavy blows by 184 Tunnelling Company, inflicted severe casualties in return. 'The enemy recovered their damaged gallery at K10 and on 23 May blew a heavy camouflet, killing eight miners attached from 14 Brigade of the 5th Division. Only one body was recovered, that of Private A. Wood [buried in Faubourg d'Amiens

British Cemetery, I.C.3], the winch man at the top of the shaft.' Seven British miners and an unknown number of German miners remain entombed. Immediately beyond (**20**) was the **Grid Iron** salient, the scene between May and July 1916 of a series of blows and counter-blows.

Between the **Grid Iron** and the **River Scarpe** there was only one other area of serious mine fighting. This straddled the road by the Bailleul Road West Cemetery (**21**). The New Zealand Engineers Tunnelling Company history records:

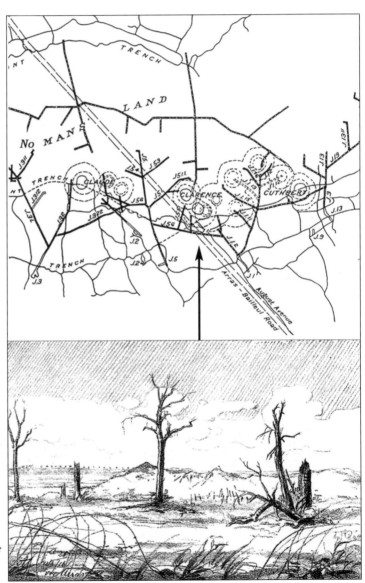

Mining plan showing Claude, Clarence and Cuthbert Craters.

Sketch by Alfons Schneider of a mine crater – probably Clarence – on the Bailleul–Arras road. (*Bayer.Haupstaatsarchive München / Jean-Luc Letho Duclos*)

On the 6th of June [1916], after an intense bombardment lasting two days, the enemy blew four big mines as a preliminary to a general attack. Three of the resulting craters were in the company's sector and one in the adjoining sector to the north. Huge craters they were – the largest 147 feet in diameter and 38 feet deep, the mounds of chalk thrown up forming conspicuous landmarks. They were christened Cuthbert, Clarence and Claude, in honour of a then popular revue.

Their effect may have helped the Germans get across no-man's-land, but the actual damage to our personnel, trenches or galleries was practically nil. The Norfolks and Warwicks suffered some casualties in the trench fighting before the Germans were driven out, but the New Zealand Tunnellers came off without a scratch.

To reach the scene of this endeavour, turn right off the D60 about 100 metres short of the junction with the D919. Bailleul Road West Cemetery is signposted. Claude was immediately north of the road at this point, Clarence immediately south, and Cuthbert a further 40 metres to the south; Claude and Clarence are still evident, although infilled; they have now become a breeding area for game birds. They are very rare survivors of what was once an area scarred by lines and groups of craters. Nigel Cave's grandfather, then CQMS of the 7th Leicesters, part of 110 Brigade, 21st Division, noted in his diary for 7 August 1916:

The Battalion went into the trenches in the front of Arras. Transport at Duissans. Just in front of the line are three massive craters, known respectively as Cuthbert, Clarence and Claude. This is a very quiet sector but means a sixteen mile march for me every day from Duissans through Arras to the trenches and back.

8 August: The enemy exploded another mine, killing eight men of D Company.

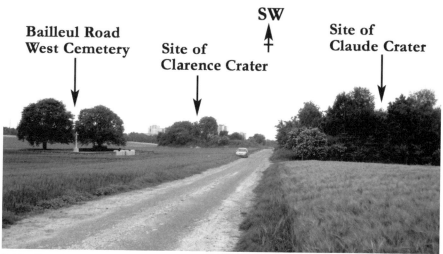

Bailleul Road West Cemetery and the sites of Clarence and Claude craters.

There are several routes from here by which you may return to central Arras; it is a matter of preference.

Tour Extension to Point du Jour Military Cemetery and Roeux

To take in the extension, continue to the junction with the D919 and turn right, towards Arras. You will then come to a succession of roundabouts of varying dimensions – keep straight on, heading towards St Laurent Blangy. After four or five of these roundabouts, by this stage in the Scarpe valley and the central area of St Laurent, take the D62 (the exit on the left (east) of the roundabout) signposted Athies. There follows a series of urban roundabouts, but at a rather bigger one there is a CWGC signpost for the 9th (Scottish) Division Memorial and Point du Jour Cemetery (first exit right). When you reach Athies, the cemetery is signposted off to the left, up the unpromising-looking Rue du Chauffour, about 100 metres before a large roundabout with a sizeable café on the right (Café des Boulistes) – so if you go too far you can return quite easily to the road. The approach road soon deteriorates into a rough, single track, but it is quite driveable. The cemetery position is 50° 18.81′N, 2° 50.17′E.

Eventually you come to a cul de sac, with the cemetery on the right. This is where Lieutenant Durant of the NZET is buried, at I.A.6. He was the first New Zealander tunnelling officer to be killed on the Western Front, becoming a casualty when assisting in a raid on 14 September 1916. As part of the development of industrial areas outside Arras there have been several discoveries of small burial grounds. In ground near here twenty members of the Lincolnshire Regiment were uncovered and in 2002 their remains removed to this cemetery. A few years ago the 9th (Scottish) Division Memorial was moved to this location from its original position on dominating ground on the N50, several hundred metres to the east. (It had to be moved because of road widening.)

Return to Athies and turn left, heading for the above-mentioned roundabout and follow the signs to Fampoux and then to Roeux. Almost immediately after crossing the A1 motorway you come to traffic lights, at which you should turn right and go over the

Roeux: view up Rue Eugene Dumont. *Souterraines* passed under the road about 100 metres from the camera position. The memorial in the foreground stands on the site of a former local cemetery.

level crossing. From this point the mapping for the Roeux *souterraine*, developed by the New Zealand Tunnellers (see Chapter 3), should enable you to explore this area.

From here you can easily return to central Arras or you might care to follow the signs for Monchy le Preux (head towards the church in Roeux to pick up the signs) and come back in to Arras along the Cambrai road.

Tour 3: The Pimple (East) – The Canadian Memorial Site – La Folie Farm and Environs
For this tour, see in particular Chapters 5 and 6 on tunnelling and Chapter 4 on subways.

The bulk of this tour is based on the Canadian National Memorial site at Vimy; it starts with a look at the German side of the Pimple (Hill 119) and ends with a short visit to the area of the Prinz Arnulf Tunnel.

NB! If you have not booked a tour for the Grange Subway – and pre-bookings are available only for groups of ten or more – then go first to the Interpretive Centre, situated near the preserved outpost line and Grange Subway area and see if you can get placed on a tour. You must keep punctually to the time allocated.

To get to a start point that is easy to find, drive to the area of the car park near the Canadian Memorial (1) (50° 22.78′N, 02° 46.20′E). Head north towards Givenchy en Gohelle; where the road takes a sharp turn to the right note that there is a café, which provides refreshments but, currently, not full-scale meals. Shortly after it there is sharp turning to the left, which you should take. The road becomes a reasonable track; though it can be rather rough, we have found it passable. There is limited space to turn around further down, but we have managed it in the past with a minibus. Continue to the junction at (2) that the Germans called *Fünfkreuzweg* (although now only three of the five roads are visible). Do not drive any further than this point – there is a barrier across the road a few hundred metres down and there is no space in which to turn around. At the junction of the track on which you arrived and the one running east down the side of the wood there is a small space in which you can get a car off the tracks.

On your immediate left there is a replacement for the 44th Battalion Memorial, the remnants of which were demolished in 2005. A local Frenchman, Monsieur F. Roger, worked to have the new plinth put up in time for the 90th anniversary of the Pimple's capture; he then added the carved front panel (see page 213). The Pimple (or Hill 119) does not seem a particularly important height as regards the fighting that took place for Vimy Ridge further to the south, but all should be revealed when looking at it from here and from (4) in the Canadian Memorial site.

Proceed to (3) along the very clear and broad farm track, which emerges at the point where Tour 2 explores the Pimple (West). Looking southeast, you will be able to see the top half of the Canadian Memorial almost immediately; there are also excellent views to the west across Souchez and to Notre Dame de Lorette. The 44th Battalion Memorial was on the other side of the hedge and was constructed on the southern lip of Irish Crater.

Return to the track; after 100 metres or so there is a large gap in the hedge on your left and you can enter the field. The now demolished 44th Battalion Memorial (3) was on the edge of the southernmost (Irish) of a line of craters: after Irish, to the north and in order, they were New Cut, Mildren, John, Broadbridge and Football (see plan on

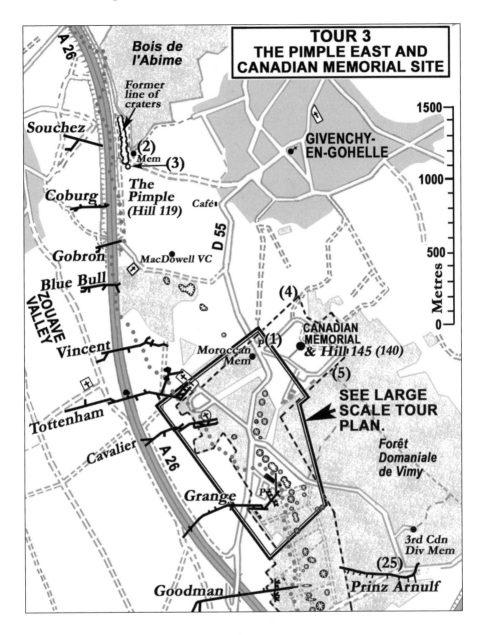

page 86 and the Trench Map with Tour 1); John was more or less on the track, itself the old road to Souchez. This field seems to be usually pasture or for haymaking, and so you should be able to get to where the crater line ran; but if not, you are close enough on the track. The Germans blew New Cut on 26 April: this had been anticipated to some extent, but it still caused casualties. 11/Lancashire Fusiliers were in the line when the mines were blown early on 26 April. They suffered five NCOs and men killed, twenty-three wounded and twenty-eight missing – presumably buried by the blast or

M. Roger's memorial. The plaque on the top reads '44th Bn Memorial. The Pimple.' The facing plaque reads:

'A LA MEMOIRE DES VICTIMES DES COMBATS DE MAI OCTOBRE 1915, COTE 119, ET DES LIBERATEURS CANADIENS 44, 46, 50 BAT. THE PIMPLE, 12 AVRIL 1917.'

taken prisoner by the Germans. They did manage, however, to secure the near lip of the crater. When these losses are combined with those incurred in the operations related to Crosbie Crater, less than three weeks later, it gives some idea of how this war underground impacted on the infantry.

Anticipating a further blast some 100 metres or so to the north, the British fired a defensive camouflet; this set the German mine off, creating the huge Broadbridge Crater. The Germans retaliated by firing two mines at 6.45 pm on 30 April, called Mildren (named after the CO of 6/London, at that time in the line) and John. In the days leading up to the German attack the 6/London battalion history records,

> The men in the front and support lines endured hell . . . the enemy's heavy mortars being particularly terrifying; four, five and six of them could frequently be seen in the sky simultaneously. The Stokes mortars replied but the 'heavies' were short of ammunition. The men replied with rifle grenades and succeeded in landing them repeatedly in the enemy's trenches, which gave them considerable satisfaction.

The German mines demolished a great chunk of the front line of 1/6th London ('The Cast-Iron Sixth') and all but four of the occupants; a whole platoon was effectively annihilated. The blasts were followed by a barrage of artillery and machine-gun fire; communications were cut and desperate confusion reigned, but the line had stabilised by the morning.

> During six terrible days the battalion had experienced a class of warfare that none wished to see again. Casualties had been heavy: twenty-four had been killed, seventeen were missing and no less than fifty-one had been wounded; but when the battalion went out of the line on May 3rd, it was by no means downhearted, and was conscious of having acquitted itself well. Many will remember the march out, made notable by Sergeant Church, who played his violin as the troops trudged along, to keep up the spirits of tried and tired men.

There is an authorised circuit of **Bois de l'Abime** (Bois de Givenchy during the war), accessed from the village. We would not recommend entering the wood from the

View from point (4) towards
the Pimple (Côte 119).

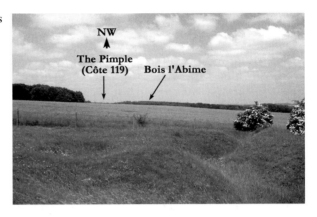

Pimple end; much of it is private and reserved for hunting and, for your own safety, especially in the hunting season, you should keep well clear. You can get glimpses of the remnants of trenches and so forth from the tracks and it is at least likely that something remains of one or more of the craters in it. (For a fuller description of the wood, see *The Battle for Vimy Ridge – 1917*, pp. 179–80.) Keep strictly to the paths laid down; access to the wood is controlled by local by-laws.

With so much to see, the Canadian Memorial site can often be a very busy place, and it does not always have a peaceful, reflective atmosphere, with the movement of vehicles and, frequently, crowds of people. The Pimple has nothing to see from the war, except the vestiges in the wood, but who could not be moved, when looking over this now tranquil area, having read some of these accounts? Before leaving it is worth considering just how many lives were lost or ruined in this relatively small area of the Ridge: French and German in 1915 and early 1916; British, Canadian and German in 1916 and 1917. It is also worth considering that there is no documentary evidence that the mines that the Germans laid for Operation Munich – never launched, but planned for early April 1917 – were ever cleared.

Return to (1). You might like to take this opportunity to visit the Memorial. Immediately you start up the approach avenue to the Memorial from the circuit road you will be going over an incline into one of the German lagers; this partially collapsed in 2005 during the renovation of the Memorial, doubtless caused by the movement of heavy trucks bringing in new stone and materials. Return towards the car park and then follow the circuit route downhill around the Memorial. The attack by the 4th (Cdn) Division on 9 April was the least successful by the divisions of the Canadian Corps and Hill 145 was not finally taken until the following day. Go to (4), situated on a bank on the footpath down to Givenchy. Look to the northwest and you should be able to make out the Pimple (it helps to look at the left edge of Bois l'Abime). Given that there would have been no woods and buildings on 9 April to obstruct either the view or fire power, it is possible to appreciate the significance of Hill 119; its defenders would have to be removed to ensure a more comfortable tenure of the hill. At the base of the Memorial, in the area of the sharp drop below the 'parade ground' area to the east, the Germans had several deep lagers, the Untere Hangstellung, essentially twin tunnels for housing reserves, and part of a defensive position known as the Hangstellung (Slope Position). This walk also reveals something of the problem facing the German defenders – the

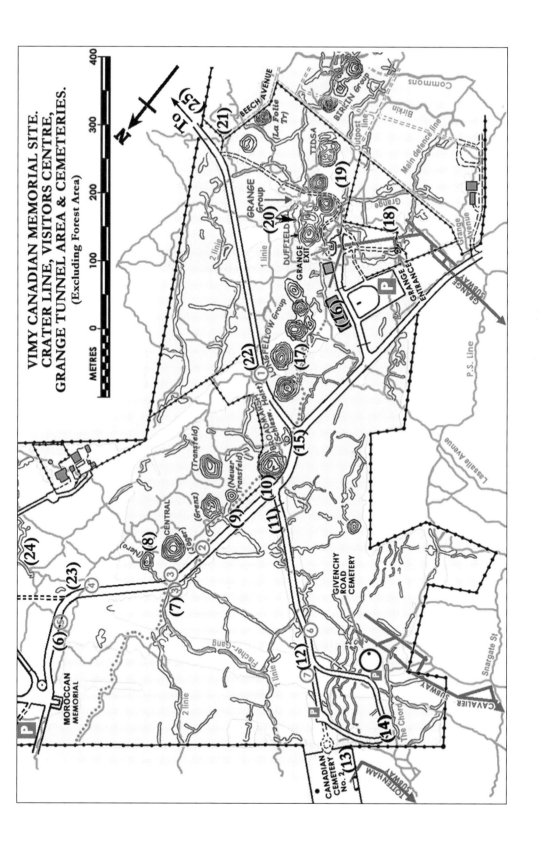

VIMY CANADIAN MEMORIAL SITE.
CRATER LINE, VISITORS CENTRE,
GRANGE TUNNEL AREA & CEMETERIES.
(Excluding Forest Area)

lack of space to hold the position in depth; once the crest of the Ridge was taken, it would be very difficult to recapture it. This also helps to explain why the Germans were so keen to push the French defenders from the line they had captured in September and October 1915, resulting in the small-scale but bitter fighting, such as the various Rupprecht operations, that characterised the months before the British arrived in the sector.

[You can go on around the circuit to (5), which provides a connection between the site and the **Forêt Domaniale de Vimy**; although it is very overgrown, there are plenty of vestiges of the fighting that took place here; by walking through the forest you are covering the whole of the 3rd (Cdn) Division's attack front.]

Return up the hill towards the car park and walk over to the Moroccan Memorial, which acts as a suitable reminder to the heroism and perseverance of the French troops of 1915, who managed to battle their way to the top of the Ridge on two occasions, only to be pushed back by equally resolute German defenders.

At the Memorial turn to the south, i.e. towards the preserved outpost line and the **Grange Subway** area. During this walk reference will be made to several wooden posts with numbers on them; these refer to a self-guided tour that is currently (2010) in preparation but they are useful markers for this tour: when these are used, the wooden marker number will be given in italics. We recommend that for this tour you start on the same side of the road as the Moroccan Memorial and return on the other side.

When you get to marker *5* (6), look west over the shell-torn landscape. The end of the woods on the right and left indicates the German front line in April 1917. Turn around and look towards the car park and the Memorial: this gives you some idea of how limited the German defensive area actually was before it began to go steeply downhill. The line captured by the Germans in May 1916 was about 80 metres behind the Moroccan Memorial, in amongst the trees now, and was maybe 200 metres from this point. The Germans adapted the old Allied trenches for their own use and made them part of their front position defensive system.

Follow the road around to the right and stop at marker *3* (7); in fact, there is a partner marker *3* on the other side of the road, a few metres north of the point (marker *2*) where the Franco-British line crossed the road. Cross the road at (7). **Nero (IV) Crater** at (8), now quite small, was 40 metres in diameter and 10 metres deep when it was fired at 1pm on 25 April. This crater was the result of a German camouflet to counter a

Jäger (Central) Crater.

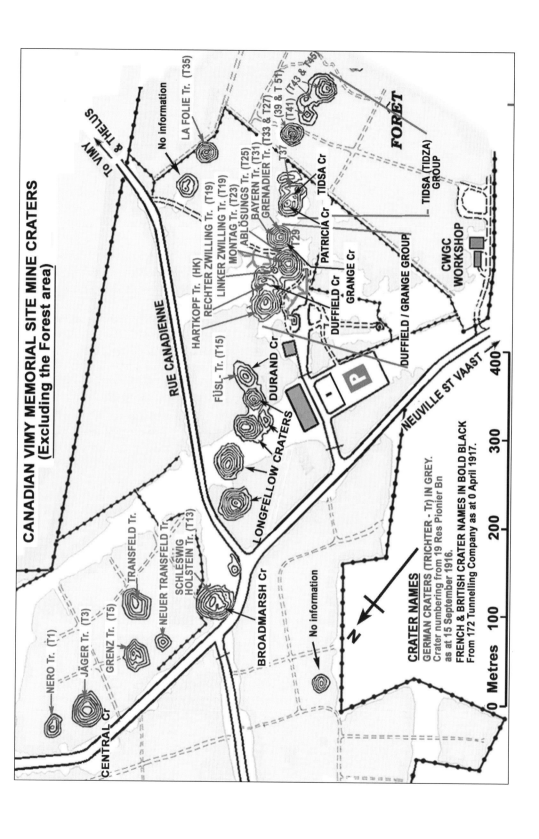

CANADIAN VIMY MEMORIAL SITE MINE CRATERS
(Excluding the Forest area)

To VIMY & THELUS

No information

La Folie Tr. (T35)

FORÊT

(T43 & T45)
(T41) (39 & T 5T)
(T33 & T27)
Grenadier Tr.
Bayern Tr. (T31)
Ablösungs Tr. (T25)
Montag Tr. (T23)
Linker Zwilling Tr. (T19)
Rechter Zwilling Tr. (T19)
Hartkopf Tr. (HK)
T37
T29

Patricia Cr
TIDSA Cr
TIDSA (TIDZA) GROUP

RUE CANADIENNE

Duffield Cr
GRANGE Cr
DUFFIELD / GRANGE GROUP

CWGC WORKSHOP

FÜSL. Tr. (T15)

DURAND Cr

LONGFELLOW CRATERS

NEUVILLE ST VAAST

NERO Tr. (T1)
JÄGER Tr. (T3)
GRENZ Tr. (T5)
NEUER TRANSFELD Tr.
TRANSFELD Tr.
SCHLESWIG HOLSTEIN Tr. (T13)

CENTRAL Cr

BROADMARSH Cr

No information

0 Metres   100   200   300   400

N

CRATER NAMES
GERMAN CRATERS (TRICHTER - Tr) IN GREY.
Crater numbering from 19 Res Pionier Bn
as at 15 September 1916.

FRENCH & BRITISH CRATER NAMES IN BOLD BLACK
From 172 Tunnelling Company as at 0 April 1917.

suspected imminent British mining attack; the camouflet – a large one of 2 tons – set off a British charge. The Germans managed to take advantage of the situation and grabbed possession of the western lip.

Just to its right – only 18 metres away when it was fired – and to the south is **Jäger (VIII) Crater**, blown at 8.30 pm on 28 April. This was substantially bigger, 52 metres in diameter and 11 deep and was the result of 6 tons of explosives. The battle to hold the crater and to fend off British counter-attacks is described in Chapter 5; it is evident from the records that the Germans also suffered heavy casualties when capturing mine craters, though in this case it is notable that they took the further, western, lip, an altogether more difficult process than taking the nearside lip. Among other things, the whole crater had to be prepared for defence and there were serious issues about ensuring that the new position was properly linked up to the existing defence systems as quickly as possible: 'The place was a hive of activity as the crater was prepared for defence, making use of copious quantities of trench stores carried forward by the companies in support. By morning the new Crater VIII and Crater IV had been linked via Sap 3 to the previous front line trench.' Reserve Jäger Battalion 9 suffered twenty killed and fifty-nine wounded in the fighting for these two craters.

The problem from the British point of view was that the new German positions made a sort of 'wall looking down this main communication trench [Centrale], which would be very serious if the Huns got an MG or a sniper's post on it'. In fact, as Johnston's account in Chapter 5 goes on to report, all attempts to dislodge the Germans failed. **Centrale** can still be traced on the ground; it will be mentioned later in the tour, but it runs back southwest from a trench that parallels the west side of the road. Today, standing close to the position, and even after the erosion of the years, it is obvious how the lips of these new craters dominated Centrale.

A few metres further on at (**9**) there are three craters: the northernmost, **Grenz**; in the centre and to the rear, a large one, **Transfeld**; and the southernmost of the group, close to the road, **Neuer Transfeld**. This latter mine was fired by the Germans just after midnight on 18 April. It destroyed 30 metres of a British gallery and permanently entombed four men (it is somewhat sobering to think that they still lie beneath your feet).

At the bend and junction (**10**) you come to the very large **Broadmarsh Crater** (Schleswig Holstein Trichter); see the photographs in Chapter 5. There was a previous mine close to here, just to the southwest, a camouflet blown by the British on 5 May. This camouflet crater was not originally held by the British, but a counter-attack the next day not only took this new one but also wrested Neuer Transfeld from the Germans (see page 76).

All this mine fighting, with blast and counter-blast, had made the Germans determined to try to push the British back and to overrun their mine shafts, thus reducing the burden that the mine warfare was causing, especially on this part of the Ridge. One German regimental history records the infantry's view of the terrors of mine warfare; doubtless their British and French counterparts would have agreed:

> These continual mine explosions in the end got on the nerves of the men. The posts in the front trenches and the garrisons of the dugouts were always in danger of being buried alive. Even in the quietest night there was the dreadful feeling that in the next moment one might die a horrible and cruel death. One stood in the front line

defenceless and powerless against these fearful mine explosions. Against all other fighting methods there was some protection. Against this kind of warfare, valour was of no avail, not even the greatest foresight . . . Some change must be brought about, the British mine shafts on Vimy Ridge must be captured.

The firing of the **Broadmarsh (Schleswig-Holstein) Crater (10)** at 9.45 pm on 21 May was part of a limited but very well resourced German assault. The crater was at the southern limit of the German attack (the south side of Momber Crater marked the northern limit). Leutnant Krüger, present at the time, records what happened:

A severe shock shook the earth and a wave-like motion began below our feet. There was a great noise from deep down then, slowly, the earth in front of us began to heave upwards into what looked like a great mountain. Suddenly it burst open and great flames, crowned with a whitish-grey smoke cloud, leapt upwards. Gradually the smoke cleared and, like a shower of meteors, clods of clay and lumps of chalk rained down upon us. It was a man-made earthquake! Gigantic! Dreadful to behold.

It was from either the Neuer Transfeld or between it and the newly formed Broadmarsh Crater that Lieutenant R.B. Jones of 8/Loyal North Lancs fought with such courage and determination that he was awarded a posthumous VC. His body was never recovered and he is commemorated on the Arras Memorial to the Missing, Bay 7.

From 21 May the front line ran along the southern lip of Broadmarsh and then west, criss-crossing the (post war) approach road to the cemeteries. By February 1917 it had been reduced to a parlous state, as shown by the photograph of one of Leutnant Grieben's pioneers making his way along the trench. Cross the road and proceed along this approach route (**11**). In the distance may be seen **Canadian Cemetery Number 2**. The area roughly between here and the field beyond the cemetery witnessed the terrible failure of a brigade-sized raid by the 4th (Cdn) Division on 1 March 1917.

There was some success at the western end of the attack, but at this end nothing at all was achieved and whatever good results there had been did not in any way justify the 600-plus casualties. So grievous was the situation after the raid was over that the Germans allowed a local armistice so that bodies and wounded could be cleared. The raid was an early test for **Cavalier** and **Tottenham Subways**, both of which were used, particularly for the evacuation of the wounded.

Ordonnant Pionier Dohl in the German first line trench about 200 metres north-west of the Broadmarsh Crater, close to the entrance to tunnel number 26. Probably January 1917. (*GPGR*)

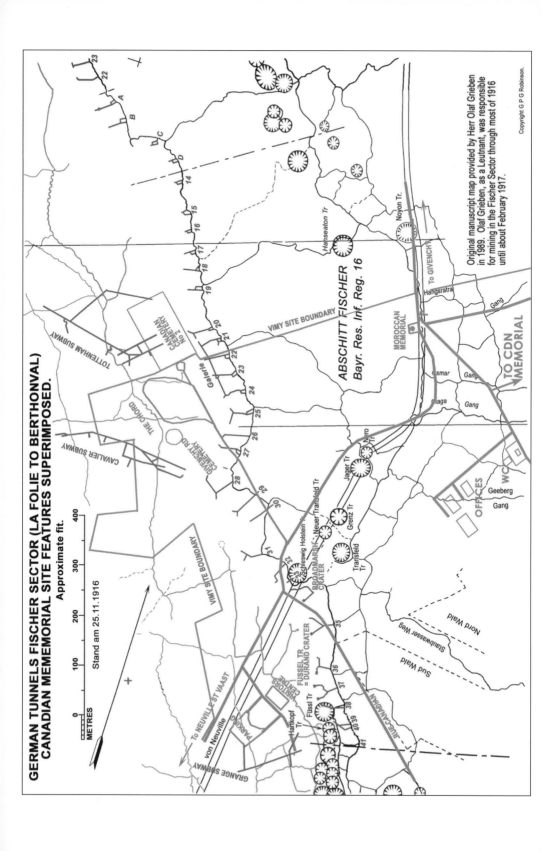

GERMAN TUNNELS FISCHER SECTOR (LA FOLIE TO BERTHONVAL)
CANADIAN MEMEMORIAL SITE FEATURES SUPERIMPOSED.

Approximate fit.

METRES

Stand am 25.11.1916

ABSCHITT FISCHER
Bayr. Res. Inf. Reg. 16

VIMY SITE BOUNDARY

CANADIAN CEMETERY No 2

TOTTENHAM SUBWAY

CAVALIER SUBWAY

THE CHORD

GIVENCHY RD.
CEMETERY

VIMY SITE BOUNDARY

Galerie

Hahseaton Tr

MOROCCAN MEMORIAL

To GIVENCHY

Hangsratra

Noyon Tr.

Gang

smar   Gang

Gang

olaga   Gang

Geeberg
Gang

OFFICES

WC

TO CDN MEMORIAL

Niro
Tr

Jager Tr

Grenz Tr

Neuer Transfeld Tr

Transfeld
Tr

Schleswig Holstein

BROADMARSH
CRATER

Nord Wald

Staubwasser Weg

Sud Wald

RUE CANADIAN

FUSSEL TR
= DURAND CRATER

VISITORS CENTRE

PARKING

To NEUVILLE ST VAAST

von Neuville

GRANGE SUBWAY

Harikopf
Tr

Flussl Tr

Original manuscript map provided by Herr Olaf Grieben
in 1989. Olaf Grieben, as a Leutnant, was responsible
for mining in the Fischer Sector through most of 1916
until about February 1917.

Copyright G P G Robinson.

With your map you can follow how the German front line twisted to and fro over the modern road. On your left, near marker 6, there were two exits from **Cavalier Subway**, to be opened up when the battle opened on 9 April. Between this marker and marker 7, at (**12**), you can see the remnants of **Centrale communication trench**, mentioned earlier, which runs diagonally eastwards north of the road and westwards south of it. At marker 7 you get an excellent view of the Memorial, and along the outer edge of the wood to your left there is a deep (German) communication trench, **Fischer-Gang**. If you turn around, the distinctive twin towers of Mont St Eloi may be seen several kilometres away.

Take the opportunity to visit **Canadian Cemetery Number 2 (13)**, a concentration cemetery with bodies brought in from as far afield as the Belgian coast in the north and the Aisne to the south; the register for this cemetery, number 1896, was the last of the French registers to be published by the CWGC. Walk to the end of the cemetery; straight ahead and slightly to the right you can see the red and white mast mentioned in Tour 1; it marks the approximate point where the German line turned to the right and then ran along to the Pimple and beyond. Further off in the distance may be seen the French National Cemetery at Notre Dame de Lorette; this may be a suitable point to consider the achievement of the French army in 1915, capturing the eastern half of that spur and advancing to beyond this point in 1915, but failing to take the prize of the Ridge and its dominant ground and at a quite frightful cost in men. In the cemetery there were two exits from **Tottenham Subway**, again emerging into No Man's Land.

Leave the cemetery and turn right, following the circular route around to **Givenchy Road Canadian Cemetery**. The trenches in the disturbed ground on your left were all in No Man's Land on 9 April. As the road bends round to the left (**14**), the Canadian front line of 9 April is on your right. Take the time to visit the small cemetery, a battlefield cemetery with 111 burials, all killed between 9 and 13 April 1917; all but two are known.

Return down the road to the junction and turn right. Right under the road junction (**15**) lies the partially cleared (and defused) **Broadmarsh Mine**. This 20,000 lb mine was laid for the 9 April attack, but was not fired. Its status was not clear – had it been defused? Had the ammonal been removed? – and it was investigated in 1997 by a specialist team which subsequently became the Durand Group. A charged mine with detonators in place can go off (as happened in Belgium in the mid-1950s), and with some types of detonator the risk arguably grows over time rather than diminishes. The presence of a potentially live mine at a major road junction in a heavily visited part of the Memorial site was not desirable, to say the least. The investigation into this mine formed the major part of a documentary, *One of Our Mines is Missing*. In fact the mine had been defused and some of the charge removed; it is now quite safe.

Proceed into the parking area and begin by visiting the **Visitors** (or Interpretive) **Centre (16)**. This gives a useful summary of the Canadian Corps at Vimy and very brief details of other Veterans Affairs Canada memorial sites in France and Belgium. You can inquire here about Grange Subway tours. This is a good time to reread Chapter 6, on the La Folie Sector, as it provides an explanation for much of what you will see near here. On the deck outside the Visitors Centre, looking up towards the Memorial, the line of craters (**17**), known as **Longfellow**, was blown by the Germans in the early hours of 23 March 1917. These new craters were probably the major reason why the

Longfellow Craters, looking towards the Durand and Duffield/Grange Group craters. The visitors' centre is on the right.

Broadmarsh mine was not fired as part of the attack on 9 April, as the extra obstacle it would cause to the infantry was thought to outweigh any tactical advantages established by blowing it. This was probably a mistake, as it turned out, but the thinking was reasonable.

The Grange Subway

For operational reasons the guided tour route (that part of it underground currently lasts about 20 minutes) through the subway is liable to change. It is strongly recommended that the visitor reads this section and examines the map carefully before going on a tour. It is a good idea, if at all possible, to try to book a tour of the subway (vimy.memorial@vac-acc.gc.ca). There are some restrictions: you cannot book a tour (as of 2010) for groups of fewer than ten people; young children are not allowed below ground; the subway is closed for over a month between early December and late January; and the subway may be closed because of storms or if it has become very wet below ground. In order to keep up with any developments, try Googling (or an equivalent) Vimy Memorial Grange Subway Tours or similar and take things from there. There is also a useful interactive site, which provides photographs of particular features in the subway, associated with a map. You can reach this site by googling VAC Canada, but it is currently quite a difficult site to navigate.

The tour usually includes an explanation of the Outpost Line and gives a brief background account of the fighting in the area from 1914 and the role of the Canadian Corps in particular.

Work has been done on the subway to make it safe, the most recent major structural work being carried out by (British) Royal Engineers in 1989 and 1990. This entailed, among other things, securing the roof, filling in a number of chambers (for example the Provost post) that had been dug out from the passageways to provide protection against collapse, blocking off inclines and installing a pump for drainage purposes. However, it should be noted that, from the authors' experience of the Goodman Subway, apart from the concrete, enhanced lighting and the chicken wire on the roof, the subway today gives a good impression of how it was then.

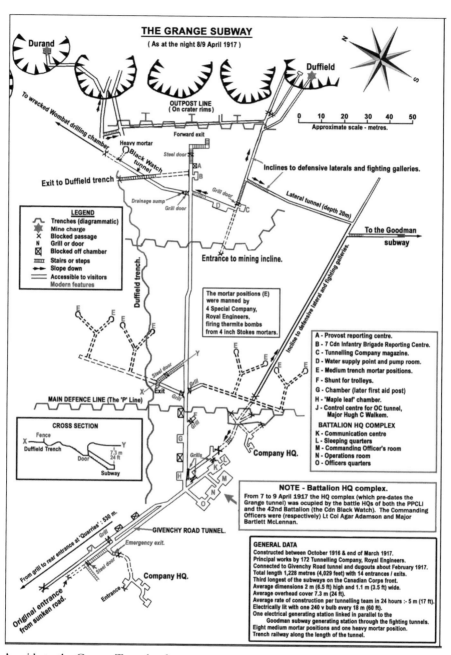

THE GRANGE SUBWAY
(As at the night 8/9 April 1917)

LEGEND
- Trenches (diagrammatic)
- Mine charge
- Blocked passage
- Grill or door
- Blocked off chamber
- Stairs or steps
- Slope down
- Accessible to visitors
- Modern features

The mortar positions (E) were manned by 4 Special Company, Royal Engineers, firing thermite bombs from 4 inch Stokes mortars.

A - Provost reporting centre.
B - 7 Cdn Infantry Brigade Reporting Centre.
C - Tunnelling Company magazine.
D - Water supply point and pump room.
E - Medium trench mortar positions.
F - Shunt for trolleys.
G - Chamber (later first aid post).
H - 'Maple leaf' chamber.
J - Control centre for OC tunnel, Major Hugh C Walkem.

BATTALION HQ COMPLEX
K - Communication centre
L - Sleeping quarters
M - Commanding Officer's room
N - Operations room
O - Officers quarters

NOTE - Battalion HQ complex.
From 7 to 9 April 1917 the HQ complex (which pre-dates the Grange tunnel) was occupied by the battle HQs of both the PPCLI and the 42nd Battalion (the Cdn Black Watch). The Commanding Officers were (respectively) Lt Col Agar Adamson and Major Bartlett McLennan.

GENERAL DATA
Constructed between October 1916 & end of March 1917.
Principal works by 172 Tunnelling Company, Royal Engineers.
Connected to Givenchy Road tunnel and dugouts about February 1917.
Total length 1,228 metres (4,029 feet) with 14 entrances / exits.
Third longest of the subways on the Canadian Corps front.
Average dimensions 2 m (6.5 ft) high and 1.1 m (3.5 ft) wide.
Average overhead cover 7.3 m (24 ft).
Average rate of construction per tunnelling team in 24 hours :- 5 m (17 ft).
Electrically lit with one 240 v bulb every 18 m (60 ft).
One electrical generating station linked in parallel to the Goodman subway generating station through the fighting tunnels.
Eight medium mortar positions and one heavy mortar position.
Trench railway along the length of the tunnel.

A guide to the Grange Tunnel today.

The conserved section of the Grange Subway comprises just over a quarter of its original length and includes a variety of features (bold letters in brackets refer to the accompanying plan) that were common to most of the principal subways. The total length of excavated subway associated with the Grange, including inclines and so forth, was just over 1200 metres; parts in the forward area, such as the Black Watch Tunnel, are closed to the public, while some 530 metres of tunnel leading to the rear exit is now blocked.

This tour indicates how the subway was used for the attack on 9 April; both before and afterwards elements of the subway would have been used for other purposes, so this is largely a snapshot of a particular day.

At the bottom of the stairs, 7.3 metres below the surface at the forward exit into the Observation (or Crater) Line, there was a Provost post [**A**] (now infilled with concrete). The Provost was linked by telephone to the Tunnel Major and to another post at the rear entrance, and between them they were responsible for controlling movement through the tunnel, protecting the entrance and processing men returning from the battlefront, sorting out the lost and strays, directing wounded, handling prisoners and, if needs be, dealing with deserters.

The chamber on the left [**B**], just past the Provost post, was 7 (Cdn) Brigade Reporting Centre, the prime purpose of which was the rapid relay of messages from the assaulting troops back to Brigade HQ, situated about 550 metres to the rear in a complex known as the Machine Gun Fort (Trench Map grid reference S27.b.1.4½, 50° 22.13′N 2° 45.90′E). Opposite the Reporting Centre an exit, now also hidden behind concrete, went up to the Duffield communication trench. A metre or so beyond this, on the right, a grill door bars access to the Black Watch Tunnel, so named because some troops of the 42nd Battalion (Canadian Black Watch) were closeted here while waiting to move forward into their assault positions. The large pit just inside the grill door was created in 1989 as a sump for draining pumps. The purpose of this tunnel, which has

The Black Watch tunnel off the Grange Subway, fitted out to appear as it might have done in 1917. This led to a heavy mortar position and a Wombat drilling chamber, destroyed when the Germans blew the Longfellow Craters.

The former water purification and supply point in the Grange Subway, now the repository of a range of tunnelling and other artefacts.

been arranged to show how it probably looked while under construction, was to establish from underground a heavy mortar position and the placement of a Wombat mine just ahead of the Observation Line. The scheme to explode a trench across No Man's Land had to be abandoned after the Germans blew what became known subsequently as the Longfellow Craters, which wrecked the Wombat drilling chamber. It is a matter for speculation whether the Wombat drilling rig is still in place.

Immediately opposite the Black Watch Tunnel a short flight of stairs leads up to a water processing chamber [D], now the venue for an array of rusting equipment. This connects with one of the tunnelling inclines leading down into the deep mining system, at the head of which is situated the miners' explosives store [C]. The tunnels at the bottom of the incline were (and still are) particularly prone to flooding so, to make a virtue out of a necessity, the engineers installed a water processing plant – probably a series of three tanks – taking and purifying the water constantly pumped up from the tunnels.

Grange Subway. A Canadian guide leading visitors along the main passageway. Note the walls reinforced with concrete.

Returning to the main tunnel, this runs straight for about 45 metres to a slight kink. The bend may have been intentional, with the purpose of preventing any enemy who entered the tunnel from firing along its length, but given that other subways ran straight it is the authors' opinion that this was a slight error by the 172 Tunnelling Company surveyor.

On the right, a short way further on, stairs lead up to an entrance-*cum*-exit into the main defence line. Just beyond, on both sides of the main passage, tunnels behind grill doors lead off to mortar emplacements [E]. Prepared from underground by sappers from 7 Company Royal Canadian Engineers, these remained concealed until broken out on the night preceding the 9 April attack. The object was to place the mortars, a short-range weapon, as close as possible to the enemy lines. For the attack a battery of eight 4-inch Stokes mortars was emplaced, manned by sappers of the 4th Special Company Royal Engineers. The original intention was to lay a smokescreen, but visibility at dawn on the day was sufficiently obscure that this was not necessary. Instead they bombarded the German lines with thermite bombs – devices that on exploding burnt and melted everything in the immediate vicinity: an extremely unpleasant Easter gift for those on the receiving end.

A little further down on the left, and now partially filled with chalk detritus, there was a shunt [F] for the tramway that ran along the tunnel. It may be presumed that at the time the rail system running through the tunnel had a switch at this point. Also along the right-hand side of the corridor there were four chambers [G, H], two of which have been blocked off with concrete. The exact purpose of each has not been determined, but one [G] appears to have been used at some stage as an aid post. There were, however, no aid posts in the tunnel at the time of the Canadian attack, the nearest such being the 42nd Battalion RAP (Regimental Aid Post) situated at the Machine Gun Fort. The other open chamber [H] has a modern vertical ventilation pipe which allows a glimpse of the distance to the surface and also boasts a carved maple leaf, one of the very few items of carved graffiti remaining, though whether this was done during or soon after the war, perhaps when the subway was prepared for public access, is not clear.

Just beyond there is something of a complex of tunnel connections. This is a junction between the subway and the Givenchy Road Tunnel, which pre-dated the Grange and connected to a battalion HQ complex, two company HQ dugouts and the main defence line. These were incorporated into the subway with some extension to the battalion command complex, with part of the earlier tunnel being abandoned. The extended battalion HQ complex is accessible to the visitor and comprises five chambers, for communications (telephones, signallers and runners) [K] and related accommodation [L], a room and office for the resident commanding officers [M], an operations room (essentially the battalion HQ office) [N] and accommodation for the battalion HQ and attached officers [O]. For several months before April 1917 this complex rotated mostly between Princess Patricia's Canadian Light Infantry (PPCLI) and the 42nd Battalion (Canadian Black Watch) as the one relieved the other in the line. Immediately prior to the attack on 9 April it must have been somewhat crowded, as both battalions shared the complex and presumably the respective commanding officers, Lieutenant Colonel Agar Adamson of the PPCLI, and Major Bartlett McLennan of the 42nd Battalion 'hot bunked' in the commanding officer's room.

Leaving the command complex and heading to the rear, the tunnel branches. That straight ahead, the Givenchy Road Tunnel, leads out to the Neuville St Vaast–Givenchy road, at the time a sunken road. A branch tunnel off this on the left, now blocked by a former emergency exit, led into a company HQ. Directly ahead steps lead up to a new entry-*cum*-exit, constructed for safety purposes in 2008, based on an original incline exit. The parallel tunnel to the right was part of the main subway construction. This passes two more blocked-off chambers and ends at a grill, beyond which the tunnel continues, half-filled with chalk debris from tunnel renovation. From this point there are about 530 metres of subway to the rear entrance; it incorporated facilities such as the power generation station. Investigations some years ago show this to be blocked by a collapse about 100 metres further along.

As already remarked, tunnel usage and design varied according to the perceptions of a division and even brigade. The Grange was structured primarily as a communication tunnel, incorporating existing command facilities. There was no provision for accommodation apart from battalion HQs and tunnel staff. Nevertheless, troops moved into the tunnel on the night of 7/8 April and were situated there for nearly 36 hours before moving into their assault positions shortly before dawn on 9 April. The first in were two companies of the 42nd Battalion, who were spread along the tunnels back to the mortar points. Following them came two companies of the PPCLI, situated back along the tunnel to about half-way to the back entrance. Two companies of the RCR (Royal Canadian Regiment) and two platoons of the 49th Battalion were located along the remainder of the tunnel. In addition there were the sappers of the Special Company, the two battalion HQs, some brigade staff, the Provost and the Tunnel Major and his staff, in all slightly under a thousand men (the various companies had a strength of about 140–150 men, below the establishment number for a variety of reasons). Most would have had to dispose themselves seated on the tunnel floor, trying to avoid being

A 1930s postcard showing the commanding officer's room in the HQ complex. The notice on the wall originally read, somewhat inaccurately, 'General's Sleeping Quarters'.

trampled upon by those who were moving to and fro. The problems of feeding and sanitary issues may well be imagined. A ban on smoking in the tunnel can hardly have elevated morale, though one wonders how many of the Canadian troops, with their disdain for authority, actually complied. It would certainly have been exceedingly uncomfortable and the atmosphere unpleasant, but for all that they were better off than their compatriots moving up through communication trenches into freezing and waterlogged positions in the forward lines.

A 7 (Cdn) Brigade Report on the operations from 9 to 12 April says of the tunnel, 'For the GRANGE Tunnel, with its branches, tramways, Trench Mortar positions, recesses for ammunition, etc., etc., facilitating supplies of every sort and saving hundreds of lives, Major Symes and the 172nd Tunnelling Company are deserving of all praise.' The report continues, 'Major H.C. Walken, Traffic Manager and Lieut. West, his assistant, did their work well'.

To repeat, it should be borne in mind that of necessity the guided tour of the Grange comprises a snapshot in time covering its primary function of supporting the attack on 9 April 1917. As with many of the other subways, it remained in use long after Vimy Ridge was taken, providing shelter and safe billets for troops and storage facilities hidden from enemy airmen. Graffiti in the Black Watch Tunnel shows that it even provided refuge for British troops in the course of the retreat to Dunkirk in 1940.

Go to (**18**), whether or not you have been able to go on the subway tour. The trench formed the front line of the Canadian main defensive system; it stretched from here just slightly south of west, into the forestry area, part of the Memorial site but closed to public access; and, slightly north of east, from here across the bottom edge of the car park and just north of the boundary fence across the other side of the road. At (**18**) you can see the earthworks associated with a heavy mortar pit, the access tunnel to which is seen as part of the tour.

Aerial view of the Grange Crater area and conserved trenches.

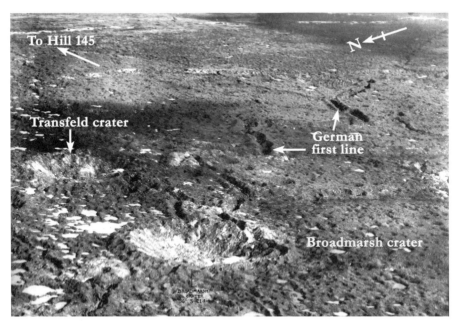

This oblique aerial view across Broadmarsh Crater gives a good idea of the terrain in March 1917. (*Durand Group*)

Walk up to the preserved trench area (**19**). This is an outpost line (or observation line or crater line) and should not be confused with a 'usual' trench system. It does provide a good example of the defences that both sides would have sought to establish after a mine had been blown in No Man's Land – that is, as a minimum, to take firm control

The conserved trenches on the Allied side of the craters in about 1935, viewed from point (**19**).

of the 'home' side of the lip. A trench line would be established below the lip and from there saps pushed forward to its crest, providing at the minimum sentry positions to give alerts to the main defensive line. Broadmarsh Crater provides a good example of the Germans carrying out this type of operation. Occasionally barbed wire and other nasties would be put into the crater to deter the enemy using them as an approach route. Any machine guns this far forward would not be targeted at the enemy immediately opposite – a machine gun is an area weapon. Such guns would be positioned to be able to fire in enfilade, in this case along No Man's Land as opposed to just across the width of it.

Cross over to the German line; you are walking between craters that comprised the Grange Group. The Durand Crater is in the trees and slightly to the right of the Visitors' Centre building. The overlapping Duffield and then Grange Group front the (wartime) exit from the Grange Subway. The original Grange Crater is on your right as you walk along the track across the crater line. Beyond Grange Crater, towards the forest, is the Tidsa Group, one of whose craters was called Patricia, after the PPCLI, which occupied it after it was fired on 19 December 1916.

The small bunker in the German line was for observation; if you get into it, you can see that it gives a good view across the width of No Man's Land, encompassing part of the Grange, Tidsa and Birkin groups of craters. The Birkin Group is in the forestry area of the site and some of the most interesting remaining features from the war are to be found in this area, almost certainly as a consequence of the fact that they have been left largely undisturbed since 1918, with the major exceptions of the forestry programme and the insertion of drives.

At (**20**) there was an entrance, now concreted over as a consequence of persistent vandalism, to two short German tunnels below the craters. Continue along the path to **Rue Canadienne**, the main route through the site from the Lens road side. As you go, notice the relative complexity of the German system of trenches compared to the Canadian side – this is because much of the Canadian system in the vicinity of the Grange Subway had to be removed as part of the public access programme. When you reach the road turn right and go to the locked gate at (**21**). There is no public access but it leads to what is known as the Beech Avenue; why this was planted is not clear, though there are plenty of reasonable hypotheses. To the left and right of this avenue there are a number of craters associated with the struggle in late 1915 and early 1916 between the French and Germans to advance a few metres.

Cross the road (carefully!) and turn left (west). The German trenches you can see to the right are from the German second line of the front-line position. At marker *1* (**22**) look back across the road at the lips of the formidable Longfellow Craters; it is easy to understand why the authorities were not keen to fire another big mine so close to it as part of a major offensive operation. Just before the road junction you cross over from what was, on 9 April, the 3rd Division's area into that of the 4th Division.

From here proceed back up towards the Memorial. At marker *4* (**23**) take the opportunity to look over the battle-ravaged ground before the Memorial; this gives some idea (minus the grass and sheep!) as to what the whole of the Ridge might have looked like in 1917 – perhaps in winter and under snow gives the best approximation. Although Vimy was never fought over again in the war, some preparations for its defence were made in the light of the anticipated German offensive in the spring of 1918; in particular, there is a very distinctive, deep trench (**24**) that leads from the site boundary with the Vimy Forest above the administrative buildings to close to the approach path to the Memorial that dates from this period.

Return to your car and head for (**25**). It is on a sharp left-hand bend, so approach carefully; there is a grassy area immediately on the left of the track which provides adequate space for a car; what it would be like in wet weather we cannot say. Walk along the track for no more than 50 metres and you will be crossing Prinz Arnulf Tunnel, from which there were numerous exits. We have investigated the area and can find no trace of these. The wooded area on your left is accessible to the public and there are earthwork remains from the war years. You might care to walk back towards the Memorial Site to visit the 3rd (Cdn) Division Memorial, near the site of La Folie Farm.

This concludes Tour 3.

Tour 4: Arras
For this tour see in particular Chapter 8.

Park in one of the ancient squares in Arras – the Grand' Place or the Place des Héros. Note that the latter is being refurbished at the moment and there is also an accompanying archaeological dig; it might still be closed in 2011. Parking is paid for by means of meters dotted around the square; there is also underground parking in the Grand' Place. Beware of the market on Saturdays – there is no parking there until the afternoon, and there are fairly frequent events when parking is either banned or very limited.

Head for the information office in the magnificently restored Hotel de Ville, which is open all day from 1 April to mid-September, with more limited opening hours in the autumn and winter months. There is a range of useful publications in English and French, including a town guide (and map). An ascent to the top of the belfry is well worth the effort for the view.

Since the opening of the Wellington Cave, the tour of the underground *boves* below the town hall takes little notice of their role in the First World War, and on occasion there are exhibitions laid out down there. However, it is a fascinating experience and well worth the entrance fee of about €5. Note that the *boves* are closed for most of January as well as for Christmas and the New Year. The tour lasts about 40 minutes and explores three floors – the first is about 4 metres below ground level, the second 8 metres below and the last 12 metres below. Originally the *boves* were quarries for the stone that built Arras; these were then adapted to become cellars (as many still are) and warehousing. It was only natural that they should become shelters for the troops during the war, providing secure accommodation and headquarters. The *boves* under the Grand' Place were almost entirely destroyed when the underground car park was built some years ago; those under the Place des Héros largely remain. There are several places in the square where the medieval stairways or first-floor cellars may be seen, such as Les Trois Luppars hotel and the hotel-restaurant Les Grandes Arcades, but these are rarely shown to visitors. Under No. 21 in the Grand' Place (just beyond Rue de Noble) there is currently a First World War artefacts shop in a *bove* and a small 'tunnel' museum.

The Rue des Dominicains, at the south end of the Grand' Place, leads to Rue Saumon, along which (on the left-hand side) is the Porte de Fer (see Chapter 8), still quite recognisable, though the doorway is much reduced. The positions of the original hinges for the bigger door are still evident.

CENTRAL ARRAS TODAY

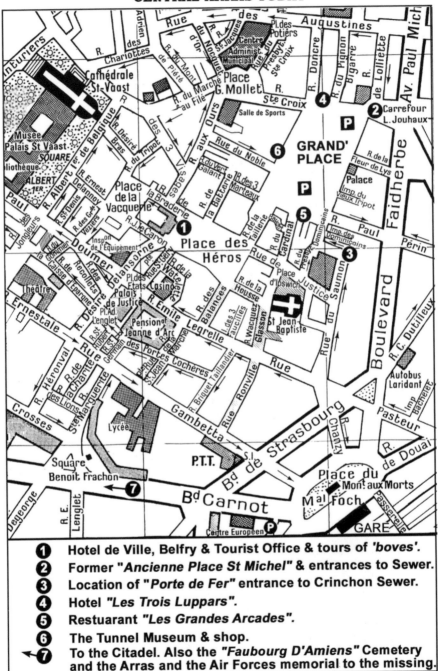

① Hotel de Ville, Belfry & Tourist Office & tours of *'boves'*.
② Former *"Ancienne Place St Michel"* & entrances to Sewer.
③ Location of *"Porte de Fer"* entrance to Crinchon Sewer.
④ Hotel *"Les Trois Luppars"*.
⑤ Restuarant *"Les Grandes Arcades"*.
⑥ The Tunnel Museum & shop.
◄① To the Citadel. Also the *"Faubourg D'Amiens"* Cemetery and the Arras and the Air Forces memorial to the missing.

The Grande Place in Arras. Les Grandes Arcades Restaurant is behind the camera position.

The Hotel de Ville and belfry in 2007, viewed from the Place des Héros (formerly La Petite Place). The tourist office is located at the front left of the building.

Second-level cellars beneath the Hotel de Ville, with an art display.

A Great War trolley chute under the Hotel de Ville, leading from street level to the first-level cellars.

From the squares drive along the Boulevard Faidherbe and the Boulevard de Strasbourg; at the lights you need to go straight ahead and then follow around to the left, on the Avenue Lobbedez, the Bapaume road. After crossing the railway line, continue straight ahead. You will pass a big Leclerc supermarket on your left (usually good for reasonably priced fuel); as you pass it get over to the left for a traffic filter in to Rue Delétoille, a narrow, one-way street at the top (south) of the Leclerc parking area. Within a few metres there is a turning on the right for the Wellington Cave; there is an entrance fee (2010) of €6.60.

The name of this cave and of others in the immediate vicinity, such as Blenheim, Nelson, Picton, Dunedin, Christchurch, Auckland, etc, come from places in New Zealand – though some might appear to be coincidentally rather undiplomatic, given that we are in France! They were part of the Ronville System, as opposed to the St Sauveur System to the east. This is an excellent opportunity to see how such systems were used by both sides during the war; a lot of money has been spent to produce a first-rate visitor experience. There is a bookshop, an exhibition area, and an audio-

The Porte de Fer (Iron Door) in 2010. Note the original hinges still in place and the recess for a former plaque. See also page 180.

Board walk in Wellington Caves.

A connecting tunnel leading to other caves and trench dump trucks on rails.

visual room. For the tour you go with a guide and an audioguide (which is included in the price) down a shaft in a glass lift to a depth of about 20 metres below the surface. Conducted by the guide, visitors are taken along well constructed board walks through high corridors, so there is no need to fear claustrophobia. Points of particular interest are highlighted and the audioguides connect automatically. Along the route there are a number of projected video vignettes portraying and relating events of the First World War period around Arras and in the caves. It is well done and the occasional historic or factual error may be readily forgiven (for example when we visited one voice-over presented the total BEF casualties for the battles of Arras as fatalities). There are some displays, one of particular interest being the absolutely clear well from which water was drawn. A large angled mirror allows a view into the depths.

It will be appreciated that the area open to visitors is only a modest part of the whole system and the works to render it safe, particularly from the possibility of chalk slabs falling, has to a degree 'sanitised' the cave, but some insight can be gained into its original workings. We were fortunate some years ago to spend time working in the system before it was developed for visitor access.

Leave the car parked and return to Rue Bapaume to visit the simple New Zealand Tunnellers' Memorial (indicated by a number of national flags) some metres further south down the Bapaume road, near an entrance to the *souterraines* from the days when the caves were used for the protection of the civil population, such as during the Second World War. About 2 kilometres down the road was the front line in 1917, in the suburb of Beaurains.

There is a lot more to Arras than its connections to the First World War, but this concludes this stage of the tours.

Tour 5: Cemeteries and Memorials

In each cemetery we have picked out some names from the registers that attracted our attention and used details from them and, on occasion, other sources to provide details of just a few of the men who fell in the service of their country. Where we have been able to identify them, members of the tunnelling companies are listed. For example, Private Bernard Chapman is buried in III.E.4 – that is, plot 3, row E, grave 4. We have used 'died' rather than 'killed' for those where it is not specifically stated in the register that they were killed in action or died of wounds or some other cause, even though we know in some of these cases that they were killed in action. Where appropriate we refer readers to relevant parts in the main part of the book where an individual or individuals can be placed with an incident described there. We have checked the registers a couple of times carefully but cannot claim to be certain that we have found every one of the tunnellers identified as such by the register in any particular cemetery.

Grave details are given using the CWGC system: thus a roman numeral indicates the plot, a letter indicates the row and the arabic number indicates the individual burial position.

In this tour, naturally, we concentrate on the tunnellers (with the exception of Notre Dame de Lorette). It is notable that, where details are given, a lot of the men from infantry regiments attached to the tunnellers were older and from mining areas. Several of the sappers were from mining areas as well.

Maroeuil British Cemetery (50° 19.69' N 02° 42.02' E)

To reach this cemetery from La Targette take the D55 to Maroeuil, passing almost immediately on your right the small La Targette British (Aux Rietz) Cemetery and the huge French cemetery, and stay on this road until it meets the D341; turn right and after a short distance – a couple of hundred metres - there is a minor road on the left (unsignposted) that leads in to Maroeuil; signal well in advance, as this can be a busy road. Drive into Maroeuil, approaching on its western side. On the left there is a French military cemetery with some British graves; take the first right turn after that cemetery, continue beyond a junction with a road coming from the right and the approach track to Maroeuil British Cemetery is 100 metres or so further on.

This is not the easiest CWGC cemetery to find, being off a track on a minor road. We would recommend that you find a place to park on the road, as the track leading to the cemetery is rough and narrow, and there is nowhere to turn around. In wet weather it can be extremely muddy, so make sure that you have appropriate footwear! This is a rarely visited cemetery and we hope that you will be able to spend some time in it.

This is a most interesting cemetery. It is placed behind the crest of a hill and so was protected from observation. It is one of the cemeteries in the area to which bodies were brought by tramways, a practice that leads, usually, to a chronological arrangement of the burials. Evidence of the existence of the tramway may be seen in the use of parts of the track as fence posts for the neighbouring properties. No graves were concentrated here after the war. There are only four unidentified graves (one of those British) among the 574 burials: 531 are from the UK, thirty from Canada, one from India (a cavalryman), one from the Chinese Labour Corps and eleven German prisoners of war.

The cemetery was started by the 51st (Highland) Division when it arrived on this front in March 1916. The 51st was a Territorial division (as opposed to a New Army or

A line of tunnellers' graves in Maroeuil Cemetery.

Regular one), which, after a slightly rocky time at High Wood on the Somme in the summer of 1916, built up a formidable reputation. The division remained associated with this cemetery, on and off and between moves elsewhere on the front, until the summer of 1918. It is no surprise, therefore, that nearly half of the burials are from that division. Almost a quarter come from the London Territorials (47th, 56th and 60th Divisions), who were on this front from July to December 1916.

This can be regarded as a tunnellers' cemetery. The register states that there are twenty-five tunnellers buried here (although rather fewer than that can be identified directly from the register). Memorials erected to the men of the 6th Seaforths, the 6th Argyll and Sutherland Highlanders and the 5th and 7th Gordon Highlanders who were killed in mine explosions still stood here when the register was first published, in 1922.

Second Lieutenant Archibald Macneill joined 9/HLI on 5 September 1914 as a private, went to France in January 1915 and was wounded at La Bassée on 13 March of the same year. He was commissioned into the Argylls and was killed on 26 March 1916, at the age of 19. (**I.A.13**)

Private William Adamson of the Highland Cyclist Battalion was killed on 1 May 1916 at the age of 18. When the war broke out he was in Argentina with his parents; he volunteered in Buenos Aires and enlisted in Dundee. (**I.D.7**)

Private Alexander Boyter, 7/Black Watch, was killed on 30 May 1916. (**I.F.8**) His mother also lost her husband, Thomas, who was 'blown up by a German mine in the North Sea'.

Private J. Kent, a 19-year-old from Sanderstead, Surrey, served in the army under the name of Barton, while his mother, Janie Gosschalk, had possibly remarried. It was unusual, but not particularly rare, for soldiers to serve under a different name. **(III.A.4.)** See also Lance Corporal Hamilton, 181 Tunnelling Company, below.

Rifleman Herbert Entwisle of 2/Queen's Westminsters was killed on 27 August 1916, his 21st birthday. **(III.E.5.)**

Corporal Malcolm Gilchrist, 1/8 Argylls, died at the age of 26 on 17 March 1917 while taking part in a bombing raid near Roclincourt. **(II.M.8.)**

Lieutenant Colonel William Macfarlane DSO was killed while in command of the 15th HLI on 19 February 1917. His DSO, won when he was a temporary major, was gazetted on 26 September 1916: 'For conspicuous gallantry during operations. Just as the relief of his company had been completed, the enemy made a strong bombing counter-attack, which drove back the relieving troops. Major Macfarlane at once led his company back to its original position, and repelled the counter-attack. He set a fine example of cool courage.' **(III.L.5.)**

Second Lieutenant Cecil Clark MM of the 1/7 Middlesex, who had been promoted from the ranks, was killed at the age of 24 'by a piece of shell whilst rescuing a wounded British airman, 24 April 1917'. **(IV.E.6.)**

Miscellaneous entries:

Private Daniel Dunnett of the 1/5 Seaforths was only 16 when he was killed on 27 March 1916 **(II.A.2)**, as was *Private H. Ingram* of the 1/7 Gordons, who died of wounds on 28 April 1916 **(II.C.3)**.

Major Eric Tyson DSO, MC, of the RFC died of wounds on 12 March 1918, aged 24. **(IV.G.16)** His DSO was gazetted on 26 September 1917 and the details published on 9 January 1918: 'For conspicuous gallantry and devotion to duty on many occasions. He has displayed the utmost fearlessness in carrying out photographic reconnaissances and artillery registration at extremely low altitudes, being continually under fire, but invariably doing excellent work and obtaining most valuable information by his great skill and daring.'

Private James Torrance of the 1/7 Black Watch was killed on 28 May 1916, aged 23. **(I.F.12)** *Sergeant William Torrance*, his brother, also of the 1/7 Black Watch, was killed less than a month later, on 22 June 1916, aged 25. **(II.G.1)** Their graves are within a few metres of each other.

THE TUNNELLERS
176 Tunnelling Company:
Sapper H. Cookson, 176 Tunnelling Company, died on 16 March 1918. **(IV.H.7)**

181 Tunnelling Company:
Private T. Hill, 17th Sherwood Foresters, attd 181 Tunnelling Company, died 16 April 1916. **(II.B.13)**

Private W. Davis, 17th Sherwood Foresters, attd 181 Tunnelling Company, from Nottingham, died on 16 April 1916, aged 37. **(II.B.1)**

Private J. Taylor, 17th Sherwood Foresters, attd 181 Tunnelling Company, died 20 April 1916. **(II.B.9)**

Lance Corporal Ernest Bracey, 181 Tunnelling Company, from Glamorgan, died 19 May 1916, aged 31. **(II.D.8)**

Private Thomas Blenkinsop, 23rd (Tyneside Scottish) Northumberland Fusiliers, attd 181 Tunnelling Company, from Annfield Plain, Co. Durham, died 29 May 1916, aged 35. **(II.E.8)**

Private James Kenny, 2/East Lancs, attd 181 Tunnelling Company, from Whitehaven and Nelson, died 8 June 1916, aged 36. **(II.F.1)**

Private E. Tetlow, 10/Duke of Wellington's, attd 181 Tunnelling Company, from Oldham, died on 8 June 1916, aged 21. **(II.E.9)**

Private Robert Williams, 2/ Northants, attd 181 Tunnelling Company, from Worksop, died 8 June 1916, aged 23. **(II.F.2)**

Lance Corporal James Hamilton (served as Smith), 181 Tunnelling Company, from West Lothian, died 29 June 1916, aged 39. **(II.H.5)**

Sapper Charles Hopkinson, 181 Tunnelling Company, of Sheffield, died on 2 July 1916, aged 25. **(II.J.5)**

185 Tunnelling Company:

Sapper W. Charlton, 185 Tunnelling Company, from Enderby, Leicestershire, died 26 April 1916. **(II.B.8)**

256 Tunnelling Company:

Second Lieutenant Sidney Faithfull, 256 Tunnelling Company, died on 15 August 1916, aged 40. He had served previously in the South African and German South West African campaigns. **(III.D.6)**

Sapper A.G. Hinton, 256 Tunnelling Company, from Cwmbran, died 15 August 1916, aged 38. **(III.D.7)**

Sapper A.G. West, 256 Tunnelling Company, from Wimbledon, died of wounds (gas), aged 36 on 15 August 1916. **(III.D.8)**

Sapper E. Clifford, 256 Tunnelling Company, died on 27 August 1916. **(III.E.3)**

Sapper George Waters, 256 Tunnelling Company, from Butterknowle, Co. Durham, was killed in action on 14 September 1916, aged 26. **(III.F.10)**

Sapper W. Gregory, 256 Tunnelling Company, from Mansfield, was killed in action on 8 October 1916, aged 24. **(III.G.15)**

Second Corporal J. Elliott, 256 Tunnelling Company, died on 17 October 1916. **(III.H.16)**

From the details in the register we can identify only nineteen of the twenty-five tunnellers that the introduction to the register states are buried here.

Ecoivres Military Cemetery (50° 20.62'N, 2° 41.18'E)
When leaving Maroeuil British Cemetery, continue to the road junction almost immediately in front of you and bear right. Continue through the small village of Bray, where the road has some sharp bends. Bray was a major light railway terminus in the build-up to the 9 April offensive and there is a modern railway line nearby, also used at the time. Along this route there were a number of hutted and tented temporary camps, housing infantry and many support troops, all sheltered from enemy fire by the hills to the right. About 200 metres after leaving Bray you will come to a large wood on your right; as you come around the bend you will see the British section of the cemetery on your left; the 'official' entrance is here. There is usually a space on the right just beyond it to pull of the road (but this road can on occasion be surprisingly busy). An alternative

is to continue to the junction, turn left and then park in the large space in front of the civil cemetery. We have found it quite easy (at least up to now) to hop over the low hedge that separates the civil from the military part of the cemetery; also, returning to the Bray road, there is disabled access to the cemetery near a CWGC maintenance area. However, be warned that the register is at the entrance on the Bray Road – i.e. at the other end of the cemetery!

The cemetery is an extension of the communal one and completely dwarfs it. Plot I is nearest the communal cemetery. There are two French plots in the British cemetery, and the French Tenth Army buried over a thousand men here (786 in this part of the cemetery). The original plan by architect Sir Reginald Blomfield was for the War Stone to be placed in the main drive leading through the cemetery, at the point where Plots 3, 4, 5 and 6 come closest together; this accounts for the slightly strange layout at the moment. Doubtless it would have been more aesthetically pleasing to have it there but perhaps practical considerations of routine grounds maintenance led to the decision not to have one at all – very unusual in a cemetery of this size.

The original register states that there are twelve unknown British soldiers in the cemetery, and lists 891 burials from the United Kingdom, 828 Canadian, four South African, two Australian (from Australian heavy artillery units) and ten German prisoners of war (the website says four).

Plots I and II in particular reflect the casualties caused by the struggle to dominate the mine war and have large numbers of burials from the 46th (North Midland), 25th and 47th (London) Divisions, the effect of the German attack on 21 May 1916 being

Ecoivres: the Cross of Sacrifice and the cemetery. Mont St Eloi is in the background.

particularly evident. The London Division casualties predominate in Plot III, A to H. Plots IV, V and VI are strongly Canadian.

The cemetery is a rather beautiful one, and normally very tranquil. Towards the top, at the entrance end, there are evocative views of the remaining twin towers of Mont St Eloi abbey, sitting on a ridge that provided the cemetery (and much else) with security from prying German eyes and shell fire.

THE TUNNELLERS

We have been able to identify thirty tunnellers or permanently attached infantry who are buried in this cemetery.

172 Tunnelling Company

Sapper J. Williams, 172 Tunnelling Company, from Bristol, was killed on 23 June 1916, aged 27. (**II.E.27.**)

Private T. Cufter, 9/Loyal North Lancs, attd 172 Tunnelling Company, died on 14 August 1916. (**III.D.28.**)

Private J. Oliver, 9/Loyal North Lancs, attd 172 [Tunnelling] Company, died 14 August 1916. (**III.D.27.**)

Sapper H. Dyson, 172 Tunnelling Company, died 14 August 1916. (**III.D.19.**)

Sapper F. Russell, 172 Tunnelling Company, died 14 August 1916. (**III.D.17.**)

Sapper G. Sell, 172 Tunnelling Company, died 14 August 1916. (**III.D.24.**)

Sapper P. Shields, 172 Tunnelling Company, died 14 August 1916. (**III.D.26.**)

Lance Corporal L. Statham, 172 Tunnelling Company, died 14 August. (**III.D.18.**)

Sapper E. Follows, 172 Tunnelling Company, from Walsall, died 31 August 1916, aged 36. (**III.F.7.**)

Sapper P. Naylor, 172 [Tunnelling] Company, from Alfreton, was killed 24 October 1916, aged 37. (**III.H.14.**)

Sapper W. Griffiths, 172 Tunnelling Company, died 3 February 1917. (**IV.C.12.**)

Sapper J. Reilly, 172 Tunnelling Company, died 3 February 1917, aged 32. (**IV.C.11.**)

Sapper W. Arrowsmith, 172 Tunnelling Company, from Aberdare, died on 6 April 1917. (**V.F.23**)

Captain Richard Brisco MC, 172 Tunnelling Company, killed 9 April 1917 (at Goodman Subway, see Chapter 6), aged 39. (**VI.E.1**)

175 Tunnelling Company

Sapper John Collins, 175 Tunnelling Company, from Redruth, died aged 24, 2 July 1916. (**III.B.3**) *Sapper S. Holborn*, 175 Tunnelling Company, from Abertillery, died 2 July 1916, aged 39. (**III.B.3**) These two men share a grave and next to them is *Sapper J. Malcolm*, 175 Tunnelling Company, of Glasgow, who died on 2 July 1916. (**III.B.2**)

The following men, of 2/13 London Regiment (2/Kensingtons), were not formally attached to 175 but were acting as a carrying party for the company; they were killed in the same incident and are buried in the same grave as Collins and Holborn – presumably they could not be individually identified and it must have been a most appalling mess: Private G. Mayhew, aged 22 (**III.B.3**); Private George Rogers, aged 23 (**III.B.3**); Private E. Smith, aged 21 (**III.B.3**); Private J. Smith, aged 25 (**III.B.3**); Private E. Thompson, aged 20 (**III.B.3**). The result of all these burials in **III.B.3** is an unusual headstone arrangement.

Sapper A. McAdam, 175 Field (sic) Company, died 21 July 1916. (**III.B.4**)

Ecoivres: the mass grave for the five privates of 13 (Kensington) Battalion, London Regiment, and two sappers of 175 Tunnelling Company killed by a shell on 2 July 1916.

The Kensingtons and Royal Engineer badges entwined.

Second Corporal W. Bassett, 175 Tunnelling Company, 14 August 1916. (**III.D.22**)

Sapper E. Cook, 175 Tunnelling Company, from Edwinstowe, Notts, died 21 August 1916, aged 23. (**III.E.14**)

Lance Corporal P. Scothern, from Clay Cross, died 21 August 1916, aged 34. (**III.E.20**)

Sapper W. Miller, 175 [Tunnelling] Company, from Cowdenbeath, died 21 August 1916. (**III.E.21**)

Sapper Thomas Walne, 175 Tunnelling Company, died on 21 August 1916, aged 26. (**III.E.19**)

Sapper Robert Glasson, 175 Tunnelling Company, from Cornwall, died 27 September 1916, aged 35. (**III.G.12**)

Sapper John Plumb, 175 Tunnelling Company, from Mansfield, died on 9 October 1916, aged 29. (**III.G.25**)

176 Tunnelling Company

Second Lieutenant Christopher Bruce, 176 Tunnelling Company, from Aberdeen and a well qualified engineer, with a BSc and an ME, died 28 March 1918, aged 33. (**VI.K.4**)

182 Tunnelling Company

Sapper E. Moxon, 182 Tunnelling Company, from Rotherham, died on 20 April 1916. **(I.E.9)**

Sapper R. Critchley, 182 Tunnelling Company, from Haydock, died on 21 April 1916. **(I.E.11)**

Sapper J. Cutts, 182 Tunnelling Company, from Hucknall, Notts, was killed on 28 April 1916, aged 35. **(I.G.7)**

255 Tunnelling Company

Private J. Barclay, 16/Royal Welch Fusiliers, attd 255 Tunnelling Company, died 12 March 1917. **(IV.F.8)**

Miscellaneous entries:

Private James Goodwill, 1/5 Lincs, died on 22 March 1916, aged 16. **(I.D.13)**

Private M. Hutchinson, 3rd Canadian Pioneers, died on 9 April 1917, aged 53. His wife lived in Sussex. **(V.C.19)**

Second Lieutenant Basil Carver, Inniskilling Dragoons, died 21 August 1916, aged 19: 'Having descended into a mine tunnel to endeavour to save his men, overcome by gas, he also fell.' **(III.E.9)** His epitaph, the often used Biblical quote 'Greater love hath no man ...' is, in his case, rendered in Latin. (See Chapter 7.)

Private Charles Clements, Inniskilling Dragoons, died 21 August 1916, aged 25. **(III.E.13)**

Private Isidore King, C Squadron, Inniskilling Dragoons, died of wounds (gas) 21 August 1916. **(III.E.11)**

Lance Corporal A. Robinson, A Squadron, Inniskilling Dragoons, killed 21 August 1916, aged 26. **(III.E.12)**

Private Percy Taylor, Inniskilling Dragoons, killed 21 August 1916, aged 22. **(III.E.10)**

Private Henry Crossley, 27 Bn CEF, died 29 March 1917, aged 21. **(IV.K.13)** Just two days later *Private Walter Crossley*, 27 Bn CEF, died 31 March 1917, aged 25. **(IV.K.12)** These brothers are buried side by side, which may have given some comfort to their grieving parents in Winnipeg.

Private D. Meteer, 2 Bn CEF, died on 1 April 1917, aged 26, and was a fisherman. **(V.A.1)** Although the register does not state this, we have established that he was the brother of *Private Charles* (not 'G' as in the register) *Meteer*, 2 Bn CEF, who died on 15 April 1917, aged 21, and was a farmer. **(VI.E.28)** They enlisted on 7 and 15 September 1915 respectively.

Private Stanley Stokes, 1 Bn CEF, was 'Killed in action at the Battle of Vimy Ridge, 9 April 1917. Aged 16. Born in London, England . . . His father served as a private in the same Battalion and also fell in the same year.' **(I.G.15)** Horace Stokes, who died on 19 September 1917, aged 40, is buried at Aix Noulette Communal Cemetery Extension. **(I.T.2)** Stanley claimed to have been born on 11 September 1897 when he joined up on 4 December 1915; in fact he was probably only a few months over 14, though he was working as a driver; his father, a horse keeper, joined up on 20 December. Although historically futile, this situation leads the mind to speculate at what had passed between the members of the family, what was said and what were the motivations; whatever, it ended in a miserable tragedy for the mother and wife, Gertrude.

Lieutenant William Withrow, 2 Canadian Pioneers, 'died of heart failure due to labours as officer i/c Topographical Section Canadian Corps Intelligence for Battle of Vimy Ridge, 4 May 1917'. This was evidently not a total surprise, as on his attestation papers (21 [?] December 1915) the medical officer originally classified him as unfit for overseas service and then amended that to fit – probably under persuasion. Withrow had been a patents examiner and was 58 when he died. **(VI.H.13)**

Driver A. Morrison, 9 Bn Canadian Field Artillery, was killed on 5 July 1917, aged 22. **(V.K.11)** His father had 'lost his life as a passenger on the *Lusitania*, torpedoed 7 May 1915'. Driver Morrison was a university student when he enlisted in December 1915, possibly motivated by his father's death.

Haute Avesnes British Cemetery (50° 19.52'N, 2° 38.07'E)

Off the N49 Arras–St Pol road, on the south side.

This cemetery is situated on the western side of the village and to the south of it, beyond buildings (2010), on a minor road heading towards Habarcq. Take the approach road into the village (noting the French cemetery on the left) and, in the centre of town, where the road bears sharply to the left, go straight on and turn almost immediately right, passing the church and main square. At the end of the road you will see a CWGC sign to the cemetery, which is out of the village, beyond a water tower on your right, on the left-hand side of the road. There is a safe turning point a few hundred metres beyond the cemetery, which lies in a pretty location and is beautifully maintained; it is evident where the 'Haute' came from in the village's name.

There were several burials in April and May 1916, in a field adjacent to the Communal Cemetery (and where there was an existing French military cemetery, already seen), which is close to the Arras–St Pol road (N39), but it was decided that this was too close to a farm. After the war the British burials were removed to Cabaret Rouge, the big post-war concentration cemetery for this part of the battlefield.

Haute Avesnes British Cemetery was opened by the 51st (Highland) Division in July 1916. Strangely, the first burial was Private H. Gradidge, 179 Company Machine Gun Corps, of the 60th (2/2 London) Division, who was killed on 3 July 1916, and a number of other early burials were also from that division. The cemetery was not much used in those early months – the last burial in Row A, the original row of burials, took place on 24 March 1917, almost nine months later; this was Private J. McLeod, 153 Company Machine Gun Corps, 51st Division. The great majority of the graves relate to the Battle

Haute Avesnes: the Cross of
Sacrifice and the cemetery.

of Arras; Field Ambulances from various divisions holding the line were established here.

There are 130 British and Dominion burials, twelve Chinese Labour Corps (who all died after the Armistice) and eight Germans. Arij Shiva, of the Indian Labour Corps, died on 15 August 1917 and is buried away from the others in Row A, effectively in a separate row, to the left of the Great Cross.

THE TUNNELLERS

There are three tunnellers buried in this cemetery, from or attached to 185 Tunnelling Company, all buried in Row A, furthest from the cemetery entrance:

Private Albert Sawyer, Royal Army Service Corps (Mechanical Transport), attd 185 Tunnelling Company, died 1 November 1916, aged 30. **(A.13)**
Second Lieutenant Jack Benjamin Joseph, 185 Tunnelling Company, was killed on 8 January 1917, aged 35. His fascinating story can be found on page 157. **(A.17)**
Private Frank Paul, 10/Glosters, attd 185 Tunnelling Company, died 11 February 1917, aged 34. **(A.19)**

Aubigny Communal Cemetery Extension (50° 20.90'N, 2° 35.40'E)

This is a large cemetery, with its origins in the fighting of 1915, when the French Tenth Army held the sector. (Note the French graves on the west side, adjacent to the communal cemetery proper.) Its size is due to the fact that there were casualty clearing stations established nearby – and this in turn was due to the convenience of road (the N49 to the south) and rail links (for onward transport of wounded to the base hospitals or the UK). Unusually, there are no unknown burials here, and the officers are buried separately, in Plots V and VI, at the northernmost end of the cemetery. There are a notable number of fallen from 5 and 16 Squadrons RFC.

There are 2,048 British burials, 666 from Canada, fifty from South Africa, four from Australia, two from New Zealand, one from the British West Indies, sixty-four German prisoners (south of Plot IV) and 227 French.

Turn off the N39 to access the village, and continue through its winding streets to the central square and then turn left at a roundabout. Continue uphill to another roundabout and the cemetery is straight ahead; you will need to park in a parking area on the left. The cemetery is not all that obvious, as it is on a bank above the road. The densely packed British section is beyond the communal and French military sections of the cemetery. On your return you have to turn right at the roundabout as there is a one-way system in the village.

THE TUNNELLERS

172 Tunnelling Company
Sapper A. McKenzie, 172 Tunnelling Company, died of pneumonia, 20 July 1917, aged 26. **(III.E.27)**
Sapper M. Moyler, 172 Tunnelling Company, died of wounds 4 February 1917, aged 33. **(I.F.56)**

176 Tunnelling Company

Private F. Sims, 1/13 London (Kensington), attd 176 Tunnelling Company, died 29 March 1918, aged 23. **(III.B.3)**

Second Lieutenant R. Martin MM, 176 Tunnelling Company (commissioned from the ranks), died 12 July 1918, aged 31. **(V.B.3)**

181 Tunnelling Company

Sapper E. Jones, 181 Tunnelling Company, died of wounds 17 April 1916, aged 38. **(I.A.47)**

184 Tunnelling Company

Sapper James Percival, 184 Tunnelling Company, died of wounds, 1 April 1917, aged 26. **(I.J.47)**

Corporal W. Simpson, 184 Tunnelling Company, died 8 June 1917, aged 38. **(III.H.9)**

185 Tunnelling Company

Sergeant A. Wiseman, 185 Tunnelling Company, died 12 April 1916. **(I.A.33)**

Sapper J. Randall, 185 Tunnelling Company, died 18 November 1916. **(I.F.3)**

Sergeant J. Robinson, 185 Tunnelling Company, died of wounds, 14 July 1916, aged 35. **(I.D.32)**

Sapper A. Allan, 185 Tunnelling Company, died of wounds 25 March 1918, aged 28. **(III.C.35)**

Sapper A. Robertson, 185 Tunnelling Company, died 25 August 1918, aged 39. **(IV.D.33)**

New Zealand Tunnelling Company

Sapper W. Edwards, NZ Tunnelling Company, died of wounds 16 September 1916. **(I.E.28)**

1 (Canadian) Tunnelling Company

Lance Corporal W. Montgomery, 1 (Canadian) Tunnelling Company, died of wounds 27 June 1918, aged 39. **(IV.L.58)** A labourer from Toronto, Montgomery joined the army on 14 July 1915. In the period before the German spring offensives of 1918, the company was given a refresher course in musketry and drill and allocated specific defensive positions; however, after the offensive failed in front of Arras, the company returned to the tasks of preparing demolitions and constructing new defence lines. Soon afterwards the Canadian 1st and 2nd Tunnelling Companies (some 1,100 men all told) were disbanded and became part of Currie's new Engineer brigades. Montgomery was among the last of 1 (Cdn) Tunnelling Company to die before it was disbanded (see Nicholson, *Canadian Expeditionary Force 1914–1919*, pp. 502–3).

Sapper M. Godas, 1 (Canadian) Tunnelling Company, died of wounds 29 August 1918. **(IV.G.30)** Given that the company had been disbanded by this stage, he should have been noted simply as Royal Canadian Engineers.

Miscellaneous entries:

Among the host of highly decorated men buried in this cemetery, one stands out: Private Claude Nunney VC, DCM, MM, of the 38th (Ottawa) Battalion CEF; he died on 18 September 1918 of wounds received during his VC action, at a casualty clearing station near Vis en Artois, and is buried in **IV.B.39**. His was a posthumous VC, gazetted on 13 December 1918, and was for his actions on 1 and 2 September 1918 during the

Aubigny CCE. The grave of Private C.J.P. Nunney VC, DCM, MM, of the 38th Battalion, Canadian Infantry. He died of wounds on 18 September 1918.

attack on the Drocourt Quéant Line, east of Vis en Artois, on the Cambrai road. He was aged 25 when he died. He was born in Dublin, but became a naturalised Canadian; he enlisted in March 1915, though apparently listed no family as next of kin.

Faubourg d'Amiens Cemetery (50° 17.22'N, 2° 45.62'E)

This is a large cemetery (over 2,600 graves) but it tends to be somewhat overshadowed by the presence of the stately Arras Memorial to the Missing and the Flying Services Memorial on its eastern side, built where originally 770 French soldiers had been buried (and some French civilians, as the town cemetery in St Sauveur was under fire) during the war.

Relatively few graves were concentrated here after the Armistice, most of which came from a cemetery in the eastern part of the town, which produced 89 out of the 207 brought in altogether. There are only ten unidentified burials, nine of whom are known to have come from the UK.

The cemetery forms a part of the Arras and the Flying Services Memorials to the Missing. It is near the Vauban citadel, which until recently was a French army barracks. (Built between 1667 and 1672, this citadel formed part of Louis XIV's 'Ne Plus Ultra' line.) It is situated on an inner ring road to the west of the city. It is not within easy walking distance of the centre and we recommend that you get directions from the town hall or make use of one of their free maps: the route to take from the main squares is Boulevard Faidherbe, right on to Boulevard de Strasbourg, on to Boulevard Carnot, keeping left on to Boulevard Vauban, which leads on to Boulevard du General de Gaulle. Soon after a right bend, keeping on the left, you will see the memorial on the left and the turning is shortly before the memorial. It is quite a simple route but there is no space here to provide an appropriate map. When you have completed your visit to the cemetery you might care to continue along the minor road by the cemetery

Faubourg d'Amiens: the exterior of the cemetery and memorials to the missing of the battles of Arras and the Air Services.

Faubourg d'Amiens: the cemetery, with the memorial to the missing of the battles of Arras in the background.

and visit the place where the Gestapo executed various members of the French resistance and others, situated in the dry moat of the citadel. It has a haunting and uncomfortable atmosphere.

THE TUNNELLERS

New Zealand Tunnelling Company

(Authors' Note: * = The register says or suggests that they were born in England; † = the register says or suggests that they were born in New Zealand; a lack of either symbol means that there was no relevant information in the register.)

Sergeant S. Vernon†, NZ Tunnelling Company, died of wounds 21 June 1916, aged 36. **(I.D.59)**

*Sapper T. Ashford**, NZ Tunnelling Company, killed 2 July 1916, aged 30. **(I.E.23)**

Sergeant J. Murphy, NZ Tunnelling Company, died of wounds 25 January 1917. **(I.F.42)**

*Sapper J. Wright**, NZ Tunnelling Company, killed 12 March 1917, aged 28. **(II.F.19)**

Lance Corporal B. Fahey, NZ Tunnelling Company, killed 20 April 1917. **(V.A.30)**

Sapper T. Turner, NZ Tunnelling Company, killed 22 May 1917. **(V.F.17)**

Sapper H. Davies, NZ Tunnelling Company, killed 24 July 1917. **(V.J.6)**

Sapper E. Davies, NZ Tunnelling Company, killed 2 August 1917. **(V.J.11)**

Sapper G. Davies† (served as Davis), NZ Tunnelling Company, 5 August 1917, aged 29. **(V.J.12)**

Sapper R. Jones†, New Zealand Tunnelling Company, killed 15 August 1917, aged 31. **(V.J.19)**

Sapper J. Healy†, NZ Tunnelling Company, died of wounds 13 September 1917, aged 33. **(V.J.28)**

Sapper J. Wesley†, NZ Tunnelling Company, killed 2 October 1917, aged 30. (**VI.A.3**)

Sapper S. Tredinnick, NZ Tunnelling Company, died of wounds, 14 October 1917. (**VI.A.8**)

Sapper M. Abbott*, NZ Tunnelling Company, killed 31 March 1918, aged 29. (**VII.C.27**)

179 Tunnelling Company

Sapper S. Chapman, 179 Tunnelling Company, killed 28 March 1917, aged 34. (**II.L.17**)

Sapper W. Graham, 179 Tunnelling Company, killed 28 March 1917, aged 30. (**II.L.20**)

Sapper P. Rowan, 179 Tunnelling Company, 28 March 1917. (**II.L.19**)

Sapper T. Cooke, 179 Tunnelling Company, 6 April 1917. (**III.O.29**)

Lance Corporal G. Wilkinson, 179 Tunnelling Company, 6 April 1917. (**III.O.30**)

Sapper C. Deakin, 179 Tunnelling Company, 17 March 1918, aged 31. (**VI.B.13**)

184 Tunnelling Company

Second Corporal J. Salisbury, 184 Tunnelling Company, died 11 April 1916. (**I.A.36**)

Sapper W. Harrison, 184 Tunnelling Company, died 17 April 1916, aged 33. (**I.A.42**)

Private A. Wood, 1/East Surrey attd 184 Tunnelling Company, killed 23 May 1916, aged 20. (**I.C.3**)

Sapper H. James, 184 Tunnelling Company, died 4 June 1916, aged 23. (**I.D.13**)

Second Lieutenant C. Sandeman, 184 Tunnelling Company, killed 4 July 1916, aged 33. (**I.E.31**)

Second Corporal J. Pilling, 184 Tunnelling Company, died 13 July 1916. (**I.E.44**)

Lance Corporal T. Poole, 184 Tunnelling Company, died 23 January 1917. (**II.C.2**)

257 Tunnelling Company

Sapper W. Roberts, 257 Tunnelling Company, died 21 March 1918, aged 28. (**VI.B.26**)

Miscellaneous entries:

Our attention was drawn to the graves of two brothers, Gunners M. (aged 20) and W. (aged 26) McIsaac of 149 Siege Battery, Royal Garrison Artillery, who both died on 11 April 1918. The sons of Malcolm and Mary McIsaac of Falkirk, they are buried side by side in **VI.E.20** and **21**.

Other tunnellers killed in the Arras area, whose graves were lost or whose bodies were never recovered, are commemorated on the adjacent Memorial to the Missing in the part devoted to the Royal Engineers.

Notre Dame de Lorette French National Cemetery and Museum (52° 24.01'N, 2° 43.16'E)

This is situated at the north end of Souchez; at the crest of the hill coming out of the town, turn left and drive up the eastern spur of Lorette hill. Parking is available on both the eastern and western sides of the cemetery. We recommend that for the view and the cemetery you park at the eastern end and then for the museum move to the western end.

THE PANORAMIC VIEW

For people using this book as a guide, an essential part of a visit here is the view offered over the western side of Vimy Ridge. There is a small orientation table across the road from the eastern entrance to the cemetery and along a path. From here one can see (on

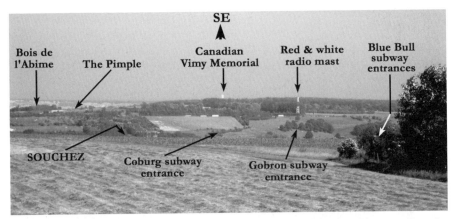

Notre Dame de Lorette: view of the northern end of Vimy Ridge from the Pimple to the Canadian Vimy Memorial. (Compare this view with that on page 70.)

Notre Dame de Lorette: view south-east to Neuville St Vaast and Maison Blanche, with Arras in the background.

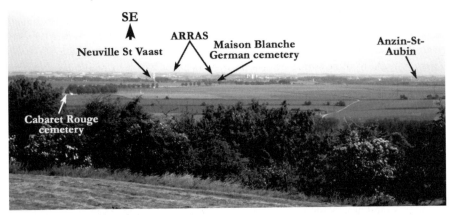

a clear day!), from north to south, the Pimple, the tops of the Vimy Memorial's pylons, Cabaret Rouge Military Cemetery, the church at Neuville St Vaast, the German Cemetery and Maison Blanche and Ecurie. The twin towers of Mont St Eloi are also visible, as are Ablain St Nazaire and Carency. This view gives an idea of the scale of the northernmost part of the attack and you can see the sectors of five front-line divisions on the opening day of the Battle of Arras, 9 April 1917. You are also looking over much of the battlefields of the three Battles of the Artois in 1914 and 1915.

THE CEMETERY AND THE OSSUARY

This is the biggest French military cemetery, with 20,000 identified graves (Verdun's Douaumont Military Cemetery, on the Verdun battlefield, has over 16,000 graves, plus some 150,000 in the ossuary there). General Barbot, mentioned in Chapter 2, occupies the first grave on the left as you enter from the eastern side; there are four mass graves – containing about 13,600 burials – and some 8,000 more are in the ossuary under the

Notre Dame de Lorette: the cemetery, Basilica and lantern tower.

lantern tower. It is astonishingly large, especially when one considers that the remains of over 12,000 soldiers from this battlefield were sent back to their families for burial and that the La Targette French Cemetery contains another 11,000 bodies. The dead were brought to these two cemeteries from all over the Artois front and they provide a clear indication of the scale of the French suffering in the battles of the Artois from autumn 1914 to the end of February 1916. In the last few years a substantial amount of money has been spent on restoring the Basilica and the Lantern Tower (so called because it has a light that shines out, like a lighthouse, over the night-time Artois landscape and is visible for many kilometres around).

THE MUSEUM
There is an excellent little museum (entry fee) and small shop at the west end of the cemetery (and nearby there is also a very good restaurant). The museum has all sorts of relics and uniforms (in excellent condition) from the war – not necessarily very well labelled and perhaps rather old fashioned in terms of display, but in our opinion none the worse for that. Another feature is a succession of life-sized dioramas, set in 'dugouts', with a commentary in French or English (make sure that you press the right button!). These are also very good. The one snag is that only a few people can see each diorama at one time, so for a mini-bus group of a dozen or so it would be best to go through this part of the museum in small groups of four or five, with an interval of about five minutes between each group. In a separate room there are about a dozen machines for viewing contemporary stereoscopic photographs, many of which are not for the faint hearted.

Appendix I

Mine Explosion Report (British), 21 August 1916

Army Form W3376

MINE EXPLOSION REPORT (BRITISH)

Third ARMY   XVII CORPS   60th DIVISION
172 TUNNELLING COMPANY RE   SECTOR P
DATE: 21.8.16   Time: 7:30 p.m.

Location and depth of Charge.	Face of P76K. Depth 76 ft.
Nature of Ground.	Chalk broken by previous blows.
Details of Charge.	6,000 lbs. Ammonal In rubber bags. Primer - 2 electric detonators in guncotton primer surrounded by commercial caps.
Tamping.	15' solid + 5' alr space + 10' solid + 5' air space + 10' solid.
Reasons and Authority for Mine.	Proximity of enemy gallery. Authority C of M.
Effects of Explosion:	
Dimensions of Crater.	Impossible to ascertain.
Underground Effects.	70-75 ft of gallery destroyed, lateral between J & K shaken but not seriously damaged.
Estimated HRR.	75 feet.
Surface effects.	Crater formed one bombing post filled in. German lip possibly slightly heightened.
Gas conditions.	Our galleries free of gas.
If against enemy gallery, estimated distance.	18 feet.
Infantry action regarding crater.	Lip re-occupied as before blow. New galleries being started from lateral to project lip.
General remarks.	Exact surface effects difficult to say owing to the blow taking place in the middle of the old craters. A lot of earth was thrown on to the enemy's side, which has probably filled in his bombing post, though it has also given him some high OPs.

(Sketch attached).   Date:23.8.16   Signed: G A Syme. Major RE

13B-A11

184 Tunnelling Company Standing Orders with regard to blows, dated 22 August 1916

STANDING ORDERS WITH REGARD TO BLOWS - Revised 22-8-16.

<u>"A" General.</u>

1.　　In the event of a blow or earth tremor of any kind felt below ground, or sudden gassing of a mine, all Officers, N.C.Os, and men are to come to the surface at once.

2.　　In the case of mines connected by laterals, the wav up will be by the downcast.

3.　　After a blow, no Officer, N.C.O. or man will go below without & Proto or Salvus apparatus, however slight the blow may have been. It is advisable to wait for half-an-hour before recommencing work.

4.　　As the men come up after a blow, all naked lights (candles) ' should at once be put out.

5.　　A C.E.A.G. lamp will be hung up in the lateral at each junction with the forward gallery for the use of rescuers. This is on no account to be used for other purposes.

6.　　In the case of a gas attack, the mine sentry (there must always be one posted), will quickly sound the gongs and get all men up from below. Smoke helmets will be immediately put on when the warning is given.

7.　　Proto men entering mines to rescue men below will wear a Proto apparatus, will carry an Oxygen Reviving apparatus and will be trained under Section arrangements in using a Reviving apparatus with a Proto set on.

8.　　Smoke Helmets are useless for Rescue work or against mine gas.

9.　　Guide ropes are to be fixed at each shaft.

10.　　Slings are to be provided at the bottom and top of shafts for hauling men up, or some similar contrivance in the case of inclines

11.　　Gas Doors where they exist, should be kept permanently shut and only opened where necessary for ventilation.

12.　　Gassed men wick be treated with the Reviving apparatus at once (in the gallery) and when brought to the surface will remain for at least half-an-hour before being removed on a stretcher. Hot Coffee should be administered. The Primus Stoves provided in the Rescue Stations are for this purpose and not for general use.

13.　　On no account should men who have been rendered unconscious move about or walk, even if able so to do- They should be carried back to the Dressing Station.

<u>"B" Gassy Mines.</u>

1.　　In the case of mines reported and found to be gassy, all men working below ground will come up and report to the Officer In charge of operations.

2.　　The Officer will decide if it is safe to work the mine or not If unsafe it will be reported as <u>"Class I Gassy."</u> If considered Safe for work on due precautions being taken it will be reported as <u>"Class II Gassy"</u>.

3.　　Mines reported <u>"Class I Gassy."</u>

(a) No man will descend, the mine without apparatus until it has been declared <u>"Class II Gassy."</u> This order particularly applies to the case of Gassed men being below.

(b) A sentry to be placed at the entrance to the mine or a notice posted to prevent anyone descending.

(c) No naked lights are to be allowed in the mine - C.E.A.G lamps or torches only are to be used.

4.　　Mines reported <u>"Class II Gassy."</u>

(a) No man or party or men are to descend without a canary or white mouse, leaving one man posted on top who should know the length of time they intend staying below. All men are to come up at once if the canary or white mouse shows signs of distress

(b) The Officer in charge will see that the means of getting the Rescue apparatus to the mine are satisfactory.

(c) That the ventilation of the mine is capable of no improvement.

5.   After a blow a mine is always to be reported "Class I Gassy" until it has been tested by a man with apparatus or canary (vide Mine Rescue Orders). Officer in charge of sections are responsible for bringing these orders to the notice of their juniors and of explaining personally to them the dangers of gas. They will ensure that a mine reported "Class I" or "Class II Gassy" is known to all ranks.

"C" Mine Rescue Orders.

1.   Close Gas Doors which are to be fixed in all laterals and branches.
2.   All men below ground are to come up at once after a blow.
3.   After a blow no man is to descend the mine without Rescue apparatus till the mine is reported clear of gas. (vide Gassy Mines
4.   The Smoke Helmets issued, by the Army afford no protection against Mine gas. They give protection against cylinder gas only (Chlorine etc).
5.   Oxygen Reviving apparatus is to be taken down the mine by the Proto men whenever possible. Proto men will use Proto appliances for Rescue work generally, Salvus plants are smaller and do not last as long.
6.   No naked lights are to to used until the mine is reported clear of gas. Rescue men will use their C.E.A.G. lamps or torches provided them.
7.   No man who has been gassed is to ascend a shaft or incline without being roped. Gassed men often collapse on reaching the fresh air or under exertion. Ropes must be available at all mines for this purpose.
8.   Men who have been unconscious should be kept in a dug-out near the shaft head or at the Rescue Station for at least two hours if possible, before being taken to the Dressing Station. Black labels will be attached to mild cases of gassing. These cases will ordinarily be returned to billets or advanced billets and will be under the supervision of the Company Medical Officer. The Red labels are for cases which have been rendered unconscious. They will be sent to Hospital through the Dressing Station and Company Headquarters warned by wire. This information will be passed to the Company Medical Officer by wire.
9.   Respiration is to be restored by Shaefer's method. Hot coffee and blankets should be ready at the Dressing Station. The storeman will be responsible that these are there and that coffee being made when they leave the Station on a call.
10.   Mine Rescue Stations will be centralised so that they are within 5. minutes of the mines they serve.

(Signed) J. Richard Gwyther, Major.
Commanding 184th Tunnelling Co., R.E.

Glossary

Abri (Fr.)	Term for a military dugout.
Adit	A mining term usually applied to a ventilation or drainage shaft, but sometimes used by the tunnellers to describe a steep entrance/exit.
Ammonal	Ammonium nitrate-based explosive with a strong lifting effect, 3½ times more powerful than gunpowder. Inert and safe to handle. Adopted in mid-1915 as the standard British mining explosive.
BEF	In the context of this book, the BEF (British Expeditionary Force) is taken to refer to British troops serving in France and Flanders.
Boyau (Fr.)	Passageway, used in the context of a communication trench.
Caltrop	Strictly a three- or four-spiked device designed to lame horses. In the context of this book a sharp metal spike embedded in the ground to impede or injure soldiers, similar to 'panji' traps.
Camouflet	A contained underground explosive charge that does not break surface. Most often employed to destroy enemy tunnels.
Carbon Monoxide (CO)	A colourless and odourless gas released on detonation of explosives.
	If inhaled, it combines with the haemoglobin in the blood displacing oxygen. If not swiftly treated, it is invariably fatal. A very serious hazard for tunnellers.
Carrière (Fr.)	A quarry, frequently applied to underground quarries – see 'Cave' and 'Souterraine'.
Catacomb	Term frequently used by German troops to describe underground quarries – see 'Carrière', 'Cave' and 'Souterraine'.
Cave	In the context of this book, a pre-First World War manmade underground cavity (or series of cavities) cut into chalk; in most cases the result of quarrying for building material, but occasionally to provide a refuge or hiding place – see 'Carrière' and 'Souterraine'.
CEF	Canadian Expeditionary Force.
Cheddite	A blasting explosive used by the French for charging mines. Similar to ammonal.
Chevaux-de-frise	Array of sharpened iron stakes generally used to block trenches.

Clay kicking	Method of digging small tunnels quickly through clay, used by sewer tunnellers. Advantage of being relatively silent. Adopted by the British tunnelling companies.
Common mine	Underground explosive charge designed to destroy enemy dugouts and surface defences.
Cordeau detonant (or detonating fuse)	A thin flexible lead tube packed with high explosive, which carries the detonating wave at a rate of around 5 km/s. Of particular value for arranging simultaneous detonation of multiple charges.
Counter-mine	Tunnels dug to defend against enemy mines. Also 'defensive mine'.
CWGC	The Commonwealth (formerly the Imperial) War Graves Commission.
Defensive mine	A gallery and charge (usually a 'camouflet' charge) aimed at attacking enemy mining galleries.
Demi-galerie	Standard French mine gallery, 1.30–1.50m high by 1m wide.
Detonator	Copper or aluminium tube, about the size of a cigarette, containing one of several very sensitive explosives. Used to initiate detonation normally via a 'primer'. Two main types, igniferous (initiated by a burning fuse) and electrical.
Entonnoir (Fr.)	Crater.
Fougasse mine	Offensive mine overcharged to bury enemy position with debris or create high crater rims.
Gallery	One of several terms describing a tunnel, most commonly one running towards the enemy lines or tunnels.
Gas door	Leather or rubberised sheet, or treated and weighted blanket, which on release provides a seal to ingress of gas. Situated in tunnels to compartmentalise them.
Geophone	A listening instrument with two microphones, constructed on the principles of a stethoscope. Sound waves through the ground are magnified and transmitted separately to each ear of the listener. By exactly balancing the pitch, a bearing can be obtained to the source of the sound.
Grafting tool	Type of spade used for clay kicking.
Guncotton	Nitro-cellulose explosive generally employed for demolitions.
Gunpowder	Traditional explosive comprising saltpetre, sulphur and charcoal used for military mining until 1915.
Imperial(s)	Term often used by Dominion troops to indicate a British formation, e.g. the 24th (Imperial) Division, or a collective term for British troops.

Incline	Sloped entrance to a tunnel used as an alternative to a vertical shaft. Frequently referred to as a 'shaft'.
Instantaneous fuse	Very fast burning fuse (about 120 ft/s, or 36 m/s). Commonly used as a 'back up' to electrical detonation circuits.
Lateral	Defensive tunnel dug parallel to the front-line trench. Used as a starting point for listening and attack galleries and interconnections between galleries. Effectively a deep underground 'trench'. Also called a transversal.
Line of least resistance	The distance of a mine to the surface used to calculate whether it would form a crater or the extent of the crater.
Mine	Explosive charge laid underground. Optionally the tunnel in which that charge is laid.
NZET	New Zealand Engineers Tunnelling Company.
Overcharged mine	Explosive charge intended to throw up debris and form high lips around the crater. See also Fougasse.
Pipe pushing	A technique employing a hydraulic ram to force a pipe horizontally through the ground and enable a tube of explosive to be inserted. Largely superseded by the Wombat drill, but remained of value for setting demolition charges below roads and railways.
Primer	A guncotton slab about the size of a cotton reel, into which a detonator can be inserted. Provides the impetus to initiate the main explosive charge.
Proto apparatus	The most commonly used of several British self-contained breathing apparatus combining an oxygen supply with a recycling system for absorbing the carbon dioxide exhaled by the user. Capable of lasting about 45 minutes. Also known as the 'Fleuss' apparatus.
Push pick	Tool used for working in clay.
Radius or spheroid of rupture	The radius of underground disintegration from the mine charge within which damage will be caused to underground workings.
Rameaux de combat (Fr.)	Offensive branch gallery usually measuring 0.80m by 0.65m.
Rojet	A listening instrument similar to the geophone.
Russian sap	Either a deep trench covered and concealed to effectively form a tunnel, or a shallow underground gallery that could be converted into a trench by breaking down the top cover.
Safety fuse	A slow burning fuse. The British Bickford fuse burned at a rate of 38 seconds per foot (125 seconds per metre).
Salvus	British self-contained breathing apparatus capable of lasting 30 minutes.

Sap	A trench dug towards the enemy. Sometimes used for a mine gallery driven towards the enemy.
Sapper	Generic term for a military engineer. Also the most junior rank in the Royal Engineers.
Seismomicrophone	An electrical sound detector usually linked to a central listening station covering an area of the mining front.
Shaft	Strictly a vertical adit or access but often used to describe inclines into tunnels or dugouts.
Slabbing	Chalk is usually layered and separated into 'bedding planes'. Where there are weak and unsupported joints, large sections can collapse in slabs.
Souterraine (Fr.)	Term strictly meaning 'underground' but extensively applied to underground quarries and sometimes to tunnels – see 'Cave' and 'Carrière'.
Soutien (Fr.)	Support, e.g. tranchée soutien = support trench
Spiling	Sheet piling technique used for tunnelling through soft or sandy ground.
Stollen	German term for a mine gallery or tunnel.
Subway	A communication tunnel providing concealed and protected access to front-line positions. Most also included some or all of the command and signals centres, accommodation and logistic facilities.
Tactical mine	A mine charge used for tactical rather than offensive purposes, e.g. to deny ground or obstruct enemy approaches, to block off enfilade fire with high lips, to provide a high rim overlooking enemy positions, etc.
Tamping	In a mining context, backfilling the gallery leading to a mine charge to prevent the force of the explosion being directed back down the tunnel.
Thermite	A mixture of finely powdered aluminium and iron oxide that produces very high temperatures on combustion. Used in mortar bombs it would ignite any combustible material in the immediate vicinity and melt metal fixtures.
Tramming	Use of wheeled trolleys to remove spoil and carry forward explosives.
Transversal	See 'lateral'.
Trichter	German for crater. Abbreviation Tr.
Tubbing	Steel cylindrical sections used for sinking shafts in wet or loose ground.

Tube(s)	Termed used in some Canadian plans and documents for subways.
Westfalit	German explosive similar to ammonal.
Wombat	A hand-operated drilling machine used by the British. Normally an 8-inch bore.
Wombat mine	A hole drilled horizontally towards the enemy about 3–6 metres below the surface, and packed with explosives; when blown, created a deep trench across No Man's Land.

Relative Measures

1 metre	3.281 ft	1 foot	0.305 metres
	1.094 yards	1 yard	0.914 metres
1 kilometre	3,281 feet	1 mile	1,609 metres
	1,094 yards		1.609 kilometres
	0.621 miles		1,760 yards
1 kilogram	2.205 lb	1 lb	0.455 kilograms
1 metric ton	1,000 kilograms	1 (imperial) ton	2,240 lb
			1,016 kilograms
1 Zenter	50 kilograms	1 cwt	120 lb
	110.2 lb		

Bibliography

Primary Sources

Canadian Corps: General Staff Corps HQ and 3rd and 4th Canadian Infantry Divisions; HQs 1, 3, 7, 8, 9, 11 and 12 Canadian Infantry Brigades and 13 (British/Imperial) Infantry Brigade, PPCLI, 38th (Ottawa) Bn, 42nd Bn (Canadian Black Watch), 49th Bn (Edmonton), Royal Canadian Regt (Toronto), 4th CMR, 54th Bn (Kootenays), 102nd Bn (Northern British Columbia – 'Pea-Soupers')

Les Armées Français dans la Grande Guerre – Tome III

Kriegsarchiv München Pion.-Bat.1 Nr.8 (WK)

First Army Mining Reports, Library of the Institute of Royal Engineers

Third Army Mining Reports, Library of the Institute of Royal Engineers

National Archives (formerly the Public Record Office)

Maps and plans, WO 153

172 Tunnelling Company War Diary, NA WO 95/244

175 Tunnelling Company War Diary, NA WO 95/404

176 Tunnelling Company War Diary, NA WO 95/244

181 Tunnelling Company War Diary, NA WO 95/405

182 Tunnelling Company War Diary, NA WO 95/488

184 Tunnelling Company War Diary, NA WO 95/245

185 Tunnelling Company War Diary, NA WO 95/336

New Zealand Tunnelling Company War Diary, NA WO 95/407

Dixon, Major H.R., MC (Assistant Inspector of Mines at GHQ, 1916–1919), 'The Lighter Side of a Tunnellers Life' (Unpublished manuscript)

Nubbert, Carol, 'To Live In Hearts We Leave Behind Is Not To Die' – a biographical study of Robert Brisco (Private papers)

Reminiscences by Col. D.C. Unwin Simpson RCE, MEIC, of Little Known Facts and Difficulties in the Construction of the Canadian Memorial on Vimy Ridge, and other Memorials in France and Belgium, photocopied typescript, Canadian War Museum [CWM], Ottawa, no date (c. 1960s)

Robinson, Lieutenant Colonel G.P.G., private papers, including correspondence with Herr Olaf Grieben and a report dated January 1989 entitled 'The Durand Mine and First World War Tunnel System in the Grange Area'

Wilson, C.R., 'Lieutenant Colonel Sir John Norton-Griffiths (1871–1930)', Royal Engineers' Museum website

Published Sources

Anon., 'German regulations for field fortifications and conclusions reached in Russia from the battles in defensive positions in Manchuria' (translated from *Militär Wochenblatt*), *Professional Memoirs. Corps of Engineers, United States Army and Engineer Department at Large*, vol. II, no. 7 (1910)

Astill, Edwin (ed.), *The Great War Diaries of Brigadier General Alexander Johnston 1914–1917* (Pen & Sword Books, 2007)

Bailey, Sergeant O.F. and Hollier, Sergeant H.M., 'The Kensingtons, 13th London Regiment', *Regimental Old Comrades Association* (1935)

Barrie, Alexander, *War Underground, The Tunnellers of the Great War* (Tom Donovan Publishing Ltd, 1961)

Barton, Peter, Doyle, Peter and Vandewalle, Johan, *Beneath Flanders Fields, The Tunnellers' War* (Spellmount Ltd, 2004)

Beattie, Kim, *The History of the 48th Highlanders of Canada (15th Battalion of the CEF)* (Southam Press Ltd, Toronto, 1932)

Bewsher, Major F.W., DSO, MC, *The History of the 51st (Highland) Division, 1914–1918* (William Blackwood & Sons, 1921)

Bygone Pilgrimage. An Illustrated History and Guide to the Battlefields 1914–1918, Arras–Lens–Douai and the Battles of the Artois. Two Years After (Naval & Military Press reprint, nd)

Cave, Nigel, *Vimy Ridge – Arras* (Pen & Sword Military, 1996, repr. 2009)

Dans La Trancheé Devant Arras, traduit de l'ouvrage d'Alfons Schneider, Édité par le Cercle Archéologique Arrageois, 1997

Faivre, Dominique, *Sur les Traces des Soldats Canadiens 1917 – Souterraine de la Maison Blanche* (Private publication, December 2001)

Fischer, Hauptmann D.R., *History of Das Reserve-Infanterie-Regiment Nr. 262 1914–1918* (Zeulenroda, 1936)

Giradet, Jean-Marie, *Roclincourt – Écurie Un Verrou Du Front D'Artois* (Le Cercle Archéologique Arrageois, 1995)

Giradet, Jean-Marie, Jacques, Alain and Letho Duclos, Jean-Luc, *La Bataille D'Arras avril–mai 1917* (Imprimerie Centrale de l'Artois, Arras, 1997)

Giradet, Jean-Marie, Jacques, Alain and Letho Duclos, Jean-Luc, *Somewhere on the Western Front, Arras 1914–18* (Éditions Degeorge, 2007)

Giradet, Jean-Marie, Jacques, Alain and Letho Duclos, Jean-Luc, *Sur l'axe stratégique Arras – Cambrai, Tilloy-les-Mofflaines, Monchy-le-Preux* (Le Cercle Archéologique Arrageois, 1999)

Graham, Captain H.W., MC, *The Life of a Tunnelling Officer* (J. Catherall & Co. Ltd, 1927). Illustrated by sketches, mainly by Lieutenant F.C.B. Cadell

Grant Grieve, Captain W. and Newman, Bernard, *Tunnellers* (Herbert Jenkins Ltd, 1936, repr. Naval & Military Press, nd)

Hussey, Brigadier General A.H. and Inman, Major D.S., *The Fifth Division in the Great War* (Nisbett & Co. Ltd, London)

Jacques, Alain, *La Bataille D'Arras, avril–mai 1917* (Imprimerie Centrale, Arras, 1997)

Jones, Simon, *Underground Warfare 1914–1918* (Pen & Sword Military, 2010)

Les Carnets de guerre de Louis Barthas, tonnelier. 1914–1918 (Editions la Decouverte, 1992)

Letho Duclos, Jean-Luc, *Saint-Laurent-Blangy dans la Grande Guerre* (Imprimerie Centrale de l'Artois, Arras)

Letho Duclos, Jean-Luc, *Saint-Laurent-Blangy, Trois Ans Au Couer Des Combats* (Le Cercle Archéologique Arrageois, 1994)

Lumb, Major A.D., MC, 'An Incident on Vimy Ridge', *TOCA Bulletin*, no. 11 (1936)

Macintyre, D.E., *Canada at Vimy* (Peter Martin Associates, Toronto, 1967)

McKee, Alexander, Vimy Ridge (Souvenir Press, 1966)

Neill, J.C. (ed.), *The New Zealand Tunnelling Company 1915–1919* (Whitcombe & Tombs Ltd, Auckland, 1922)

Plummer, Captain B.D., MC, 'France and Flanders Revisited', *Tunnellers Old Comrades Association Bulletin*, no. 4 (1929)

Riebike, Otto, *Unsere Pioniere im Weltkriege* ('*Our Engineers in the World War*') (Kyffhauser Verlag, Berlin, 1925)

Scott, Major General Sir Arthur B. and Middleton Brumwell, P., *History of the 12th (Eastern) Division in the Great War* (Nisbet & Co. Ltd, 1923)

Sheldon, Jack, *The German Army on Vimy Ridge 1914–1917* (Pen & Sword Military, 2008)

Sheldon, Jack and Cave, Nigel, *The Battle for Vimy Ridge – 1917* (Pen & Sword Battleground Europe Series, 2007)

Taboika, J. Victor, *Military Antiques and Collectables of the Great War, A Canadian Collection* (Service Publications, Ottawa)

Topp, C.B., DSO, MC, *Regimental History of the 42nd Battalion CEF (Royal Highlanders of Canada) in the Great War* (Gazette Printing Co., nd but c. 1932)

Trounce, Captain H., *Fighting the Boche Underground* (Charles Scribner's Sons, New York, 1918)

Zschokke, Bruno, *Handbuch der militärischen Sprengtechnik für Offiziere aller Waffen* (Verlag von Veit & Co., Leipzig, 1911)

Selective Index